Protecting Geographical Indications in Africa

Protecting Geographical Indications in Africa

MARIUS SCHNEIDER
Founder and Director, IPvocate Africa Legal Advisers, Mauritius

NORA HO TU NAM
Partner, IPvocate Africa Legal Advisers, Mauritius

OXFORD
UNIVERSITY PRESS

Great Clarendon Street, Oxford, OX2 6DP,
United Kingdom

Oxford University Press is a department of the University of Oxford.
It furthers the University's objective of excellence in research, scholarship,
and education by publishing worldwide. Oxford is a registered trade mark of
Oxford University Press in the UK and in certain other countries

© Marius Schneider and Nora Ho Tu Nam 2024

The moral rights of the authors have been asserted

All rights reserved. No part of this publication may be reproduced, stored in
a retrieval system, or transmitted, in any form or by any means, without the
prior permission in writing of Oxford University Press, or as expressly permitted
by law, by licence or under terms agreed with the appropriate reprographics
rights organization. Enquiries concerning reproduction outside the scope of the
above should be sent to the Rights Department, Oxford University Press, at the
address above

You must not circulate this work in any other form
and you must impose this same condition on any acquirer

Public sector information reproduced under Open Government Licence v3.0
(http://www.nationalarchives.gov.uk/doc/open-government-licence/open-government-licence.htm)

Published in the United States of America by Oxford University Press
198 Madison Avenue, New York, NY 10016, United States of America

British Library Cataloguing in Publication Data

Data available

Library of Congress Control Number: 2024931141

ISBN 9780192864468

DOI: 10.1093/9780191955082.001.0001

Printed and bound by
CPI Group (UK) Ltd, Croydon, CR0 4YY

Links to third party websites are provided by Oxford in good faith and
for information only. Oxford disclaims any responsibility for the materials
contained in any third party website referenced in this work.

Authoring a book is often a collaborative journey and this book is no exception.

To our families.

Foreword

The African continent is renowned for the abundance of its cultural, floral, agricultural, and handicraft heritage, a reputation that also extends to the richness of its traditional knowledge, folklore, and genetic resources. This immense wealth is currently insufficiently exploited for various reasons, one of which is the lack of expertise regarding the technical and legal tools needed for the valorization and exploitation of the continent's heritage.

Indeed, how can it be that Africa is the main exporter of many agricultural raw materials (coffee, cocoa, cashew nuts, etc.), yet collects less than one-third of the income generated? This situation demonstrates that the wealth generated depends more on the value added than on the volume of product sold.

Creating added value is precisely the role assigned to the intellectual property system, and particularly to the system of geographical indications. Geographical indications are defined by the Bangui Agreement (2015) in its Annex VI as 'indications that serve to identify a product as originating from a place, region or country, in cases where the quality, reputation or other specific characteristic of the product can be essentially attributed to such geographical origin'.

The Member States of the African Intellectual Property Organization (OAPI) understood very early on the strategic importance of creating added value based on the origin of the product. As early as 1977, provisions on appellations of origin were introduced into the Agreement Establishing an African Intellectual Property Organization.

Building on this heritage, OAPI has been working to promote geographical indications as a tool for rural and artisanal development for several years. It is therefore with great pleasure that I welcome this excellent book on geographical indications in Africa.

The Member States of the OAPI, through various declarations (Ouagadougou and Abidjan) and accession to the Lisbon Agreement, have sparked the adoption of special initiatives such as the Project to Support the Implementation of Geographical Indications (PAMPIG[1]). The OAPI's accession to the Geneva Act of the Lisbon Agreement on Appellations of Origin is part of this impetus.

The recent accession to the Geneva Act by several African states reflects the desire to exploit geographical indications as a tool for economic development.

---

[1] Acronym for *Projet d'appui à la mise en place des indications géographiques dans les États membres de l'OAPI*.

The development of geographical indications is one of the areas of interest of the African Union, which has taken the initiative of the continental strategy, as the authors rightly note.

This book offers a great opportunity to understand how the geographical indications system works in Africa. Indeed, the authors have not merely provided a brief description of the system but also a critical analysis of the related legal framework.

Regarding the legal framework, it cannot be said that African countries have moved away from what is being done at the international level. In the absence of a tradition in the field of geographical indications, African OAPI member countries have aligned their legislation with existing models, including the French model, which has been highly influential. The first registrations of geographical indications in OAPI member states were, indeed, obtained with the support of French experts through the PAMPIG project.

Finally, I would like to thank and congratulate the authors, who are great practitioners of intellectual property law, for making available a book whose usefulness is evident. One may hope that, as awareness of the topic increases, the number of African geographical indications will rise, allowing African producers to benefit from the recognition they richly deserve.

Denis Bohoussou
Director General of the African Intellectual Property Organization

Preface

The adventure of writing this book was sparked by our love for Africa, the desire to guide owners of geographical indications (GIs) on the continent,—and this is no secret—our shared appreciation of good food and drink. The first driver behind this venture is our passion for Africa. Africa is a vibrant and dynamic continent, home to diverse cultures, traditions, agricultural areas, and natural resources. This has led to the creation of a wide variety of high-quality products, respectful of traditions and the local culture. Unfortunately, while consumers clamour for products with a true origin story, many farmers and producers in Africa are unable to tap into this demand. African farmers and producers are often relegated to raw material producers and seldom have the opportunity to export transformed and finished products, on which margins are higher. Even when finished products are exported and marketed internationally, farmers and producers may not be the ones benefiting economically from their labour. GIs and their numerous touted benefits, ranging from price premiums to the development of rural areas, the revitalization of agricultural communities, and the expansion of tourism, are one possible solution to the problems faced by African farmers and producers and, more broadly, rural communities. We thus sought to explore GIs from an African perspective, examining their possible advantages and benefits to African producers and farmers. Any mechanism adopted to protect African GIs must respect international and continental commitments while remaining suited to the local economic and developmental context.

The second reason behind this book is to help right holders of GIs in effectively protecting and enforcing their rights in Africa. Often, right holders are uncertain how to protect GIs and to combat counterfeits and other infringing products in Africa. This affects right owners who suffer from a reduction in their market share, and consequently their profits, and consumers who might be tricked into paying more for substandard and adulterated products. This book thus aims to set out the available protective mechanisms and enforcement remedies for GIs in the various African states.

Last but not least, the authors value high-quality products and the role of local products as portals into a country's culture. The unique food, drink, and handicraft of a country often reflect its unique history, lifestyles, and beliefs. Through these highly localized products, one is allowed a glimpse into long-held traditions.

How to use this book

This book is divided into two parts. The first part of the book, Part A, provides an introduction to GIs and the questions raised by their protection in three chapters. It is possible to read each chapter individually or all three chapters together to obtain a comprehensive overview of GIs in Africa. The second part of the book, Part B, covers eleven African countries and the two regional IP organizations. The chapters have been structured to be self-standing, and readers may consult only the particular chapter on the country of interest. The chapters in Part B all follow the same structure, allowing readers to find answers to the same questions across various jurisdictions quickly and easily. Thus, a comparative approach to the legislation, the registration procedure, and the enforcement mechanisms available is possible. This structure has been devised specifically to aid practitioners.

Acknowledgements

We would like to thank our families for their support in authoring this book.

We are deeply appreciative of our colleagues and friends who have taken the time to review the chapters and whose suggestions have enriched the book. All omissions and mistakes remain ours. Our thanks also to our friends and staff at Oxford University Press for their help and patience. Finally, we celebrate producers all over Africa, custodians of the cultural heritage and traditions of the continent. This book would not exist without them.

Contents

Table of Cases   xxi
Table of Legislation   xxiii

1. Introduction to Geographical Indications with a Focus on Africa   1
2. International Legal Framework for the Protection of Geographical Indications in Africa   19
3. Geographical Indications and Trade Marks   33
4. The African Regional Intellectual Property Organization   47
5. The African Intellectual Property Organization   55
6. Algeria   73
7. Angola   87
8. Botswana   97
9. Democratic Republic of the Congo   109
10. Egypt   117
11. Ethiopia   129
12. Kenya   141
13. Mauritius   159
14. Morocco   173
15. Nigeria   189
16. South Africa   201
17. Conclusion   227

Index   237

Detailed Contents

Table of Cases   xxi
Table of Legislation   xxiii

1. Introduction to Geographical Indications with a Focus on Africa   1
   1. Definition of GIs   8
   2. GIs and Development   10
   3. GIs and Traditional Knowledge   15

2. International Legal Framework for the Protection of Geographical Indications in Africa   19
   1. International Legal Framework for the Protection of GIs   19
   2. African Continental Initiatives for GIs   25
   3. Protection under Regional/Bilateral Trade Agreements   29

3. Geographical Indications and Trade Marks   33
   1. Conflict between Trade Marks and GIs   34
   2. GIs Considered as Generic in Other Countries   42
   3. Homonymous GIs   45
   4. Concluding Remarks   46

4. The African Regional Intellectual Property Organization   47
   1. Legislation on GIs   50
   2. Registration of GIs Domestically   51
   3. Looking Forwards   53

5. The African Intellectual Property Organization   55
   1. Legal Framework   57
   2. Regional Legislation on GIs   58
   3. Registration of GIs   59
      3.1 GIs   59
      3.2 Collective and certification marks   59
   4. Registrability of Names   60
      4.1 GIs   60
      4.2 Collective and certification marks   60
   5. Procedure and Requirements for Registration   61
      5.1 GIs   61
      5.2 Collective and certification marks   63
   6. Term of Protection   64
      6.1 GIs   64
      6.2 Collective and certification marks   65

- 7. Rights of the Owner and Enforcement Mechanisms against Infringers — 66
  - 7.1 GIs — 66
  - 7.2 Collective and certification marks — 67
- 8. Customs Enforcement — 70
- 9. Bilateral Agreements — 71

6. Algeria — 73
- 1. Legal Framework — 76
- 2. Domestic Legislation on GIs — 77
- 3. Registration of GIs Domestically — 77
  - 3.1 Appellations of origin — 77
  - 3.2 Collective marks — 78
- 4. Registrability of Names — 78
  - 4.1 Appellations of origin — 78
  - 4.2 Collective marks — 79
- 5. Procedure and Requirements for Registration — 79
  - 5.1 Appellations of origin — 79
  - 5.2 Collective marks — 81
- 6. Term of Protection — 81
  - 6.1 Appellations of origin — 81
  - 6.2 Collective marks — 82
- 7. Rights of the Owner and Enforcement Mechanisms against Infringers — 82
- 8. Customs Enforcement — 84
- 9. Bilateral Agreements — 85

7. Angola — 87
- 1. Legal Framework — 88
- 2. Domestic Legislation on GIs — 89
- 3. Registration of GIs Domestically — 90
- 4. Registrability of Names — 90
- 5. Procedure and Requirements for Registration — 91
- 6. Term of Protection — 93
- 7. Rights of the Owner and Enforcement Mechanisms against Infringers — 93
- 8. Customs Enforcement — 94
- 9. Bilateral Agreements — 95

8. Botswana — 97
- 1. Legal Framework — 98
- 2. Domestic Legislation on GIs — 99
- 3. Registration of GIs Domestically — 99
  - 3.1 GIs — 99
  - 3.2 Collective marks — 100
- 4. Registrability of Names — 100
  - 4.1 GIs — 100
  - 4.2 Collective marks — 100

5.	Procedure and Requirements for Registration	101
	5.1 GIs	101
	5.2 Collective marks	102
6.	Term of Protection	103
	6.1 GIs	103
	6.2 Collective marks	104
7.	Rights of the Owner and Enforcement Mechanisms against Infringers	104
	7.1 GIs	104
	7.2 Collective marks	105
	7.3 Unfair competition	106
8.	Customs Enforcement	107
9.	Bilateral Agreements	108

9. Democratic Republic of the Congo — 109

1.	Legal Framework	110
2.	Domestic Legislation on GIs	111
3.	Registration of GIs Domestically	111
	3.1 Appellations of origin and indications of source	111
	3.2 Collective marks	112
4.	Registrability of Names	113
5.	Procedure and Requirements for Registration	113
	5.1 Appellations of origin and indications of source	113
	5.2 Collective marks	113
6.	Term of Protection	114
	6.1 Appellations of origin and indications of source	114
	6.2 Collective marks	114
7.	Rights of the Owner and Enforcement Mechanisms against Infringers	115
	7.1 Appellations of origin and indications of source	115
	7.2 Collective marks	115
8.	Customs Enforcement	115
9.	Bilateral Agreements	116

10. Egypt — 117

1.	Legal Framework	118
2.	Domestic Legislation on GIs	119
3.	Registration of GIs Domestically	120
	3.1 GIs	120
	3.2 Collective and certification marks	120
4.	Registrability of Names	120
5.	Procedure and Requirements for Registration	121
	5.1 GIs	121
	5.2 Collective and certification marks	122
6.	Term of Protection	123
7.	Rights of the Owner and Enforcement Mechanisms against Infringers	123
	7.1 GIs	123
	7.2 Collective and certification marks	124

	8. Customs Enforcement	126
	9. Bilateral Agreements	127
11. Ethiopia		129
	1. Legal Framework	132
	2. Domestic Legislation on GIs	133
	3. Registration of GIs Domestically	134
	4. Registrability of Names	134
	5. Procedure and Requirements for Registration	135
	6. Term of Protection	137
	7. Rights of the Owner and Enforcement Mechanisms against Infringers	137
	8. Customs Enforcement	139
	9. Bilateral Agreements	140
12. Kenya		141
	1. Legal Framework	143
	2. Domestic Legislation on Geographical Indications (GIs)	144
	3. Registration of GIs Domestically	145
	4. Registrability of Names	146
	5. Procedure and Requirements for Registration	146
	6. Term of Protection	148
	7. Rights of the Owner and Enforcement Mechanisms against Infringers	149
	8. ACA Enforcement	157
	9. Bilateral Agreements	157
13. Mauritius		159
	1. Legal Framework	160
	2. Domestic Legislation on GIs	161
	3. Registration of GIs Domestically	161
	3.1 GIs	161
	3.2 Collective and certification marks	162
	4. Registrability of Names	162
	4.1 GIs	162
	4.2 Collective and certification marks	162
	5. Procedure and Requirements for Registration	163
	5.1 GIs	163
	5.2 Collective and certification marks	164
	6. Term of Protection	165
	6.1 GIs	165
	6.2 Collective and certification marks	166
	7. Rights of the Owner and Enforcement Mechanisms against Infringers	167
	8. Customs Enforcement	170
	9. Bilateral Agreements	171

14.	Morocco	173
	1. Legal Framework	175
	2. Domestic Legislation on GIs	176
	3. Registration of GIs Domestically	178
	3.1 GIs	178
	3.2 Collective and certification marks	178
	4. Registrability of Names	179
	4.1 GIs	179
	4.2 Collective and certification marks	179
	5. Procedure and Requirements for Registration	180
	5.1 GIs	180
	5.2 Collective and certification marks	182
	6. Term of Protection	182
	6.1 GIs	182
	6.2 Collective and certification marks	183
	7. Rights of the Owner and Enforcement Mechanisms against Infringers	183
	7.1 GIs	183
	7.2 Collective and certification marks	186
	8. Customs Enforcement	186
	9. Bilateral Agreements	187
15.	Nigeria	189
	1. Legal Framework	191
	2. Domestic Legislation on GIs	191
	3. Registration of GIs Domestically	193
	4. Registrability of Names	193
	5. Procedure and Requirements for Registration	193
	6. Term of Protection	196
	7. Rights of the Owner and Enforcement Mechanisms against Infringers	197
	8. Customs Enforcement	200
	9. Bilateral Agreements	200
16.	South Africa	201
	1. Legal Framework	203
	2. Domestic Legislation on GIs	204
	3. Registration of GIs Domestically	205
	3.1 Prohibited marks	205
	3.2 GIs and designations of origin	206
	3.3 Collective and certification marks	207
	4. Registrability of Names	208
	4.1 GIs and designations of origin	208
	4.2 Collective and certification marks	210
	5. Procedure and Requirements for Registration	210
	5.1 GIs and designations of origin	210
	5.2 Collective and certification marks	214

6. Term of Protection 217
    6.1 GIs and designations of origin 217
    6.2 Collective and certification marks 218
  7. Rights of the Owner and Enforcement Mechanisms against Infringers 218
  8. Customs Enforcement 223
  9. Bilateral Agreements 224

17. Conclusion 227

Index 237

Table of Cases

EUROPEAN UNION

Comité Interprofessionnel du Vin de Champagne v GB, Judgment, C-783/19,
  ECLI:EU:C:2021:713 36–37
*Consorzio per la tutela del formaggio Gorgonzola v Käserei Champignon
  Hofmeister GmbH & Co. KG and Eduard Bracharz GmbH.,* Judgment,
  C-87/97, ECLI:EU:C:1999:115 .... 36–37, 229
*Council of the European Union, Belgium (intervening) and ors (intervening) v
  Front populaire pour la libération de la saguia-el-hamra et du rio de oro
  (Front Polisario)* [2016], Case C-104/16 P 187
*Federal Republic of Germany, Kingdom of Denmark v Commission of the European
  Communities ('Feta II'),* Opinion of Advocate General Ruiz- Jarabo Colomer
  [2005] Joined cases C-465/02 and C-466/02, ECLI:EU:C:2005:636 1
*Federal Republic of Germany, Kingdom of Denmark v Commission of the European
  Communities ('Feta II'),* Judgment [2005] Joined cases C-465/02 and C-466/02,
  ECLI:EU:C:2005:636 42–43
Scotch Whisky Association v Michael Klotz, Judgment, C-44/17, ECLI:EU:C:2018:415 36
*Syndicat interprofessionnel de défense du fromage Morbier v Société Fromagère
  du Livradois,* Case C-490/19, ECLI:EU:C:2020:1043 227
*Windsurfing Chiemsee Produktions-und Vertriebs GmbH v Boots-und Segelzubehor
  Walter Huber and Franz Attenberger* [1999] ETMR 585 207

NATIONAL JURISDICTIONS

Kenya

*Agricultural And Processed Food Products Export Development Authority (APEDA)
  V. Krish Commodities Limited* (No.338 of 2013) High Court of Kenya 148

Mauritius

Beau Bebe v Comanu Ltee And Pharmacie Nouvelle Ltee (2003) SCJ 208 169
Unilever Plc v Manufrance (Ile Maurice) Ltee (2003) SCJ 167 169

Nigeria

Banire v. NTA-Star TV Network Ltd [2021] LPELR-52824 (CA) 198
Beech Group Limited v Esdee Food Product Nigeria Limited [1999] FHCLR 477 198
Fan Milk International A/S v Mandarin Oriental Services B.V
  (Suit No FHC/ABJ/CS/791/2020) 19, 191
Fan Milk Inter-national A/S v Mandarin Oriental Services B.V
  (Suit No FHC/ABJ/CS/792/2020) 19, 191
Procter and Gamble Company v Global Soap and Detergent Industries Limited
  (2012) LPELR-8014(CA) 191

South Africa

Century City Apartment Property Services CC and Another v Century City Property Proprietors' Association 2010 (3) SA 1 (SCA) 207
Long John International Ltd v Stellenbosch Wine Trust (PTY) Ltd and others 1990 (4) SA 136. 221
Milestone Beverage CC and Others v The Scotch Whisky Association and Others (1037/2019) [2020] ZASCA 105. 222
Tie Rack plc v Tie Rack Stores (Pty) Ltd & Another, 1989 (4) SA 427 (T) 221–22

United States

Interprofession du Gruyère et al. v. U.S. Dairy Export Council et al., Civil Action No. 1:20-cv-1174 (E.D. Va. December 15, 2021) 3–4

WORLD TRADE ORGANIZATION PANEL

Australia - Certain Measures Concerning Trademarks, Geographical Indications and Other Plain Packaging Requirements Applicable to Tobacco Products and Packaging – Report of the Panels, WT/DS435/R; WT/DS441/R; WT/DS458/R; WT/DS467/R (28 June 2018) 35
European Communities - Protection of Trademarks and Geographical Indications for Agricultural Products and Foodstuffs - Complaint by Australia - Report of the Panel, WT/DS290/R (15 March 2005). 34–35, 38–39
European Communities - Protection of Trademarks and Geographical Indications for Agricultural Products and Foodstuffs - Complaint by the United States - Report of the Panel, WT/DS174/R (15 March 2005) 34–35, 37–39

Table of Legislation

INTERNATIONAL TREATIES AND CONVENTIONS

Acte de Bamako (2015) 55, 58, 70–71
Agreement Establishing an African
   Intellectual Property Organization
   1977 (ARIPO)................vii, 47
   Art 2........................48–49, 57
   Art 2(i)...........................57
   Art 2(4) 57–58
   Art 7(1) 47–48
   Art 10............................49
   Art 18............................58
Arusha Protocol for the Protection of
   New Varieties of Plants 47–48
Banjul Protocol *see* Banjul Protocol
   on Marks
Harare Protocol.................47–48
Swakopmund Protocol on Protection
   of Traditional Knowledge and
   Expressions of Folklore Harare
Agreement of Bangui 1977 (OAPI),
   amended 1999 and 2015 ....25, 50, 55
   Annex I (patents) 55
   Annex II (utility models)............55
   Annex III (marks)..........55, 59–60,
                                67–68, 70
   Art 2............................64
   Art 2(2) 59–60
   Art 2(3) 59–60
   Art 3..........................60, 64
   Art 6............................67
   Art 41..........................65–66
   Art 45(1) 65–66
   Art 49 I..........................67
   Art 50(1) 67–68
   Art 50(2) 67–68
   Art 50(5) 67–68
   Art 51............................68
   Art 52............................68
   Art 53............................68
   Art 54..........................68–69
   Art 55..........................68–69
   Art 56............................69
   Art 57 I..........................70
   Art 59............................70
   Art 60............................70
   Art 62.1 70
   Art 63............................70
   Annex IV (industrial designs)..........55
   Annex V (commercial names) 55
   Annex VI (geographical
     indications) ....viii, 55, 59, 67
   Art 1..........................59, 61
   Art 2............................59
   Art 3(1) 60
   Art 3(2) 60
   Art 3(3) 71
   Art 4............................59
   Art 5............................65
   Art 6(2) 66
   Art 6(3) 66
   Art 6(5) 65
   Art 8............................62
   Art 20(1) 66
   Art 21(1) 65
   Art 22(2) 67
   Art 22(4) 67
   Art 23............................67
   Annex VII (literary and artistic
     rights)..........................55
   Annex X (plant variety rights)..........55

REGULATION RELATING TO USE AND MANAGEMENT OF PGI LOGO OF OAPI

Arts 3 and 21 66
Agreement on the Creation of the
   Industrial Property Organization for
   English-Speaking
   Africa (1976) (Lusaka
   Agreement).................47–48
Agreement on Trade-Related
   Aspects of Intellectual
   Property Rights (1994) 3–4, 9–10,
                     19, 21–22, 28, 29–30,
                     32, 35, 39, 42–43, 46,
                     58–59, 66, 77, 89, 99, 111,
                     116, 119, 133, 138, 144–45,
                     161, 176, 187–88, 191, 221,
                     224–25, 227–28, 232

xxiv TABLE OF LEGISLATION

Art 3 . . . . .21–22, 111
Art 4 . . . . .21–22, 111
Art 5 . . . . .21–22, 111
Art 16(1) 38–39
Art 17 38–39
Arts 22–24 . . . . .22, 30–31
Art 22 . . . . 22-24, 33, 99–100, 144–45
Art 22(1) 9, 22, 59, 78, 112,
  144–45, 161, 178
Art 22(2) 22–23
Art 22(2)(b). 35, 94
Art 22(3) 23, 34–35, 103–4
Art 22(4) 23–24, 45
Art 22(7) 23
Art 23 . . . . 23–24, 144–45, 192
Art 23(1) 23–24, 94
Art 23(2) 23–24, 34–35
Art 23(3) 23–24, 45, 165
Art 23(4) 23–24, 65, 165–66
Art 24 . . . . .23–24, 144
Art 24(1) 24
Art 24(3) 24, 38–39
Art 24(4) 24, 34–35, 103
Art 24(5) 24, 34–35, 37, 38,
  60, 65, 121
Art 24(6) 24, 42, 44, 162
Art 24(8) 24
Art 24(9) 24
Art 50 138
ARIPO *see* Agreement Establishing
  an African Intellectual Property
  Organization
Banjul Protocol on Marks 47–48,
  50–52, 99
  s 5*bis*(1) 51–52
  s 6*bis*(2) 52
  s 8(1). 52
General Agreement on
  Tariffs and Trade. 37–38
Geneva Act of the Lisbon Agreement
  on Appellations of Origin and
  Geographical Indications
  (2015). . . . . vii, 21, 58–59,
  62, 71, 77
Lisbon Agreement for the Protection of
  Appellations of Origin and their
  International Registration
  (1958). . . . . vii, 8–9, 20–21,
  39, 42–43, 44–45,
  55, 58–59, 76, 77, 79,
  80, 89, 99, 111, 119, 133,
  144, 161, 176, 191, 204, 227–28

Art 2 78
Art 2(1) 8–9
Art 3 20–21
Art 5 20–21
Art 5(3) 39
Art 6 44–45
Lusaka Agreement *see* Agreement on the
  Creation of the Industrial Property
  Organization for English-Speaking
  Africa (1976)

MADRID AGREEMENT FOR
THE REPRESSION OF FALSE OR
DECEPTIVE INDICATIONS OF
SOURCE ON GOODS

1891 (amended 26 April 1970) . . .8–9, 20,
  42–43, 77, 89, 99,
  111, 119, 133, 144, 161,
  191, 204, 227, 230–31
Art 1 20
Art 1(1) 8–9, 20
Art 4 44
Madrid Protocol for the International
  Registration of Trade Marks 2007
  (Madrid System). . . . 58–59, 71, 77, 89,
  144, 146, 161,
  176, 230–31
Marrakesh Agreement Establishing the
  World Trade Organization (1994)
  Annex 1C. 3
OAPI *see* African Intellectual Property
  Organization (OAPI)
Paris Convention for the Protection of
  Industrial Property 1883 (amended
  28 September
  1979) 19, 20–22, 42–43, 58–59,
  77, 89, 99, 111–12, 119,
  133, 144, 161, 176, 191, 204, 221
Art 1(2) 8–9
Art 10 8–9
Art 10*bis*. 22–23, 35
Art 10*bis*(2) 35
Art 10*bis*(3)(iii). 22–23, 35

ECONOMIC PARTNERSHIP
AGREEMENTS (EPAS)

African, Caribbean, and Pacific
  (ACP)–EU Partnership
  Agreement 2000 (Cotonou
  Agreement) 29–31
Art 46(1) 29–30

African, Caribbean, and Pacific
 (ACP)–EU Partnership
 Agreement (2023) 29–31
 Art 12(4) 29–30
East African Community (EAC)–
 EU EPA (2014) 31
 Art 3...........................31
 Art 89(d)(ii)......................31
EU Economic Partnership
 Agreement with the
 Cariforum nations 29
EU–Egypt Association Agreement
 (2004)........................127
 Art 23(1) 127
EU–Mauritius, Madagascar, Seychelles,
 and Zimbabwe (2009) 171
EU–Morocco (2015) 187
EU–South Africa on Trade in
 Wine (1999) 224–25
EU–Southern African Development
 Community (SADC)
 EPA (2016) 30–31, 108,
                             204–5, 225, 226
 Art 16........................30–31
 Art 16(3) 30–31
 Art 16(4) 30–31
 Protocol 3 South Africa-EU 30–32

FREE TRADE AGREEMENTS AND AREAS

African Continental Free Trade
 Area Agreement 2019
 (AfCFTA) 27, 28, 233
 Protocol on Intellectual Property.....28
EU–Republic of Korea Free Trade
 Agreement (2009) 29
EU–Vietnam Free Trade
 Agreement....................31–32
US–Morocco Free Trade Agreement
 (2004)............ 32, 39–40, 187–88
 Art 15.2(4).................32, 187–88
 Art 15.3(1).................32, 187–88
 Art 15.3(2).......... 32, 39–40, 187–88

EU legislation

Council Regulation (EEC) No 2081/92
 of 14 July 1992 on the protection
 of geographical indications and
 designations of origin for
 agricultural products
 and foodstuffs 4–6, 37–39

Art 14(2) 37–38, 39
Art 14(3) 37–39
Council Regulation (EC) No 510/2006
 of 20 March 2006 on the protection
 of geographical indications
 and designations of origin for
 agricultural products and
 foodstuffs................39, 85, 227
 Art 14(2) 39
Regulation (EU) No 1151/2012 of the
 European Parliament and of the
 Council of 21 November 2012 on
 quality schemes for agricultural
 products and foodstuffs
 [2012]...................... 4–6,
                              35–36, 227
 Art 5(1) 4–6
 Art 5(2) 4–6
 Art 6(4) 40–41
 Art 13(1)(a)....................36
 Art 13(2) 44–45
 Art 14(1) 40–41
 Art 14(2) 40–41
 Art 41(2) 42–43
Regulation (EU) No 1308/2013 of the
 European Parliament and of the
 Council of 17 December 2013
 establishing a common organisation
 of the markets in agricultural
 products [2013]
 Art 103(2)(a).....................36
Regulation (EU) 2017/1001 of the
 European Parliament and of the
 Council of 14 June 2017 on the
 European Union trade mark [2017]
 Art 3..........................4–6
Regulation (EU) 2019/787 of the European
 Parliament and of the Council of
 17 April 2019 on the definition,
 description, presentation, and labelling
 of spirit drinks, the use of the names
 of spirit drinks in the presentation
 and labelling of other foodstuffs, the
 protection of geographical indications
 for spirit drinks, the use of ethyl
 alcohol and distillates of agricultural
 origin in alcoholic beverages, and
 repealing Regulation (EC) No 110/
 2008
 Art 21(3) 44–45
 Art 35(2) 40–41
 Art 36(1) 40–41
 Art 36(2) 40–41

NATIONAL LEGISLATION

Algeria

Customs Code on the importation of counterfeit goods
  Art 22 84
Decree regarding procedures for registration and publication of appellations of origin and establishing fees No 76–121, 16 July 1976 77
Decree fixing the system of quality of agricultural products or products of agricultural origin No 13–260, 7 July 2013 .... 77, 78, 80–81
  Art 2 78
  Art 5 80–81
  Art 28 80–81
Law 8–16 on agricultural orientation, 3 August 2008 77
Order of 5 May 2016 laying down the rules relating to the procedure for recognition of Appellations of origin, geographical indications, and quality agricultural labels
  Art 2 80–81
  Art 4 80–81
  Art 19 80–81
Ordinance of 4 Joumada El Oula 1423 corresponding to 15 July 2002 on the application of Article 22 of the Customs Code on the importation of counterfeit goods
  Art 2 84
Ordinance regarding procedures for the registration and publication of appellations of origin no 76–65, 16 July 1976 ...... 77, 78, 79, 80, 82, 83
  Art 1 77
  Art 3 79
  Art 4 .... 79, 82
  Art 6 77
  Art 7 .... 79, 80
  Art 7(9) 79
  Art 21 83
  Art 23 82
  Art 28 83
  Art 30 83
Ordinance regarding the protection of marks No 03–06, 19, July 2003 .... 77, 78
  Art 2 78
  Art 23 81

  Art 25 82
  Art 26 83
  Art 32 83

Angola

Code of Administrative Procedure approved by Law No 31/22 of 30 August 2022. 89
Code of Contentious Administrative Procedure approved by Law No 33/22 of 1 September 2022 89
Customs Code. 94–95
  Art 19(1)(p) 94–95
  Art 71(1)-(3) 94–95
Industrial Property Code of 1940 89
Law No 9/89 (Law on Crimes against the Economy) 94
Law No 3/92 of 28 February 1992 on Industrial Property Law 89, 90, 94–95
  Art 30 91
  Art 30(1) 90
  Art 30(30) 90
  Art 31(2) 91
  Art 35 .... 90, 92
  Art 61(1) 90
  Art 62 90
  Art 70 93
  Art 73 94
  Art 77 94
Law No 29/22 of 29 August 2022, the 'Organic Law on the Organization and Functioning of The Courts of Common Jurisdiction 88
  Art 10 88–89
Penal Code
  Art 46 94
  Art 448 94
Resolution No 2/21 of the Judiciary Superior Council, published on 4 March 2021. 88–89

Botswana

Industrial Property Act No 8 of 2010 99
  s 2 99–100
  s 74 99
  s 74(1)(d) 99
  s 74(2) 100–1
  s 75 103
  s 81(1) 105
  s 81(2) 106

s 81(2)........................106
s 82..........................228
s 82(1)(d)..................103, 106
s 83(5).......................106
s 90.........................102–3
s 90(1)........................99
s 91(1).......................104
s 105.........................103
s 106(2).............100, 102, 103–4
s 108(2)......................102
s 110(1)......................102
s 111(1)......................104
s 111(3)......................105
s 112.........................103
s 113(1).....................103–4
s 114(1).....................106–7
s 114(3)......................107
s 134(4)......................105
s 134(5).....................106–7

Industrial Property
Regulations 2012
   s 53........................102

Democratic Republic of Congo

Code of Commerce 115
Customs Code..................115–16
   Art 77....................115–16
   Art 78(2) 116
   Art 82....................115–16
Law No 82– 001 of January 1982 on
   Industrial Property........111, 114
   Art 3.....................111–12
   Art 24(2) 113
   Arts 101–5..................111
   Art 133.2 100
   Art 140...................113–14
   Art 141.....................112
   Art 142...................113–14
   Art 147.....................114
   Art 148.....................115
   Art 149.....................114
   Art 151.....................114
   Art 161..................113, 115
   Art 159.....................112
Ordinance Law No 41/ 63 of
   24 February, 1950 regulating
   unfair competition............115
Penal Code 115

Egypt

Decree No 770/ 2005, art. 28 126

Law No 82 of 2002 pertaining to
   the Protection of Intellectual
   Property Rights............119, 124
   Art 67(8) 120–21
   Art 69......................120
   Art 70......................120
   Art 90......................123
   Art 104...................119–20
   Art 105.....................121
   Art 108...................120–21
   Art 110..............120–21, 122
   Art 111.....................121
   Art 112.....................124
   Art 113.....................124
   Art 114.....................123

Unfair Competition Law
   Art 66......................125

ETHIOPIA

Civil Code
   Art 2057....................139
Constitution of Ethiopia (1994) 133–34
Criminal Code 139
   Art 720.....................139
Trade Competition and Consumers
   Protection Proclamation
   (Proclamation
   No 813/ 2013)..............138–39
   Art 8.....................138–39
   Art 8(1) 138–39
   Art 8(2)(e)................138–39
   Art 14(1) 138–39
   Art 22....................138–39
   Art 22(1) 138–39
   Art 22(15) 138–39
Trademark Registration and Protection
   Proclamation 501/2006 133–34,
                                    138, 139
   Art 2(1) 134
   Art 2(12) 134
   Art 6(1)(e).................134
   Art 6(1)(g).................136
   Art 6(2) 134–35
   Art 18(1) 135
   Art 18(2) 134
   Art 18(3) 135
   Art 18(4) 137
   Art 20(1) 137
   Art 20(2) 137

Art 26 138
Art 30(3) 137
Art 39 138
Art 39(1) 138
Art 39(2) 138
Art 41(1) 139
Art 41(2) 139
Art 42(1) 139–40
Art 42(2) 139–40

Kenya
Anti Counterfeit Authority
s 2 153
s 32 .... 153, 154–55
s 33(1) 153
s 35(1) 154–55
s 35(3) 154–55
s 35(5) 154–55
Competition Act 156–57
s 55(b)(iii) 156–57
Penal Code 155, 156
s 380 156
s 381(1) 156
  Trade Descriptions Act
s 7(1)(a) 156
s 9(1)(e) 156
s 15 156
Trade Marks Act (2002) 144–45, 156
s 5 153
s 7(1) 150
s 12(d) 146
s 21(2) 148
s 40 145
s 40(2) 147
s 40(3) 150
s 40(4) 150
s 40(5)(a) 150–51
s 40(5)(b) 150–51
s 40(6) 151
s 40(7) 146–47, 148
s 40A 145
s 40A(2) 147
s 40A(4) 148
s 40A(5) 146
s 58B(1) 152
s 58B(3) 152
s 58B(4) 152
s 58C 152
s 58D(1) 153
s 58E(1) 153
s 58G 151
s 58H(1) 153

First Schedule
s 1(1) 147
s 4(1) 149
Weight and
  Measures Act 156
Trade Marks Rules
Rule 39 146–47
Rule 40 148

Mauritius
Civil Code
Art 1382 168
Art 1383 168
Courts Act ....
S 74 168–69
District and Intermediate Courts
  (Civil Jurisdiction) Act 168–69
Industrial Property
  Act (2019) 161, 170
s 2 .... 161, 162
s 91(2)(b) 162
s 91(2)(f) 162
s 98(1) 167–68
s 98(3) 168
s 101(5) 167
s 102(5) 167
s 105 166
s 105(1) 165
s 105(2) 162
s 106 166
s 106(3) 163
s 108(1) 164
s 109 167–68
s 110(1) 165
s 110(1)(a) 167–68
s 110(2) 165–66
s 111 165
s 112(1) 166
s 113 166
s 137 167–68
s 139 167–68
Patent Industrial Designs and
  Trademark Act 2002 170
Protection against Unfair
  Practices (Industrial Property
  Rights) Act 168, 170
Rules and regulations
IPA Regulations by Government
  Notice No 36 of 2022 161
  reg 109s 165
Supreme Court
  Rules 2000 168–69

Morocco

Decree No 2.75.321 of 12 August 1977 regulating wine- making and the stocking, circulation, and trading of wines 176–77
   Art 19(3) 176–77
Law No 13–83 on the repression of fraud in goods 185
   Art 1 185
   Art 4 185
Decree No 1955–98 of 8 October 1998 relating to the general conditions of production of controlled designation of origin 176–77
Law No 17–97 as amended and completed by Law Nos 23–13 and 3–05 .... 176, 177, 178, 179, 180, 181, 183, 184, 185
   Art 133(a) 179–80
   Art 134........................179–80
   Art 135(c) 181
   Art 137(d) 181
   Art 161..........................183
   Art 166........................178–79
   Art 170..........................182
   Art 180.......................178, 179
   Art 181.......................178, 179
   Art 182..........................183
   Art 184..........................183
   Art 202.......................183–84
   Art 203..........................184
   Art 231..........................185
Law No 25–06, related to distinctive signs of origin and quality of food and agricultural and fish products 176, 178, 179, 180, 181–82, 185
   Art 2 178
   Art 8 180
   Art 9 180
   Art 12 181
   Art 16 176
   Art 24 179
   Art 33 182
   Art 37 185
   Art 38 185
Law No 133–12 relating to the Distinctive Signs of Handicraft Products promulgated by the Dahir of 27 April 2016....... 174–75, 177, 178
   Art 3 177
   Art 6 181–82
   Art 9 179
   Art 11 181–82

Law on Industrial Property
   Art 176.4 186
Order No 869–75 of the Minister of Agriculture and Agrarian Reform regulating the designation of origin regime for wines of 15 August 1977 176–77

Nigeria

Constitution of the Federal Republic of Nigeria (1999)
   s 12 191
Merchandise Marks Act Cap M10 Laws of the Federation of Nigeria 2004 ....198, 199
   s 2(1)............................199
   s 3(1)............................199
   s 3(2)............................199
   s 3(3)............................199
   s 4..............................199
National Agency for Food and Drug Administration and Control Act 1993 (as Amended) Spirit Drinks Regulations 2019......192
   Art 5(1) 192
National Agency for Food and Drug Administration and Control Act 1993 (as Amended) Wine Regulations 2019 ....192, 200
Trade Malpractices (Miscellaneous Offences) Act 198, 200
   s 1(a)............................200
Trademarks Act of the Federal Republic of Nigeria 1990 .....192, 198
   s 3 198
   s 9(1)(d).........................193
   s 31(2)(a) 196
   s 31(2)(b) 196
   s 34(5)..........................196
   s 43(1)..........................193
   s 43(3)..........................197
   s 43(4)..........................197
   s 43(5)..........................198
   s 43(6)..........................198
   s 60 198
   s 61 198
   s 67(1)..........................193
First Schedule
   s 3(1).......................196–97

Trademarks Regulations

    reg 42 193–94

South Africa

Adjustment of Fines Act No 101 of
    1991 221
Agricultural Product
    Standards Act
    No 119 of 1990 . . . . 202–3, 204–5,
                                        211, 218–19
    s 3(1)(a) 218–19
    s 11(2). 221
    s 11(2)(a) and (b) 218–19
    s 6. 218–19
    s 6A. 218–19
Consumer Protection Act 221
    s 29(b)(i) 221
Counterfeit Goods Act No 37 of
    1997 224
Foodstuffs, Cosmetics and
    Disinfects Act No 54 of
    1972 219–20
Liquor Products Act No 60
    of 1989 . . . . 202–3, 204, 205, 222
    S 12. 222
    s 12(1). 222
    s 13A. 205
    s 13A(2) 205
Merchandise Marks Act
    No 17 of 1941 . . . . .202–3, 204, 221
    s 1 221
    s 15 . . . . 202–3, 204, 205–6, 221, 223
    s 15(3). 221
Protection, Promotion, Development
    and Management of Indigenous
    Knowledge Act No 6 of
    2019 . . . . 204, 205
Trade Marks Act No 194 of
    1993 . . . . 202–3, 204, 205, 207,
                                        210, 222, 223
    s 9. . . . . .210, 215
    s 10 . . . . .210, 215
    s 10(2). 207
    s 10(13). 207
    s 21 216
    s 34(1). 223
    s 34(2). 223
    s 34(3). 223
    s 36 223
    s 42(1). 207–8
    s 43(1). 208
    s 59(2). 216

Regulations

Agricultural Products Standard Act:
    Regulations: Protection of
    geographical indications used on
    agricultural products intended
    for sale in South Africa.
    No R447 of 2019 . . . . . 204–5, 206, 208,
                                210–11, 214, 217, 221
    reg 1 206
    reg 2(1). 206
    reg 3(1). 219–20
    reg 3(2). 219–20
    reg 3(2)(a)(iv) 219–20
    reg 4(1). 209, 210–11
    reg 4(1)(e) 209
    reg 4(1)(f) 209
    reg 4(2). 211
    reg 4(4). 211–12
    reg 4(5). 211–12
    reg 4(6). 211–12
    reg 6(1). 210–11
    reg 6(2). 212
    reg 6(2)(a) 211
    reg 6(3). 212
    reg 7(1). 214
    reg 7(2). 217–18
    reg 7(3). 214
    reg 8 212
    reg 9 212–13
    reg 10 213
    reg 11(1). 213
    reg 11(3)-(5) 213–14
    reg 13(2). 214
    reg 14(3). 217
    reg 15(1). 217
    reg 15(2). 217–18
    reg 15(4). 217
    reg 15(5). 218
    reg 16(1). 217
    reg 16(3). 217
    reg 17(1). 219–20
    reg 18(4). 207
    reg 19 219–20
    reg 20(1). 220
    reg 20(2). 218
    reg 21 221
    reg 21(6). 220

United States

Lanham (Trade Mark) Act of 1946, 15 USC
    ss 1051 *et seq* 6–7
    s 1052(e)(2) 6–7

1
Introduction to Geographical Indications with a Focus on Africa

Africa may well be the birthplace of brands and geographical indications (GIs). As far back as Ancient Egypt, the provenance of goods was indicated on certain products. The ancient Egyptians are believed to be the inventors of wine labels. From 1770 to 1550 BC, Egypt dominated the wine trade, introducing standardized amphorae and protective seals to allow wine to travel better. Standardized containers, however, made it difficult to distinguish between wines, leading the ancient Egyptians to adopt a labelling system, indicating the place of production, the vintage, the producer's name, and the style of the wine.[1] This is the origin story of linking products, craftsmanship, and a place of provenance.

Over the centuries, the linking of specific commodities with unique characteristics to their place of origin grew unabated. The cedars of Lebanon and gold from Ophirare are mentioned in the Old Testament as denominations of quality goods originating from a locality. Classical Greek authors also referenced Corinthian bronze and Carrara marble as prestigious goods originating from a particular region.[2] In the Middle Ages, guild members used the mark of the guild to show that products were crafted in respect of specific requirements, which, in turn, indirectly safeguarded the place of production. In certain instances, the sign was constituted of the initial of the town's name or its coat of arms. Even after guilds were abolished, rules promoting the specialities of certain areas, such as soap from Marseille, steel from Westphalia and the Rhineland, and forges from Austria, remained.[3] The English language is itself proof of this link between origin and product: Damask cloth from Damascus, denim cloth from Nîmes (contraction of the French term 'de Nîmes'), and currants from Corinth are now household words for these products.[4]

Africa is intertwined with the birth of the French *Appellation d'origine contrôlée* (AOC). An AOC is a product whose main production steps occur within a defined geographical area, which gives the product its characteristics and whose production

---

[1] Adam Teeter, 'The First Wine Label Was Invented in Egypt' (*VinePair*, 14 March 2016) <https://vinepair.com/wine-blog/the-first-wine-label-was-invented-in-egypt> accessed 16 August 2023.
[2] Joined cases C-465/02 and C-466/02 *Federal Republic of Germany and Kingdom of Denmark v Commission of the European Communities*, Opinion of Advocate General Ruiz-Jarabo Colomer [2005] ECLI:EU:C:2005:276, para 5.
[3] ibid paras 7–9.
[4] Roderick Thirkell White, 'Locus Classicus: Origin Brands in Roman Luxury Markets, c. 100 BC–c. AD 130' (PhD thesis, University College London 2017) 52.

follows a well-established technique. The French AOC helped shape the current European policy on GIs. In the first half of the nineteenth century, France started to take measures to prevent consumers from being misled as to the origin of natural and manufactured products, particularly in the wine sector. In 1855, the first classification of *cru* in the sense of an area or plot of land exhibiting typical characteristics was published in France on the occasion of the *Exposition Universelle* of 1855. In the late nineteenth century, France faced a phylloxera plague, which destroyed French wine production and led to an increase in the domestic demand for wine from Italy and Spain. The French government promoted wine produced in Algeria, then a French colony, to combat the influx of foreign wine. As a result, Algeria soon became one of the largest wine producers in the world. However, Algeria's success turned sour for French wine makers when French wine production picked up again. French wine producers perceived cheaper Algerian wines and adulterated wines as unfair competition and demanded quality regulations, including a label clearly stating the origin of the grapes. In 1905, France thus enacted its first appellation law, separating wine regions by geography, grape type, and the process of making wine. In so doing, the law reinforced the notion of *terroir* whereby natural factors such as the soil, the climate, the topography, and traditional techniques impact the style and taste of wine.[5] *Terroir* highlights the link between the essential characteristics of the land and the qualities of the product. Over the next few decades, regional boundaries were drawn up; referred to as appellations, they were codified into the modern AOC system in 1935.[6]

Whether in relation to wine or other products, local producers have always sought protection from, and exclusion of, perceived lower-quality copies of their products. AOCs came into existence because French wine producers lobbied the government to protect their interests. With the emergence of globalization allowing for the easy movement of people and goods across borders, the sharing of knowledge, and production at lower costs in other countries, these issues have only gained in importance. Local production techniques and recipes have been taken abroad by migrants leaving Europe for the 'New World'. More recently, manufacturers from emerging economies, essentially in Asia, have started the production of spirits, wines, and other food products reflecting an occidental lifestyle increasingly adopted by local consumers. As a result, producers from certain areas are more than ever keen to collectively protect their products, know-how, and acquired reputation. GIs are seen as a possible solution to keep such imitators, both domestic and foreign, from unfairly competing against high-quality local products. Thus grew the concept of the GI: a collective right belonging to a group of

---

[5] Digeso Joanne, 'The Beginning of French Wine Law in Champagne, Bordeaux and Southern France' (*SommWine*, 12 August 2020) <www.sommwine.com/beginning-of-french-wine-law>.

[6] Joshua Malin, 'Tipsy History: The Great Boom & the Epic Bust of the Algerian Wine Industry' (*VinePair*, 27 August 2014) <https://vinepair.com/wine-blog/tipsy-history-boom-bust-algerian-win>.

producers, protecting a name used for identifying and commercializing products with a specific geographical origin and possessing qualities or a reputation that are due to that origin. The right recognizes the link between the product's qualities, characteristics, or reputation and the place of origin.[7]

In recent years, GIs have come under the spotlight. This is due to their inclusion not only in the World Trade Organization (WTO) Agreement on Trade-Related Aspects of Intellectual Property Rights (TRIPS)[8] but also, at a multilateral level, in bilateral/plurilateral agreements such as free trade agreements (FTAs), and scholarly circles.

Discussions on GIs today emanate not only from Europe, which as the birthplace of the modern GI system was at the forefront of the negotiations for the inclusion of GIs in the TRIPS Agreement,[9] but also from other countries, including developing countries. Discussions, however, do not equate with agreement, and few areas of intellectual property rights are as controversial as GIs.

Contrary to what one might think, the inclusion of GIs in the TRIPS Agreement has yet to lead to a global consensus on how GIs should be protected. What is commonly agreed is that GIs must be protected against misleading and confusing use and unfair competition. How this happens, and the extent of such protection, remains open to debate. The two main positions are exemplified by Europe (often referred to as the 'Old World' in this context) and the United States (part of the so-called 'New World'). The divergent approaches of the European Union (EU) and the United States are one of the few areas of intellectual property (IP) where their policies openly collide.[10] Given its long history and the economic importance of GI products, which represent 15.5 per cent of EU food and beverage exports, [11] Europe has a keen interest in preserving the geographical names of its products (in particular, wine and cheese) and preventing the New World from freeriding on the reputation of those names and producing what Europe considers subpar replicas. European countries have chosen to protect GIs through a *sui generis* system that reflects the cultural, historical, and economic importance of GIs. With a *sui generis* system, it is possible to tailor provisions to best suit GIs, such as providing for the coexistence or priority of GIs over prior registered identical or similar trade marks

---

[7] World Trade Organization, 'Geographical indications' (*World Trade Organization*, nd) <www.wipo.int/geo_indications/en>.
[8] TRIPS: Agreement on Trade-Related Aspects of Intellectual Property Rights, 15 April 1994, Marrakesh Agreement Establishing the World Trade Organization, Annex 1C, 1869 UNTS 299, 33 ILM 1197 (1994) (TRIPS Agreement).
[9] Dwijen Rangnekar, 'The Socio-Economics of Geographical Indications, A Review of Empirical Evidence from Europe' (International Centre for Trade and Sustainable Development (ICTSD) and United Nations Conference on Trade and Development (UNCTAD) 2004) 15.
[10] Vicente Zafrilla Díaz-Marta and Anastasiia Kyrylenko, 'The Ever-Growing Scope of Geographical Indications' Evocation: From Gorgonzola to Morbier' (2021) 16(4–5) JIPLP 442.
[11] European Commission Directorate-General for Agriculture and Rural Development, 'Study on Economic Value of EU Quality Schemes, Geographical Indications (GIs) and Traditional Specialities Guaranteed (TSGs): Final Report' (2021) 18.

and protecting GIs in perpetuity from genericity. On the other hand, the United States and other New World countries, such as Australia, have long argued that GIs are an attempt to monopolize names that are now generic because they have been used for centuries in the New World by migrants from Europe.[12] The pre-existing trade mark system is favoured to avoid the creation of a double standard that would afford preferential rather than fair treatment to some to the detriment of others. The *Gruyère* case, decided in December 2021 before a Virginia court in the United States, is a good illustration of the position of both parties. Two professional groups representing cheese producers from Switzerland and France had applied to register the name *Gruyère*—registered as a GI in Switzerland[13] and the EU[14]—as a certification mark in the United States, one criterion being that *Gruyère* can only be applied to *Gruyère* cheese from the Gruyère region in Switzerland and France. The United States Patent and Trademark Office refused the application, leading to an appeal before the Virginia Court of Appeal. The Court of Appeal ruled that Gruyère, regardless of its location of production, has been labelled and sold as such in the United States. Customers understand Gruyère as a type of cheese. The Court concluded that the term is therefore 'generic to cheese purchasers in the United States'.[15]

One of the EU agricultural policy aims is to promote regional specialty foods in the EU and internationally.[16] To achieve this goal, in 1992, the EU enacted the EU Council Regulation on the Protection of Geographical Indications and Designations of Origin (Regulation No 2081/92).[17] This regulation provided for two types of GI designation: Protected Designation of Origin (PDO) and Protected Geographical Indication (PGI). Although Regulation No 2081/92 is no longer in force, the current Regulation No 1151/2012 retains a rather similar definition of these two GI designations.[18] The label 'PDO' identifies a product

---

[12] Irene Calboli, 'Geographical Indications between Trade, Development, Culture, and Marketing: Framing a Fair(er) System of Protection in the Global Economy?' in Irene Calboli and WeeLoon Ngloy (eds), *Geographical Indications at the Crossroads of Trade, Development, and Culture Read: Focus on Asia-Pacific* (CUP 2017) 8.

[13] In Switzerland, *Gruyère* was granted its Protected Designation of Origin (*Appellation d'origine contrôlée*) on 6 July 2001: 'Protected Designation of Origin (AOP)' (*Le Gruyère Switzerland AOP*, nd) <www.gruyere.com/en/le-gruyere-aop/protected-designation-of-origin-aop>.

[14] In the EU, *Gruyère* was granted a protected geographical indication in 2013: 'Un terroir, une histoire' (*Gruyere France*, nd) <www.gruyere-france.fr/un-terroir-une-histoire.html> and European Commission, 'eAmbrosia the EU Geographical Indications Register' (*European Commission*, nd) <https://ec.europa.eu/info/food-farming-fisheries/food-safety-and-quality/certification/quality-labels/geographical-indications-register/details/EUGI00000014024>.

[15] *Interprofession du Gruyère and others v US Dairy Export Council and others*, Civil Action No 1:20-cv-1174 (ED Va 15 December 2021) 15. Note that Swiss *Gruyère* is still protected as a certification mark in the United States under registration no 85118515 LE GRUYÈRE SWITZERLAND AOC.

[16] Christian Häberli, 'IP in EU Agriculture: Geographical Indications' (*European Centre for International Political Economy*, April 2022) <https://ecipe.org/blog/ip-in-eu-agriculture-geographical-indications>.

[17] Council Regulation (EEC) No 2081/92 of 14 July 1992 on the protection of geographical indications and designations of origin for agricultural products and foodstuffs [1992] OJ L 208 24 July 1992.

[18] Regulation (EU) No 1151/2012 of the European Parliament and of the Council of 21 November 2012 on quality schemes for agricultural products and foodstuffs [2012] OJ L 343 14 December 2012

complying with the following requirements: it originates in a specific place, region, or (exceptionally) country; its quality or characteristics are essentially or exclusively due to a particular geographical environment with its inherent natural and human factors; and all its production steps take place in the defined geographical area.[19] A PGI identifies a product that originates in a specific place, region, or country whose given quality, reputation, or other characteristic is essentially attributable to its geographical origin and where at least one of the production steps takes place in the defined geographical area.[20] PDOs are the products with the strongest links to their geographical origin, with the requirement that every part of the production, processing, and preparation process takes place in the designated area and its requirement for the quality or characteristics to be essentially or exclusively due to the geographic environment.[21] Reputation alone, which may be due to a long-standing history rather than a physical connection, is not a permissible ground for PDO registration. Surprisingly, although the requirements are more stringent for a PDO, there are more PDOs than PGIs registered in the EU.[22] Those GI designations are protected in perpetuity against existing and future trade marks. The *sui generis* GI system at Union level coexists with the availability of national and Union-wide trade mark registration, including certification[23] and collective marks.[24] Producer associations will often also protect their GIs as collective marks as it extends the scope of protection and simplifies enforcement and the extension of the protection into third countries. In addition, the GI system only protects a name. Hence, producer associations

---

(Quality Schemes Regulation). A political agreement was reached in October 2023 by the European Parliament and Council of the EU to reform the protection of agricultural products, wines and spirits through a single regulation that would replace all related existing regulations The political agreement must now be formally approved by the EU co-legislative bodies. European Innovation Council and SMEs Executive Agency, 'New Regulation on EU Geographical Indications for Wine, Spirit Drinks and Agricultural Products' (IP Helpdesk, 6 November 2023)
 https://intellectual-property-helpdesk.ec.europa.eu/news-events/news/new-regulation-eu-geographical-indications-wine-spirit-drinks-and-agricultural-products-2023-11-06_en.

[19] Quality Schemes Regulation (n 18), art 5(1).
[20] ibid art 5(2).
[21] Specific rules apply to wines granted a PGI or PDO. For wines granted a PDO, the grapes must come exclusively from the geographical area where the wine is made, whereas for a GI, at least 85 per cent of the grapes used have to come from the geographical area where the wine is actually made: European Commission, 'Geographical Indications and Quality Schemes Explained' (*European Commission*, nd) <https://agriculture.ec.europa.eu/farming/geographical-indications-and-quality-schemes/geographical-indications-and-quality-schemes-explained_en#pdo>.
[22] As of 14 June 2023, e-Ambrosia listed 1,943 PDOs against 1,602 PGIs registered by EU member states: European Commission, 'eAmbrosia the EU Geographical Indications Register' (n 14).
[23] In the EU, certification marks cannot certify origin: Regulation (EU) 2017/1001 of the European Parliament and of the Council of 14 June 2017 on the European Union trade mark [2017] OJ L 154, 16 June 2017, art 3.
[24] Names of craft and industrial products also benefit from GI-protection in the EU since the entry into force of the Regulation (EU) 2023/2411 on the protection of geographical indications for craft and industrial products on 16 November 2023.

using a figurative sign containing the GI must necessarily protect the device as a collective mark.[25]

The United States has adopted a different approach to protecting GIs through the certification mark as incorporated in US law by the Lanham (Trade Mark) Act of 1946.[26] A geographic word, name, symbol, or device, which otherwise would be considered primarily geographically descriptive, can be registered as a certification mark.[27] The certification mark is owned by one person, in the case of a GI often a legal person, but used by others, often producers, to certify the origin and main ingredients of the product. The owner may not use the mark but is required to monitor and control use of the mark by others effectively. Upon request, the certification mark owner must certify goods or services that satisfy the standards or conditions required under the mark. There are three types of certification mark indicating either: (a) regional or other origin; (b) material, mode of manufacture, quality, accuracy, or other characteristics of the goods/services; or (c) that a member of a union or other organization performed the work or labour on the goods/services. There is no government influence, but consumers trust the sign as a symbol of quality. Certification marks coexist, with federal statutes adopted by states to protect specific products. Some states have adopted laws that prescribe minimum standards for certain products, such as *Kona Coffee* in Hawaii and Indian River *Navel Oranges* in Florida. The Alcohol and Tobacco Tax and Trade Bureau oversees labelling requirements for wines, beers, and spirits. A defined domestic grape-growing region having a name, distinguishing features, and a delineated boundary may thus be protected as an American Viticultural Area. An appellation of origin is required under certain conditions on wine labels. These systems coexist with collective marks and the 'normal' trade mark regime. Geographic terms or signs are not registrable as trade marks if they are geographically descriptive or geographically mis-descriptive of the goods' origin. However, where a geographic sign is used in such a way as to identify the source of the goods/services, and, over time, consumers recognize it as identifying a source, the geographical sign can be protected as a collective mark or trade mark.[28] Finally, the United States recognizes the common law certification mark, which applies to unregistered designations that are understood as reliable indications of regional origin by purchasers and

---

[25] Alexander von Mühlendahl, 'Trade Marks and Geographical Indications Future Perspectives Collective Marks and Geographical Indications' (PowerPoint Presentation for the European Union Intellectual Property Office Trade Marks and Geographical Indications: Future Perspectives (Intermediate level) course) <https://euipo.europa.eu/knowledge/course/view.php?id=3342>.

[26] Lanham Act, 15 USC ss 1051 et seq.

[27] ibid s 1052(e)(2) exempts certification marks indicating regional origin from refusals based on geographic descriptiveness.

[28] United States Patent and Trademark Office (USPTO), 'Geographical Indication Protection in the United States' (*USPTO*, nd) <www.uspto.gov/sites/default/files/web/offices/dcom/olia/globalip/pdf/gi_system.pdf>.

that have been used substantially and exclusively in the United States for a significant time.[29]

The respective approaches of the EU and the United States are a good illustration of the divergent systems regarding the protection of GIs present in the world today. While the means of protection are widely (and, at times, bitterly) debated, there is consensus on the potential advantages derived from protecting products having a specific geographical origin and possessing qualities or a reputation due to that origin.. GIs have been promoted as the solution to rural devitalization, as being capable of preserving local heritage and traditional know-how while creating opportunities in trade, employment, and tourism.[30] GIs, by allowing consumers to buy locally produced products, minimize the carbon footprint of consumption. In fact, everyone seems to benefit from a GI: the producer can apply higher prices against cheap, high-volume production of agricultural goods, while the consumer benefits from a product satisfying minimum quality standards. A study published by the Food and Agriculture Organization of the United Nations found a price premium of more than 120 per cent for Cameroonian *Penja Pepper* and even 500 per cent for producers of *Taliouine Saffron* from Morocco.[31] It was estimated that, in 2017, the average value premium rate for GI products in the EU stood at 2.11 compared to a non-GI product.[32] It is therefore no wonder that the numerous benefits attached to GIs have attracted the attention of developing countries, including African countries, and much has already been written on how and why developing states should promote GIs domestically and the products that could benefit from a GI.[33] This book therefore neither dwells on the potential benefits of GIs for developing states nor on identifying potential candidates for GI protection. Instead, it looks at how GIs may be protected in Africa and the available enforcement mechanisms by studying the two main regional IP organizations in Africa: the African Intellectual Property Organization (OAPI, acronym for *Organisation Africaine de la Propriété Intellectuelle*) and the African Regional Intellectual Property Organization (ARIPO) as well as eleven other African states—Algeria, Angola, Botswana, the Democratic Republic of Congo, Egypt, Ethiopia, Kenya, Mauritius,

---

[29] USPTO, 'Geographical Indications' (*USPTO*, nd) <www.uspto.gov/ip-policy/trademark-policy/geographical-indications>.

[30] European Parliament, 'Motion for a European Parliament Resolution on the possible extension of geographical indication protection of the European Union to non-agricultural products' (2015/2053(INI)) para 2.

[31] Emilie Vandecandelaere and others, 'Strengthening Sustainable Food Systems through Geographical Indications: An Analysis of Economic Impacts' (Food and Agriculture Organization of the United Nations (FAO) 2018) 14.

[32] Directorate-General for Agriculture and Rural Development (n 11) 102.

[33] See, eg Michael Blakeney and others (eds), *Extending the Protection of Geographical Indications: Case Studies of Agricultural Products in Africa* (Routledge 2012); United Nations Conference on Trade and Development (UNCTAD), *The Case for Geographical Indication Protection of the Mozambique White Prawn* (UN 2022) and African Union Commission Department of Rural Economy and Agriculture, 'Continental Strategy for Geographical Indications in Africa 2018–2023' (African Commission Department of Rural Economy and Agriculture 2023).

Morocco, Nigeria, and South Africa. Of course, this is not intended as a slight on countries not reviewed in this book. Many other African countries have adopted laws and regulations concerning GIs, such as Ghana, Zimbabwe, and Uganda. Instead, the choice of countries was motivated by the need to represent all regions of the continent as well as cultural, legal, and linguistic diversity. In addition, in all eleven states chosen, there is a sizeable middle and/or upper class with the means to purchase GIs and other high-quality products. The economic growth in Africa and its rising middle and upper class is a reality: household consumption in Africa has increased faster than the continent's gross domestic product (GDP), which itself has consistently outpaced the global average. Consumer expenditure has grown at a compound annual rate of 3.9 per cent since 2010, from USD 1.4 trillion in 2015 to an expected USD 2.5 trillion by 2030.[34] If one adds in the importance of brand recognition and commercial origin to African buyers, the young and growing population, and rapid urbanization, there is no doubt that Africa presents exciting opportunities for high-value products on the continent. Even in low-income countries, there are pockets of wealth where domestic and foreign high-end goods are in demand. The demand for high-end goods is recognized by various economic actors that are either entering the continent or expanding their presence. Nowhere is it more visible than in the alcohol industry, where the prospects for growth brought about by increasing income and a growing demand for premium products have been highlighted by the major players. For example, *Irish Whiskey*, whose fifth largest export market is South Africa, has highlighted future growth in Africa, in particular East Africa.[35]

This chapter offers an introduction to GIs with a focus on Africa. It interrogates the link between GIs and development and traditional knowledge. Chapter 2 looks at the protection of GIs at the international, continental, and regional levels. Cognizant of the newcomer status of GIs, Chapter 3 looks at the conflicts between trade marks and GIs. Part B of the book deals with the regional and country chapters. Each country chapter examines how foreign and domestic GIs may be protected in the specific country: the registration system available, the registration requirements, and the enforcement mechanisms open to right holders.

1. Definition of GIs

In the simplest terms, GIs are distinctive signs that link the quality and reputation of a product to its place or area of production. In the legal sphere, various concepts

---

[34] Landry Signé, *Africa's Consumer Market Potential: Trends, Drivers, Opportunities, and Strategies* (Africa Growth Initiative at Brookings 2018) 1.
[35] Drinks Ireland Irish Business and Employers' Confederation (IBEC), 'Irish Whiskey Industry Targets Africa for Future Sales Growth' (*Drinks Ireland IBEC*, 3 March 2021) <www.ibec.ie/drinksirel and/news-insights-and-events/news/2021/03/03/irish-whiskey-industry-targets-africa>.

are used to describe and discuss GIs. In its treaties focused on GIs, the World Intellectual Property Organization (WIPO) uses the terms 'indications of source' and 'appellations of origin'. The term 'indications of source' is thus used in articles 1(2) and 10 of the Paris Convention for the Protection of Industrial Property of 1883 (Paris Convention)[36] and the Madrid Agreement for the Repression of False or Deceptive Indications of Source on Goods of 1891 (Madrid Agreement on Indications of Source).[37] Neither of these treaties defines the term 'indications of source', although a definition may be inferred from article 1(1) of the Madrid Agreement on Indications of Source.[38] An indication of source is an indication of origin to a country or part of a country, that is 'made in . . .'. There is no requirement for a special quality or characteristics.[39] The term 'appellation of origin' is defined in the Lisbon Agreement for the Protection of Appellations of Origin and their International Registration, of 1958[40] (Lisbon Agreement). An appellation of origin is the 'geographical name of a country, region, or locality, which serves to designate a product originating therein, the quality and characteristics of which are due exclusively or essentially to the geographical environment, including natural and human factors'.[41]

The TRIPS Agreement administered by the WTO uses the term 'geographical indication(s)', defined as identifying 'a good as originating in the territory of a member, or a region or locality in that territory, where a given quality, reputation or other characteristic of the good is essentially attributable to its geographical origin'.[42]

A comparison of the three terms shows that an indication of source is the most comprehensive concept, referring to the place of origin of the product without implying any specific quality. An indication of source cannot qualify as a GI under the TRIPS Agreement. There exist greater similarities between an appellation of origin and a GI, such as the requirement of quality and characteristics that are essentially attributable to the place of origin of the product. This requirement is highly reminiscent of the French concept of *terroir*, which has infused the discussions on GIs. Still, there are differences, with appellations of origin being more narrowly defined than GIs. The link to the place of origin must be stronger for an

---

[36] Paris Convention for the Protection of Industrial Property, as amended on 28 September 1979, entered into force on 3 June 1984, <https://wipolex.wipo.int/en/details.jsp?id=1263>.
[37] Madrid Agreement for the Repression of False or Deceptive Indications of Source on Goods, as amended on 26 April 1970, entered into force on 15 July 1892, <www.wipo.int/treaties/en/ip/madrid>.
[38] The article reads: 'All goods bearing a false or deceptive indication by which one of the countries to which this Agreement applies, or a place situated therein, is directly or indirectly of the said countries.'
[39] WIPO, 'Standing Committee on The Law of Trademarks, Industrial Designs and Geographical Indications Sixth Session' (12–16 March 2001) (WIPO, 'Sixth Session') para 4.
[40] Lisbon Agreement for the Protection of Appellations of Origin and their International Registration, as amended on 28 September 1979, entered into force on 5 November 1983, <www.wipo.int/wipolex/en/treaties/textdetails/12586>.
[41] ibid art 2(1).
[42] TRIPS Agreement (n 8) art 22(1).

appellation of origin than a GI. The quality or characteristics of a product protected as an appellation of origin must result exclusively or essentially from its geographical origin. Usually, this means that the production and processing must take place in the specific region. For a GI, it is sufficient for either quality, reputation, or other characteristics to be attributable to the geographical origin. The addition of reputation for a GI is also a differentiating factor. While appellations of origin are very much focused on the land providing these characteristics and quality, which lead to the reputational advantage, a GI may stem from a mere mental link between the product and its perceived quality, that is the reputation.[43] In summary, all appellations of origin are GIs, but some GIs are not appellations of origin.[44]

This book will use the term 'GI' as an umbrella term for the various legal mechanisms and terms used to identify a product's origin and the link between the particular characteristics of the product and its origin. Where terms such as appellation of origin, PDO, PGI, certification mark, or collective mark are used, these will reflect the use of the specific term in the relevant domestic law.

2. GIs and Development

While discussions are still ongoing at multilateral, bilateral, and domestic levels as to the most appropriate legal framework to protect high-quality origin products, consumers are showing an undeniable interest in such goods. Consumers, especially in developed countries, demand authentic and sustainable products and want to know 'the story behind the product'. GIs have the potential to respond to this demand. GIs are collective rights belonging to a group of producers in a given geographical area who craft their products in the respect of the product specification. GIs allow producers and producer communities to tell a story collectively, often highlighting generations-old traditions and illustrating the harmonious use of a region and its resources by humans. The collective nature of GI rights contributes to this discourse of authenticity, which consumers demand.[45] GIs also speak to the desire of consumers for sustainability. Producers of GIs cannot delocalize their production, unlike industry captains, who can look for the cheapest country to produce their commodities— and GI producers must carefully use local resources in order to preserve their production area. Africa is uniquely placed to take advantage of consumer interest in authentic and sustainable products. The rich history and diversity of agricultural areas, natural resources, and traditions has endowed

---

[43] Daniel Gervais, 'Traditional Innovation and the Ongoing Debate on the Protection of Geographical Indications' in Peter Drahos and Susy Frankel (eds), *Indigenous Peoples' Innovation: Intellectual Property Pathways to Development* (ANU Press 2012) 125.
[44] WIPO, 'Sixth Session' (n 38) para 7.
[45] Monique Bagal and others, *Manual for Geographical Indications in Africa* (2nd edn, European Union Intellectual Property Office 2023) 10.

the African continent with unique products. Consumer curiosity as to the characteristics, place of origin, and production methods of the products may thus allow locally produced goods to access broader domestic and foreign markets, provided that African producer groups can 'tell the story behind the African products'.

Due to the link between GIs, tradition, local knowledge, and natural resources, GIs often originate from rural areas. The ability of GIs to develop rural areas and revitalize agricultural communities are among their most flaunted advantages. For the authorities, creating a GI does not simply aim to increase tax revenue through increased sales and proceeds of a specific product; it also aims to solve many of the issues faced in rural and often remote areas. These include poverty and unemployment, demographic changes, declining towns, isolation, and lower economic growth compared to the rest of the country. Notably, those issues are present in both developed and developing countries. In Africa, the percentage of the population living in urban areas is expected to rise from 40 per cent in 2015 to 60 per cent in 2050, driven largely by rural–urban migration.[46] By increasing farmers' and producers' incomes, a GI may retain the population and prevent migration from rural to urban areas. A good example is *Taliouine Saffron* in Morocco, whose registration as a GI in 2010 was motivated by the aim to increase development in a poor region and thereby stop rural migration.[47]

A GI allows producers to differentiate their products from globalized, mass-produced goods and market them as niche and exclusive. A GI builds on growing consumer interest in 'authentic', 'traditional', and 'wholesome' food. This should, in turn, allow producers and other actors involved to charge a price premium. Local producers may further use the 'glow' of a GI to enhance their reputation and sell directly to consumers, thereby cutting out the middleman and competing more effectively against big corporations.[48] In other instances, GI producers may use the collaborative momentum of the association to establish a minimum annual price, similar to what is currently the case for *Penja Pepper* in Cameroun.[49] These should all lead to increased revenue for producers.

As demand for the protected goods rises, employment within the GI industry and the broader tourism and culture industry should also increase. GIs are often perceived as nostalgic, wholesome, and authentic products, drawing consumers and tourists to the local region. The Champagne wine region, which gives its name to one of the most well-known GIs in the world, is a major tourist attraction in France. Likewise, tourism in Darjeeling in India has benefited from its association

---

[46] Joseph Teye, 'Urbanization and Migration in Africa' (United Nations Expert Group Meeting for the Review and Appraisal of the Programme of Action of the International Conference on Population and Development and Its Contribution to the Follow-Up and Review of the 2030 Agenda for Sustainable Development 2018) 1, 4.
[47] Vandecandelaere and others (n 30) 13.
[48] Rangnekar (n 9) 16.
[49] Vandecandelaere and others (n 30) 106.

with the famous tea, and South Africa has successfully established several wine routes as tourist attractions.[50] Ancillary industries in the region, such as packaging factories, real estate, transport, and even legal services, also benefit from the economic boom created by a successful GI. In Cameroun, it was reported that the grant of the GI *Oku White Honey* led to greater recognition of the area and an increased number of tourists. People involved in selling materials for hive construction, providing transport, and the labourers employed for harvesting also reported benefiting from the GI.[51] Further, the availability of skilled employment encourages the settlement and retention of young people, thereby fighting one of the major issues faced by rural areas, which is the outflow of young adults with only an ageing population remaining. Promoting a GI has spillover effects upon a region, capitalizing on and enhancing the goodwill in a locality.

For lesser-known products and those originating in developing countries, a GI, with its associated image of quality control through traceability, food safety, and product excellence, enhances consumer confidence. This allows lesser-known products to access global spaces.[52] It also diminishes search costs for the consumer, signalling that the product is of high quality and worthy of purchase. GIs also provide a buffer for developing countries, protecting them from market fluctuation: many developing countries' economies are highly reliant on producing a single raw and low-value product such as coffee beans, cocoa, tea, or rice, and such commodities are susceptible to market fluctuation. The trade marking and licensing initiative launched by the government of Ethiopia with regard to three valuable coffee regions, Harrar, Sidamo, and Yirgacheffe, was motivated by the desire to counter the low and declining price of coffee and allow farmers to benefit from the true value of regional specialty coffee.[53] In 2018, while farmers in the Fero region of Ethiopia received only USD 1.45 per pound of coffee, which amounted to only USD 1 once production costs were accounted for, *Fero Coffee* was sold at USD 26 per pound in the United States.[54] The trade marking initiative thus aimed to reclaim the premium of regional speciality coffees for Ethiopia. Finally, a GI, by providing for proper regulatory and enforcement mechanisms, can ensure that small producers benefit from their know-how and the added value of the GI, rather than being sidelined or even having their product misappropriated by bigger and more powerful producers. In this way, a GI empowers small producers by granting legal

---

[50] South Africa Visit Our Winelands, 'South African Wine Routes Map' (*South Africa Visit Our Winelands*, nd) <www.visitwinelands.co.za/uploads/files/South_African_Wine_Routes_Map_Visit_Winelands.pdf>.

[51] Verina Ingram and others, 'To Label or Not? Governing the Costs and Benefits of Geographic Indication of an African Forest Honey Value Chain' (2020) 3(X) Frontiers in Forests and Global Change <http://10.3389/ffgc.2020.00102>.

[52] Titilayo Adebola, 'Geographical Indications in the Era of the African Continental Free Trade Area (AfCFTA)' (2022) 17(9) JIPLP 5.

[53] Maria Brownell, 'Coffee Trademark Licensing for Farmers: Brewing a Farmer-Owned Brand' (2009) 14(2) Drake J Agric L 296.

[54] ibid 292.

rights to those producers (often low-income agricultural workers) and ensuring that they benefit from these rights.[55]

Still, for all their touted benefits for local development, GIs are no magic pill. The passing of adequate laws and the creation of a GI do not, of themselves, produce economic value and revitalize rural areas. An increase in net producer income will only occur if there is a demand and recognition for the products bearing the GI and if the GI is structured in such a way as to ensure fair distribution of any premium. Much work must be done to promote the product to potential consumers, retailers, and the media. Some products may already be commanding a premium, and the registration of a GI solidifies their position as high-quality products and ensures that consumers obtain the right product for that higher price.[56] Such products benefit from a competitive advantage in the marketplace. For other products, there is either no willingness on the domestic market to pay for a premium[57] or there is no readily available foreign market.[58] In this case, a GI can only be successful if a strong marketing campaign is launched to create demand and increase awareness of the product. In Tunisia, the *Fig of Djebba* became an AOC in 2012. Prior to the launch in 2013 of a project designed to increase consumer awareness and appreciation of the product, consumers in Tunisia were unaware of the product. Prices for the *Fig of Djebba* increased by 142 per cent between 2014 and 2019 due to a comprehensive action plan. This included labelling the product to strengthen its identity as an AOC, promotional activities such as tastings in supermarkets, and greater mediatization of the product.[59] It is, furthermore, important to note that a GI does not exist in isolation, but its economic impacts will depend on other domestic conditions. A GI will only be successfully exported if the relevant facilities are in place and administrative support is provided through simplified export procedures. The GI *Oku White Honey* was chosen in part due to its potential as a 'high-value export product'. Once registered as a GI, regrettably, those interested in exporting the honey abandoned the project due to high transport costs, complicated and expensive permits, and difficulty in complying with quality testing.[60]

---

[55] Surbhi Jain, 'Effects of the Extension of Geographical Indications: A South Asian Perspective' (2009) 16(2) APDJ 80.
[56] For example, a study by UNCTAD found that Bhutanese red rice, prior to any GI registration, was already fetching premium process in export markets: UNCTAD, 'Why Geographical Indications for Least Developed Countries?' (UNCTAD 2016) 20.
[57] Although there are, at times, talks of a GI for Papua New Guinea coffee, it is neither a well-known coffee nor one praised by coffee connoisseurs: Jain (n 54) 85. It is therefore highly doubtful whether a GI would command higher prices.
[58] The registration of *Feni*, a liquor from Goa, India, did not create a demand for the product internationally, which remains limited to Goa's diaspora. This is at odds with the idea of launching *Feni* as a global liquor: Justin Hughes, 'The Limited Promise of Geographical Indications for Farmers in Developing Countries?' in Calboli and Ng-loy (n 12) 83.
[59] Organisation des Nations Unies pour le Développement Industriel, 'La mise en oeuvre d'une indication géographique pour la promotion du développement local: Le cas de la figue de Djebba AOC en Tunisie' (Organisation des Nations Unies pour le développement industriel 2021) 12, 13.
[60] Ingram and others (n 50) 13.

Often, the economic success of EU GIs, with sales of GIs estimated by an EU Commission study in 2021 at EUR 74.7 billion in 2017, is touted as an example of what is achievable.[61] It is crucial to analyse those figures further to obtain a more realistic approach to the benefits of GIs for low-income countries: around 58 per cent of EU GIs (calculated per value) are sold in the country where they are produced. Around 20 per cent are sold within the EU, and only 22 per cent are sold in non-EU countries. Of this 22 per cent, most of this trade is concerned with wine and spirits.[62] This data is worthy of consideration. GIs are often seen as an export tool when the statistics for EU GIs tend to show otherwise: the real market is domestic. Further, not to say that many developing countries do not have quality wine and spirits to offer, but often, GIs in developing countries relate to agricultural products. The export value of agricultural products is low. Wine alone accounts for 50 per cent of the total sales value of GIs sold outside the EU.[63] The same EU Commission study also found sales value to be highly concentrated among a limited number of GIs: for 41 per cent of GIs, the sales volume was under EUR 1 million, accounting for 0.5 per cent of the total sales value of EU GIs.[64]

Similarly, by June 2023, the EU had 3,547 registered GIs in the then 27 member states.[65] It would be foolish to believe that GIs have allowed for rural development in every locality. GIs may lead only to modest returns and, at times, similar returns to non-GI goods. This is particularly true for raw materials and non-processed agricultural products.[66] Countries considering which products to register as a GI must consider this information to ensure the highest possible rate of return. For African countries, where products that have the potential to be registered as GIs are often raw materials and non-processed agricultural products, this information helps select the right product for registration as a GI. Otherwise, there is a risk that the returns on a specific GI will not exceed the costs of creating a quality-control framework and marketing the products.

As mentioned earlier, GIs allow producers to enter a niche market and build upon their differentiation. A differentiated product, however, also means that not all producers will be able to produce the GI-labelled product. GIs, due to the specifications articulated in the production of the goods, represent a barrier to entry that some producers will not be able to overcome. In developing countries, where rural farmers are unlikely to have access to the appropriate infrastructure to abide by strict quality-control measures, the creation of a GI could have the unintended consequence of locking them out and creating excessive competition over land and

---

[61] Directorate-General for Agriculture and Rural Development (n 11) 16.
[62] ibid 19.
[63] ibid 19.
[64] ibid 22.
[65] European Commission, 'eAmbrosia the EU Geographical Indications Register' (n 14) 3.
[66] Calboli (n 12) 22.

the exploitation of natural resources. Bigger foreign companies may be those most able to comply with quality, sanitary, and phytosanitary specifications, thereby alienating small farmers. A monopoly by powerful actors and the exclusion of weaker sections of the supply chain would nullify the development benefits of a GI.[67] In fact, the movement for creating a GI is sometimes pushed only by the big players, without considering whether smaller players will be able to abide by any future rules. True representation of all actors is essential but far from guaranteed.

Still, there are undoubtedly numerous success stories, both for well-established GIs such as *Roquefort* and *Queso Manchego* and for newly established GIs such as *Figs of Djebba* from Tunisia and *Kampot Pepper* from Cambodia, which are already demanding a premium on the market. Registration as a GI also elevates the value of a product: there has been a suggestion that Nestlé might integrate *Penja Pepper* into its Maggi cube.[68] At the same time, one must be cognizant that the registration of a GI is only the first step in ensuring the development of poorer and marginalized rural communities. A GI may even exclude those targeted communities if one is not careful.

3. GIs and Traditional Knowledge

There is no internationally binding instrument focused on traditional knowledge, although traditional knowledge is important for many worldwide. Traditional knowledge provides food and medicine to millions in the developing world. It is part of the cultural identity and unites the community. There is, further, no binding definition as to what constitutes traditional knowledge. This quote by WIPO, however, provides a good working definition of traditional knowledge:

> [I]ntellectual activity in a traditional context, and includes the know-how, skills, innovations, practices and learning that form part of traditional knowledge systems, and knowledge embodying traditional lifestyles of indigenous and local communities or contained in codified knowledge systems passed between generations and continuously developed following any changes in the environment, geographical conditions and other factors. It is not limited to any specific technical field, and may include agricultural, environmental and medicinal

---

[67] Jain (n 54) 80. A study on Banaras textile from India found that small producers or individual artisans reaped limited benefit from the GI registration and that benefits accrued primarily to merchants and traders: Rosemary J Coombe and S Ali Malik, 'Rethinking the Work of Geographical Indications in Asia: Addressing Hidden Geographies of Gendered Labor' in Calboli and Ng-loy (n 12) 90.

[68] Cameroon Report.com, 'Nestlé Wishes to Integrate Penja's Pepper in Its Maggi Cube Formula' (*Cameroon-report.com*, 15 May 2018) <https://cameroon-report.com/economie/agriculture/nestle-wishes-to-integrate-penjas-pepper-in-its-maggi-cube-formula>. How much of this talk will translate in actual implementation remains to be seen.

knowledge, and any traditional knowledge associated with cultural expressions and genetic resources.[69]

One aspect of GIs that greatly interests developing countries is their ability to preserve and reward traditional knowledge.[70] There are several similarities and connecting points between the two concepts. Both GIs and traditional knowledge protect accumulated knowledge from a specific locality and/or community. They reflect the value placed by a community on a product due to its origin and history. Products identified as GIs often result from years of knowledge passed down within a specific community in a particular region, whether for agricultural products or handicrafts. Rather than innovation, GIs and traditional knowledge both highlight traditional cultural values and knowledge. GIs attribute value to traditional principles, traditional practices, and reputation, allowing community members to translate their knowledge into livelihood and income. As this translates into increased income, younger members may be persuaded to carry forward such traditional practices, ensuring the continuation of traditional lifestyles.

The nature of GIs as a collective right is well suited to the protection of traditional knowledge. Traditional knowledge is often held and shared by all in the community, making it unsuitable for other contemporary forms of IP right such as trade marks or patents. A GI allows a group to retain control over its knowledge and sets down the rules for production while allowing all to benefit economically from the shared knowledge. No institution or individual is exerting a monopoly over the knowledge, which remains in the community. At the same time, a GI excludes those outside the community from freeriding on the knowledge accumulated over the years or from using it in a derogatory manner. A GI cannot be assigned, thus protecting the community against being cast aside. Furthermore, there is no time limitation on GIs: the protection may remain in place for as long as it benefits the community.

Another interesting aspect of using GIs to protect traditional knowledge is that the GI system allows the community to take control of its products and regulate production on its terms. Rather than the government or any other institution deciding on who may have the right to claim traditional knowledge belonging to a community, the community sets its own internal set of rules. The indigenous community can evolve those rules as per its requirements.

However, a GI not a replacement for an appropriate protective legal framework for traditional knowledge. GIs tend to protect goods, applying only to commercially exploitable forms of expression. GIs cannot adequately protect processes, techniques, and cultural expressions or intangible rights such as dances,

---

[69] WIPO Intergovernmental Commission (IGC) Secretariat, 'The Protection of Traditional Knowledge: Revised Objectives and Principles' (WIPO Doc WIPO/GRTKF/IC/18/5 2011) Annex 18.
[70] We use the broader term 'traditional knowledge' as it encompasses indigenous knowledge.

costumes, and poetry. For these intangible forms of knowledge, states must ensure other effective measures to prevent their unauthorized fixation, disclosure, or exploitation.

While GIs and traditional knowledge have several similarities, they differ in an important aspect. GIs ultimately aim to promote the commercialization of accumulated knowledge. By contrast, traditional knowledge aims to preserve, safeguard, and develop this accumulated knowledge to pass it down to future generations. These differing aims may lead to a host of issues. A successful GI may result in an intensification of the exploitation, particularly for agricultural products. While this may procure increased income, it may also trigger overexploitation of the land. Successful commercialization may further lead to changes to the traditional product to increase efficiency or render it more suited to contemporary market demand.[71] These are in direct opposition to the long-term safeguarding aims of traditional knowledge.

Furthermore, the traditional knowledge embodied in a GI may still be misappropriated. A GI prevents the use of a specific designation; however, nothing prevents the misappropriation of the knowledge to produce similar products without the protected designation. It is further essential that the benefits of any GI protecting traditional knowledge accrue to the rightful owners and not to those who have unlawfully or unethically exploited indigenous communities' knowledge. In South Africa, the knowledge of the medicinal properties of *Rooibos* was first held by the San hunter-gatherers and Khoi pastoralist indigenous peoples. During colonization, the San and the Khoi indigenous peoples were dispossessed of their traditional knowledge, culture, and land.[72] Apartheid further marginalized the 'coloured', a racial group with a mix of origin, including San and Khoi peoples, mixed-race people, and slaves or workers from other countries. By the time *Rooibos* was gaining in popularity and being protected, 93 per cent of the cultivable land was owned by commercial white farmers, and the majority of the production was concentrated on large farms.[73] Coloured farmers were marginalized: *Rooibos* wild harvesters (mainly from 'coloured' communities) were even prevented from selling their wild tea by the Rooibos Council.[74] The original knowledge owners were thus deprived of the commercial benefits arising from the exploitation and protection of *Rooibos*. Following a process started in 2010, a benefit-sharing agreement between the South Africa San Council, National Khoisan Council, and Rooibos Council was signed in 2019. An annual levy of 1.5 per cent of the price paid by tea processors for unprocessed *Rooibos* is allocated to

---

[71] Gervais (n 42) 134–35.
[72] Camille Meyer and Kiruben Naicker, 'Collective Intellectual Property of Indigenous Peoples and Local Communities: Exploring Power Asymmetries in the Rooibos Geographical Indication and Industry-Wide Benefit-Sharing Agreement' (2023) 52(9) Res Policy 4.
[73] ibid 4.
[74] ibid 5

a government-managed fund. The fund is equally distributed between two trusts held by the San and Khoi peoples.[75]

Still, a GI may contribute indirectly to the protection of traditional knowledge by making the exploitation of the product economically valuable, thereby ensuring that the skills and knowledge surrounding the production are passed on to future generations.[76]

Further to this general introduction on GIs with a focus on Africa, highlighting the historical development of the concept, including on and by the continent, explaining the terminology, presenting the possible benefits to development, and pointing out certain parallels between traditional knowledge and GIs, the authors will proceed to a review of the international legal framework for the protection of GIs in Africa.

[75] ibid 7
[76] Rangnekar (n 9) 18.

2
International Legal Framework for the Protection of Geographical Indications in Africa

In the second part of the book, we examine how African countries, either domestically or through regional organizations, protect geographical indications (GIs) in their countries. This GI protection exists within the greater international framework of the World Intellectual Property Organization (WIPO) and the World Trade Organization (WTO)-administered treaties as well as bilateral and multilateral agreements, which we examine in this chapter.

1. International Legal Framework for the Protection of GIs

The first international convention on GIs was the Paris Convention for the Protection of Industrial Property (Paris Convention) adopted in 1883. As mentioned in Chapter 1, the terms 'indications of source' and 'appellations of origin' were used instead of 'geographical indication'. Although the focus is on geographical origin, there is no requirement for linked qualities or characteristics. The Paris Convention obliges states to prohibit or seize upon importation, or within the country, any product bearing a false indication. This relatively simple obligation is, however, complicated by the absence of a clear definition of what constitutes a false indication or appellation and the absence of a list of protected names in each country. Courts have to determine, on a case-by-case basis, the status of protected names. In addition, the Paris Convention protects against false indications but not against accurate indications that unfairly benefit from the reputation of an existing indication. Albeit timid, the Paris Convention represented the first step in the international protection of GIs. As of February 2024, fifty-one (out of fifty-four) African countries were party to the Paris Convention.[1]

---

[1] Eritrea, Ethiopia, Somalia, and South Sudan are not parties to the Paris Convention. Considering that nearly all British Commonwealth states follow the dualist approach, the authors recommend checking the local laws on the domestication of international treaties before relying on a state party being party to an international convention, including the Paris Convention. By way of illustration, in *Fan Milk International A/S v Mandarin Oriental Services B.V* (Suit No FHC/ABJ/CS/791/2020) & *Fan Milk Inter-national A/S v Mandarin Oriental Services BV* (Suit No FHC/ABJ/CS/792/2020), the Federal High Court of Nigeria (Abuja Judicial Division) found that neither the Paris Convention nor the

The Madrid Agreement for the Repression of False or Deceptive Indications of Source on Goods (Madrid Agreement) adopted in 1891 was meant to address these failings, expanding its range of action to include both false and deceptive indications of source. Member states must seize on importation any product bearing a false or deceptive indication that directly or indirectly indicates a state party or place situated therein as being the country or place of origin of the product.[2] The Madrid Agreement still does not define the term 'indication of source', although article 1(1), by stating the duty of member states, clarifies the term: 'a false or deceptive indication [. . .], or a place situated therein, is directly or indirectly indicated as being the country or place of origin'. As of February 2024, there were thirty-six member states to the Madrid Agreement, including four African countries: Algeria, Egypt, Morocco, and Tunisia. The number of ratifications is so low that the impact of the Madrid Agreement is limited.

Another attempt at an international treaty focused on GIs was made through the Lisbon Agreement for the Protection of Appellations of Origin and their International Registration (Lisbon Agreement) concluded in 1958. Any member of the Paris Convention may accede to the Agreement. The Lisbon Agreement applies to appellations of origin and provides for an international registry for appellations of origin administered by the International Bureau of WIPO. Applications for registration may only be made by the appointed national authority,[3] meaning that member states must appoint a national authority to liaise with the International Bureau. It also means that the initiative to register an appellation under the Lisbon Agreement lies with the domestic authorities only.[4] Once an appellation is protected in the register maintained by the International Bureau, member states to the Lisbon Agreement must protect the appellation in their country unless they declare that they cannot ensure its protection within one year of the receipt of WIPO's notification and provide an indication of the grounds to the refusal.[5] One cannot appeal or request a review of such a decision. Once an appellation is protected, member states must protect the appellation against 'any usurpation or imitation, even if the true origin of the product is indicated or if the appellation is used in translated form or accompanied by terms such as "kind", "type", "make", "imitation", or the like'.[6]

Agreement on Trade-Related Aspects of Intellectual Property Rights (TRIPS) is applicable in Nigeria as it has not been domesticated.

[2] Madrid Agreement, art 1. Note that while national courts retain the ability to decide which appellations, on account of their generic character, do not fall within the provisions of the Madrid Agreement, regional appellations concerning the source of products of the vine are excluded from this reservation (art 4).
[3] Lisbon Agreement, art 5.
[4] Daniel Gervais, 'Traditional Innovation and the Ongoing Debate on the Protection of Geographical Indications' in Peter Drahos and Susy Frankel (eds), *Indigenous Peoples' Innovation: Intellectual Property Pathways to Development* (ANU Press 2012) 128.
[5] Lisbon Agreement, art 5.
[6] ibid art 3.

States may choose how they will protect the appellation and the remedies to be adopted in case of an infringement. With thirty member states as of February 2024 (ten being from Africa, namely Algeria, Burkina Faso, Cape Verde, Congo, Gabon, Ghana, Ivory Coast, Morocco, Togo, and Tunisia), one cannot say that the Lisbon Agreement has been a resounding success. It is far from having created a worldwide registration system. By June 2020, there were 1,027 registrations in force. Among the probable reasons for the low rate of accession is that the Agreement is only open to countries that protect appellations of origin 'as such'[7] and not under unfair competition, trade mark, or consumer protection laws, for example.[8]

Conscious of the limitations posed to an international registration valid only in a few countries, the Lisbon Union—comprising the member states of the homonymous Agreement—proposed a series of reforms, including allowing for the registration of GIs in addition to appellations of origin. This culminated in the Geneva Act of the Lisbon Agreement on Appellations of Origin and Geographical Indications, which was adopted on 20 May 2015 and entered into force in February 2020. Under the Geneva Act, holders of GIs and appellations of origin may file one application and pay one set of fees for protection in other contracting states. Intergovernmental organizations, under certain conditions, may also join. Transborder applications (ie GIs covering the territory of two neighbouring states) are accepted. The neighbouring states may file joint or separate applications. There is no requirement for how GIs and appellations of origin are protected so long as the protective standards are respected. This is left to the appreciation of contracting states. As of February 2024, there were twenty-one members, with the African Intellectual Property Organization (OAPI), Burkina Faso, Cape Verde, Congo, Gabon, Ghana, Ivory Coast, Mali, Sao Tome and Principe, Senegal, Tunisia and Togo from Africa.[9]

Although these international conventions have introduced the topic of GIs at the multilateral level, it is undeniable that the WTO Agreement on Trade-Related Aspects of Intellectual Property Rights, 15 April 1994 (TRIPS Agreement) had the most influence on the protection of GIs around the world. Coming into force on 1 January 1995, the TRIPS Agreement sets out minimum standards of protection for intellectual property. It also provides that member states should comply with the substantive obligations of the Paris Convention. With 164 members, the impact of the TRIPS Agreement is far-reaching. Every member of the WTO, except for least-developed countries, must apply the provisions of TRIPS. Least-developed countries need not apply the provisions of the TRIPS Agreement, other than articles 3, 4, and 5, until 1 July 2034, or until they cease to be a least developed country,

---

[7] See the Lisbon Agreement, art 1(2), which provides for the protection of appellations of origin 'recognised and protected as such in the country of origin'.
[8] Carlos Correa, 'Protection of Geographical Indications in Caricom Countries' (Caricom 2022) 9.
[9] Some member countries (Burkina Faso, Congo, Gabon, Ivory Coast, Mali, Senegal and Togo) are also members of the OAPI.

whichever comes earlier.[10] Ten African states are not members of the WTO. Among the African countries not members of the WTO, Eritrea does not wish to accede. Algeria, Comoros, Ethiopia, Equatorial Guinea, Libya, Sao Tome and Principe, Somalia, South Sudan, and Sudan are not yet members but are at different stages of the application process to become WTO members.

The GI section of the TRIPS Agreement comprises articles 22–24. The GI section falls within the wider framework of the TRIPS Agreement and its resulting obligations: compliance with the provisions of the Paris Convention, availability of enforcement measures, national principle, and most-favoured-nation treatment.

Article 22 defines a GI and provides the minimum protection for all GIs. Under article 22, protection is afforded to all indications that fall within the TRIPS definition, that is 'indications which identify a good as originating in the territory of a Member, or a region or locality in that territory, where a given quality, reputation or other characteristic of the good is essentially attributable to its geographical origin'.[11] Protection is afforded to all goods, not just to food, wine and spirits, which often are the main concern of GIs. Services are widely held to be excluded from the TRIPS Agreement as article 22 uses the term 'products'. Since the TRIPS Agreement only provides for a minimum level of protection, nothing prevents member states from including services as GIs.[12] However, a distinction is drawn in the protection afforded between all products, wines and spirits, and wines only.

Members shall provide for the legal tools for interested parties to prevent 'the use of any means in the designation or presentation of a good that indicates or suggests that the good in question originates in a geographical area other than the true place of origin in a manner which misleads the public as to the geographical origin of the good' or 'any use which constitutes an act of unfair competition within the meaning of Article 10*bis* of the Paris Convention (1967)'.[13] There are three cumulative requirements under the first section of article 22(2): (a) the use of a word, phrase, or symbol indicating or suggesting that a product comes from a geographic region; (b) the fact that the product does not come from that region; and (c) that this false use misleads the public. Article 22(2) does not apply to the false use of an indication that does not mislead the public. Whether the public is misled is determined by the courts. There have been some concerns about this provision, which

---

[10] WTO, 'WTO Members Agree to Extend TRIPS Transition Period for LDCs until 1 July 2034' (*World Trade Organization*, 29 June 2021) <www.wto.org/english/news_e/news21_e/trip_30jun21_e.htm>. The following African countries are members of the WTO and classified as least developed countries: Angola, Benin, Burkina Faso, Burundi, Central African Republic, Chad, the Democratic Republic of the Congo, Djibouti, Gambia, Guinea, Guinea Bissau, Lesotho, Liberia, Madagascar, Malawi, Mali, Mauritania, Mozambique, Niger, Rwanda, Senegal, Sierra Leone, Tanzania, Togo, Uganda, and Zambia. They are eligible for an extended transition period to apply the TRIPS Agreement. Some of these countries are, however, members of the OAPI and apply the TRIPS-compliant provisions as provided for under the Bangui Agreement.
[11] TRIPS Agreement, art 22(1).
[12] Correa (n 8) 10.
[13] TRIPS Agreement, art 22(2).

allows freeriding since one could use a GI for a product so long as the true indication is provided and thereafter argue that no consumer was misled. The burden of proof lies with the plaintiff to prove either that the consumer is misled or that there was an act of unfair competition.[14] As for an act of unfair competition under Article 10*bis* of the Paris Convention, WTO members must prohibit any 'indications or allegations the use of which in the course of trade is liable to mislead the public as to the nature, the manufacturing process, the characteristics, the suitability for their purpose, or the quantity, of the goods'.[15] These two provisions certainly overlap.[16] Note that article 22 does not specify the legal means for the protection of GIs, and member states are free to determine the appropriate implementation mechanism.

Under article 22(3) of the TRIPS Agreement, WTO member states must, either *ex officio* or at the request of an interested party, refuse or invalidate the registration of a trade mark that contains or consists of a GI with respect to goods not originating in the territory indicated if the use of the indication in the trade mark for such goods in that member state is of such a nature as to mislead the public as to the true place of origin.

The use of homonymous GIs is prevented when—though literally true as to the territory, region, or locality in which the goods originate—they falsely represent to the public that the goods originate in another territory.[17]

Wines and spirits benefit from a higher level of protection under article 23. Member states must provide the legal means to prevent the use of a GI for a wine or spirit not originating in that place, 'even where the true origin of the goods is indicated or the geographical indication is used in translation or accompanied by expressions such as "kind", "type", "style", "imitation" or the like'.[18] Similar to what is provided for in article 22, member states shall refuse or invalidate a trade mark that contains or consists of a GI, subject to the exceptions provided under article 24.[19] The use of the GI need not be misleading; the burden of proof does not lie with the plaintiff.[20] Article 23(3) of the TRIPS Agreement relates to homonymous GIs for wines where member states must determine the practical conditions under which the homonymous indications in question will be differentiated from each other, taking into account the need to ensure equitable treatment of the producers concerned and that consumers are not misled. Each country can determine the conditions applicable to differentiate the two indications. This also adds to a level of legal uncertainty as every country will establish, through their courts, whether the

---

[14] Surbhi Jain, 'Effects of the Extension of Geographical Indications: A South Asian Perspective' (2009) 16(2) APDJ 80, 74–5.
[15] Paris Convention, art 10*bis* (3)(iii).
[16] Correa (n 8) 10.
[17] TRIPS Agreement, art 22(4).
[18] ibid art 23(1).
[19] ibid art 23(2).
[20] Jain (n 14) 73.

use is misleading.[21] Homonymous GIs for products other than wines, including spirits, are protected under article 22(4) and not article 23(3). Finally, article 23(4) obliges member states to enter into negotiations concerning the establishment of a multilateral system of notification and registration of GIs for wines to facilitate their protection.

Article 24 is a bit of a mixed bag, providing for international negotiations and exceptions to the GIs obligation. Article 24 applies to all products, including wine and spirits, except for article 24(4), which is exclusive to wines and spirits, and article 24(6), which provides a specific exception to grape varieties. Under article 24(1), member states agree to continued negotiations to increase individual GIs' protection. The provisions of the GI section are to be kept under review by the Council for TRIPS. Any matter affecting compliance with the obligations under these provisions may be drawn to the attention of the Council. Member states may not use the provisions of TRIPS to diminish the protection of GIs that existed in their country immediately prior to the date of entry into force of the WTO Agreement.[22] Subsections 4–9 provide for exceptions in the protection of certain terms, particularly with regard to the additional protection for GIs for wines and spirits. Under article 24(4), there is no obligation to prevent continued and similar use of a GI identifying wines or spirits from another member state where that GI was used in a continuous manner with regard to the same or related goods or services in the territory of that member either for at least ten years preceding 15 April 1994 or in good faith preceding that date. Where a trade mark similar to a GI has been applied for or registered in good faith or its rights acquired through use in good faith either before the date of application of the GI provisions in the country or before the GI is protected in its country of origin, the trade mark registration shall remain valid and be entitled to be used.[23] Generic terms are non-protectable. A member state need not apply the relevant GI provisions where the indication is identical with the term customary in its common language as the common name for such goods or services or with the customary name of a grape variety existing in its territory for products of the vine.[24] The GI provisions shall in no way prejudice the right of any person to use, in the course of trade, that person's name or the name of that person's predecessor in business, except where such name is used in such a manner as to mislead the public.[25] Finally, a member state need not protect GIs that are not, or cease to be, protected in their country of origin or have fallen into disuse in that country.[26]

---

[21] TRIPS Agreement, art 23(3).
[22] ibid art 24(3).
[23] ibid art 24(5).
[24] ibid art 24(6).
[25] ibid art 24(8).
[26] ibid art 24(9).

2. African Continental Initiatives for GIs

GIs are not a new addition to the African legal landscape. As early as 1977, GIs were included in the Bangui Agreement, which governs the formation of the OAPI. Yet, the first registered GI in the OAPI only occurred in 2006 with *Champagne*, and the first GI from the OAPI region, *Penja Pepper*, was registered only in 2013. The number of products from OAPI countries recognized by the Organization as GIs has increased over the past years, including such names as *Ananas Pain de Sucre du Plateau d'Allada* and *Chapeau de Saponé*. This aligns with the increased interest in GIs expressed over the past two decades.

At the continental level, one must highlight the 'Continental Strategy for the Geographic Indications (GIs) in Africa for the period 2018 to 2023' (Continental Strategy) developed by the Department of Rural Economy and Agriculture (DREA) in collaboration with the African Union (AU) member states, Regional Economic Communities (RECs), and technical and development partners. Adopted by the African Union in October 2017 and endorsed as a specific deliverable of the AU–EU Summit in November 2017,[27] the Continental Strategy looks at the potential of GIs to respond to Africa's vision for the future. The AU hopes that creating an enabling environment for GI development in Africa will foster inclusive and gender-equitable sustainable rural development while increasing food security.[28] This should help achieve safe and quality nutrition on the continent, improve African livelihoods, and fulfil United Nations (UN) development goals, in particular ending hunger and reducing poverty.[29] The Continental Strategy's vision is to be guided by internal and external coherence. Internal coherence means ensuring adaptation and appropriation by AU member states by building on existing GI networks and experiences at the regional level with the OAPI and the African Regional Intellectual Property Organization (ARIPO), partnering with RECs and stakeholders at the national level, and adopting a participative approach, transparency, and the search for consensus. External coherence is coordinating and partnering with international stakeholders such as the UN agencies and other donors and ensuring conformity with international instruments such as the TRIPS, the Lisbon, and the Madrid Agreements.[30] The Continental Strategy, however, does not prescribe how GIs must be protected. It is, furthermore, a non-binding instrument.

---

[27] Pan-African Geographic Indications Information Hub, 'Endorsement of the African Union Continental Strategy for Geographical Indications in Africa 2018–2023' (*Pan-African Geographical Indications Information Hub*, 30 November ny) <https://africa-gi.com/en/pan-african-gi/news/endorsement-african-union-continental-strategy-geographical-indications-africa>.

[28] African Union Commission Department of Rural Economy and Agriculture, 'Continental Strategy for Geographical Indications in Africa 2018–2023' (African Union Commission Department of Rural Economy and Agriculture nd) 50.

[29] ibid 70.

[30] ibid 51.

The Continental Strategy provides an extensive overview of the work undertaken in the field of GIs in Africa over the past two decades, highlighting training, awareness-raising events, and technical assistance projects such as the *Projet d'Appui à la Mise en Place des Indications Géographiques dans les États Membres de l'OAPI* (PAMPIG).[31] PAMPIG was funded by the French Development Agency and supported the establishment of GIs in OAPI member countries. The project, which ran from 2010 to 2014, allowed for the registration of the first three GIs in sub-Saharan Africa: *Penja Pepper* and *Oku White Honey* (both from Cameroun) and *Ziama Macenta Coffee* from Guinea.[32] PAMPIG 2 ran from 2018 to 2022 and aimed to register six new GIs from the OAPI region: *Sugar Bread Pineapple*; *Gari Sohui of Savalou* (both were registered); *Red Cocoa*, *Fogo Wine*, *Attieké des Lagunes*, and *Baoulé Cloth*. Another example of past work highlighted in the Continental Strategy is the International Trade Centre and WIPO project for branding and protecting *Zanzibar Clove*.[33]

The Continental Strategy has great aspirations for Africa. It views GIs as an important tool to achieve improved socio-economic development in Africa and higher quality of life for Africans. At the same time, the Continental Strategy must be complemented with well-crafted, practical, achievable action plans and commitments that will promote African interests.[34] Implementing activities have already begun. In March 2019, three initiatives were decided on: the preparation of a training and technical assistance programme to develop GIs in Africa, the establishment of an African GI website,[35] and the identification of potential GIs in different African countries.[36] A consultative committee, composed of the African Union Commission, OAPI, ARIPO, and the European Commission, has also been established to guide the implementation of the strategy. The Food and Agriculture Organization, WIPO, the French Agricultural Research Centre for International Development, and European Union Intellectual Property Office are invited as observers.[37]

However, there is still a lack of detail as to how the aims of the Continental Strategy, which go beyond the mere establishment of GIs, are to be achieved. For example, a strategy is needed for the production of a GI to result in a gender-equitable

---

[31] ibid 2–4.
[32] ibid 2–3.
[33] ibid 3.
[34] Titilayo Adebola, 'Geographical Indications in the Era of the African Continental Free Trade Area (AfCFTA)' (2022) 17(9) JIPLP 6.
[35] Pan-African Geographical Indications Information Hub, 'Outputs' (*Pan-African Geographical Indications Information Hub*, nd) <https://africa-gi.com/en/pan-african-gi/outputs>.
[36] Flora IP, 'On the Continental Strategy for Geographical Indications in Africa: An Interview with Ms Diana Akullo' (*FLORA IP*, 12 May 2020) <www.floraip.com/2020/05/12/on-the-continental-strategy-for-geographical-indications-in-africa-an-interview-with-ms-diana-akullo>.
[37] Gerardo Fortuna, 'EU–Africa Move in Step on Geographical Indications Revolution' (*EURACTIV*, 17 December 2020) <www.euractiv.com/section/agriculture-food/news/eu-africa-move-in-step-on-geographical-indications-revolution>.

sustainable rural development. Such results do not automatically ensue from the creation of a GI. Likewise, a strategy is needed to promote African GIs locally and abroad. There will be no poverty reduction through the sale of more expensive niche products if there is no demand for such products, whether locally or abroad.[38] Hopefully, prior to the drafting a new strategy for the year 2024 onward, the AU will take stock of the impact, the benefits and lacunas of the 2018-2023 Continental Strategy.

The Continental Strategy must be seen in the broader context of the ambitions and projects of the AU. The Continental Strategy was crafted at a time when the AU was pushing for implementing programmes under Agenda 2063 'Aspirations for the Africa we want'. Agenda 2063 is the long-term blueprint for the continent's sustainable development and inclusive economic growth. Adopted by the AU Assembly of Heads of State and Government, Agenda 2063 highlights seven aspirations and sets out a collective plan to implement these over the next fifty years.[39] One of these aspirations is 'An integrated continent, politically united based on the ideals of Pan-Africanism and the vision of an African Renaissance'. One of the most publicized means of realizing this aspiration is the African Continental Free Trade Area (AfCFTA).

The AfCFTA is open to all fifty-five AU member states to establish a single continental market where goods, services, and people can move freely. Today, only Eritrea has not signed the Agreement. There are eight interrelated general objectives, which can be broadly summed up as follows: AfCFTA aims to expand intra-Africa trade; enhance competitiveness of economies; support the sustainable and inclusive economic transformation of Africa; and promote industrial development through diversification and regional value chain development, agricultural development, and food security. It is the world's largest free trade area by the number of participating countries and is expected to boost Africa's income by USD 450 billion by 2035 while adding USD 76 billion to the world's economy.[40]

The AfCFTA was adopted in March 2018 with the protocols on trade in goods. The Agreement came into force on 30 May 2019 following ratification by twenty-four countries, and trading under the Agreement was due to start on 1 January 2021, following a six-month delay due to the COVID-19 pandemic.[41] In practice,

---

[38] Adebola (n 34) 7.
[39] The seven aspirations are: (1) A prosperous Africa based on inclusive growth and sustainable development; (2) An integrated continent, politically united, based on the ideals of Pan Africanism and the vision of Africa's Renaissance; (3) An Africa of good governance, respect for human rights, justice and the rule of law; (4) A peaceful and secure Africa; (5) An Africa with a strong cultural identity, common heritage, values and ethics; (6) An Africa whose development is people-driven, relying on the potential of African people, especially its women and youth, and caring for children; and (7) Africa as a strong, united, resilient, and influential global player and partner.
[40] Adebola' (n 34) 4.
[41] David Thomas, 'What You Need to Know about the African Continental Free Trade Area' (*African Business*, 10 February 2022) <https://african.business/2022/02/trade-investment/what-you-need-to-know-about-the-african-continental-free-trade-area>. Countries that have yet to ratify the Agreement are unconcerned by the start of trade under the AfCFTA regime.

delays in finalizing tariffs and rules of origin have, again, led to a delay in the operationalization of the Agreement. Many areas still need to be sorted out, and these negotiations have been divided into three phases. Phase 1 concerns trade in goods and services and culminated in the adoption of the Agreement itself and protocols on trade in service, trade in goods and settlement of disputes. Some details are, however, still under negotiation. Phase 2 negotiations concerning intellectual property rights (IPR), investment, competition policy, and e-commerce/digital trade, as well as women and youth in trade, is undergoing consultations, drafting, and negotiations. Phase 3 concerns e-commerce and will start upon completion of phase 2.

Of particular interest to the topic of GIs is the AfCFTA protocol on intellectual property under Phase 2. A final draft was adopted in October 2022 at the Extraordinary Meeting of the Council of Ministers in Gabon.[42] It was later approved by the African Union at the 36th Ordinary Session of the Assembly of the Union held on 18–19 February 2023, paving the way for its implementation.[43] The Protocol applies to all categories of IPRs, including GIs. It provides that all state parties must protect GIs under a *sui generis* system, which may be complemented by additional protective mechanisms including certification marks, collective marks, or unfair competition laws.[44] Additional obligations for all IPRs will be provided for in the Annexes to the Protocol. These are still being drafted.

In imposing a *sui generis* system, the AfCFTA protocol on intellectual property goes further than the TRIPS Agreement. Since a *sui generis* system is compulsory, the African Union should consider the possibility of a continental filing system. A unitary system would encourage more filings thanks to simplified formalities, lower costs, and a harmonized enforcement system. A continental system also makes sense given the current low number of GI applications in many African countries. Contrary to trade marks, there is a limit to the number of products' names that may be registered as a GI by every country, and each country setting up their own filing system might not be the most efficient use of already limited domestic resources. In addition, a continental system would recognize GIs that are spread over different countries. One must remember that boundaries in Africa were arbitrarily drawn and do not reflect how various cultures and peoples inhabited the land.[45]

---

[42] AfCFTA, 'The Extraordinary Meeting of the Council of Ministers Responsible for Trade' (*AfCFTA*, nd) <https://au-afcfta.org/2022/10/the-extraordinary-meeting-of-the-council-of-ministers>.

[43] Assembly of the Union, 'Draft Decisions, Declarations, Resolution and Motion' (*African Union*, 18–19 February 2023) <www.afdb.org/sites/default/files/documents/resolutions_36th_ordinary_session_african_union_assembly_19_february_2023.pdf>.

[44] Draft AfCFTA Protocol on IPRs, art 9(1).

[45] Frederic Perron-Welch, 'Implications of the African Continental Free Trade Area for Trade and Biodiversity: Policy and Regulatory Recommendations' (UNCTAD 2021) 10.13150/RG.2.2.32493.10725, 26–27.

3. Protection under Regional/Bilateral Trade Agreements

Unsurprisingly, the EU calls for the insertion of GIs in its free trade agreements (FTAs). The EU sees GIs as a tool to consolidate the reputation and niche market of its products while ensuring that it maintains the value of its agricultural exports, particularly as it competes with goods produced in countries with lower production costs.[46] Starting in the late 1990s and early 2000s, no doubt influenced by discussions and agreements at the multilateral level and by the fact that there is no global GI registry, the EU advocated for new or expanded IP protection provisions in its trade agreements with third countries. The first such Agreement was the Economic Partnership Agreement with the Cariforum nations[47] (EUCariforum). The EUCariforum differed significantly from previous FTAs by highlighting intellectual property as another commodity of trade with the potential to engage and foster economic development. There was, however, no specific provision on GIs, which are included within the broader IPR. Negotiations to include GIs are, however, ongoing.[48] EUCariforum was soon followed by the EU–Republic of Korea FTA signed in 2009, one of the first bilateral trade agreements incorporating the explicit TRIPS-plus mandate of the Global Europe strategy whereby trade agreements should deepen Europe's economic relationships and global competitiveness. From there on, there has been an ever more robust focus on GIs by the EU.

In Africa, the protection of GIs was included under the African, Caribbean, and Pacific (ACP)[49]–EU Partnership Agreement signed in June 2000, also known as the Cotonou Agreement. The Cotonou Agreement provided for the parties to 'ensure an adequate and effective level of protection of intellectual, industrial and commercial property rights, and other rights covered by TRIPS including protection of GIs, in line with the international standards'.[50] The Partnership Agreement highlights the importance of adhering to TRIPS, while stating that the conclusion of agreements aimed to protect GIs for products of particular interest to either party may be considered. Cooperation between the Parties entails capacity-building assistance for intellectual property law, such as the preparation of laws and regulations; the prevention of the abuse of IPR by rights holders and the infringement of such rights by competitors, and the establishment and reinforcement of domestic and regional offices and other agencies, including support for regional intellectual

---

[46] Jain (n 14) 66.
[47] Cariforum countries comprise fifteen Caribbean states along with the Dominican Republic.
[48] European Commission, 'ACP–EU Partnership' (*European Commission*, nd) <https://trade.ec.europa.eu/access-to-markets/en/content/eu-cariforum-economic-partnership-agreement>.
[49] The African countries in the ACP group are Angola, Cape Verde, Comoros, Benin, Botswana, Burkina Faso, Burundi, Cameroon, Central African Republic, Chad, Congo (Brazzaville), Congo (Kinshasa), Cote d'Ivoire, Djibouti, Eritrea, Ethiopia, Gabon, Gambia, Ghana, Republic of Guinea, Guinea-Bissau, Equatorial Guinea, Kenya, Lesotho, Liberia, Madagascar, Malawi, Mali, Mauritania, Mauritius, Mozambique, Namibia, Niger, Nigeria, Rwanda, Sao Tome and Principe, Senegal, Seychelles, Sierra Leone, Somalia, Sudan, Swaziland, Tanzania, Togo, Uganda, Zambia, and Zimbabwe.
[50] ACP–EU Partnership Agreement (n 48) art 46(1).

property organizations involved in enforcement and protection. The Cotonou Agreement has now expired. A new ACP–EU Agreement was approved by the EU on 20 July 2023 and is open for signature. It will apply for the next twenty years.[51] Under article 12(4) of the new Agreement, parties shall

> build capacities to promote the registration and protection of geographical indications (GIs) for both African and European agricultural and food products. They shall undertake actions to support the implementation of the African Union's Continental Strategy for Geographical Indications in Africa, as well as support local communities to take full advantage of geographical indications to move up regional and global value chains.

The Cotonou Agreement provided for negotiating trade and development agreements known as Economic Partnership Agreements (EPAs) between ACP countries divided into seven groups and the EU. This is still the case under the new Agreement. The focus on GI and TRIPS-Plus obligations in Africa starts with the EU and the Southern African Development Community (SADC) EPA. Although the EPA is labelled as between the EU and the SADC, in reality, the EPA is between Southern African Customs Union (SACU) members (Botswana, Lesotho, Mozambique, Namibia, South Africa, and Eswatini) plus Mozambique, rather than all sixteen member states of the SADC.[52] The EPA provisionally came into force for SACU members on 10 October 2016 and has been provisionally applied by Mozambique since 4 February 2018. Article 16 of the EU–SADC Agreement under the heading 'Cooperation on Protection of Intellectual Property Rights' provides for the protection and enforcement of IPR with an explicit focus on GIs. All parties must cooperate with regard to GIs in accordance with articles 22–24 of the TRIPS Agreement. Parties 'recognise the importance of GIs and origin-linked products for sustainable agriculture and rural development'.[53] This recognition is supplemented by a duty to 'respond to reasonable requests to provide information and clarification to each other on GI and other IPR-related matters'.[54] The explicit reference to GIs within the general provisions on IP illustrates the additional importance placed on GIs.[55] The EU–SADC EPA also includes a bilateral protocol, on the

---

[51] European Council and Council of the European Union, 'Post-Cotonou Agreement' (*European Council and Council of the European Union*, 24 July 2023) <www.consilium.europa.eu/en/policies/cotonou-agreement>.
[52] The member states are: Angola, Botswana, Comoros, Democratic Republic of Congo, Eswatini, Lesotho, Madagascar, Malawi, Mauritius, Mozambique, Namibia, Seychelles, South Africa, United Republic Tanzania, Zambia, and Zimbabwe. EPAs with other member states are being negotiated as part of other subregional groups.
[53] EU–SADC EPA, art 16(3).
[54] ibid art 16(4).
[55] Liam Sunner, 'How the European Union Is Expanding the Protection Levels Afforded to Geographical Indications as Part of Its Global Trade Policy' (2021) 16(4–5) JIPLP 6.

protection of GIs and the trade in wines and spirits, between South Africa and the EU. South Africa protects 251 EU GIs covering wine, spirits, and food in return for the protection in the EU of 105 GI names from South Africa, 102 being for GIs for wines.[56] This will be discussed in more detail in Chapter 16 on South Africa.

The East African Community (EAC)–EU EPA also contains provisions on IPR, although the content of these obligations must be further negotiated. Although the EPA is labelled as between the EU and the EAC, in practice, the EPA is between Burundi, Kenya, Rwanda, Tanzania, Uganda and the EU. The three other members of the EAC, South Sudan, the Democratic Republic of Congo and Sonalia that joined the EAC after the negotiations may join the Agreement after it has entered into force. Under article 3, parties undertake to conclude the negotiations on IPR within five years of entry into force of the Agreement. The EU undertakes to contribute to the development of appropriate legal and regulatory instruments and the protection of IP rights in the area of inland fisheries and aquaculture development.[57] The EAC–EU EPA negotiations were concluded on 16 October 2014. Kenya is the only EAC state that has signed and ratified the Agreement. Rwanda signed the Agreement in September 2016. For the EPA to enter into force, the three remaining EAC members (Burundi, Tanzania, and Uganda) must sign and ratify the Agreement. In practice, this is unlikely to happen. Tanzania, in particular, has clearly signified its reluctance to sign the EPA, which it considers goes against its interest.[58]

The increased focus on GIs by the EU is intended to provide for effective enforcement in case of infringements and a better commercialization of protected goods.[59] The exportation of GI-labelled products is a significant source of revenue for European-based companies, and commercialization is more likely to succeed in an environment where competing products are tightly regulated. *Kalamata Olives* from Greece are more likely to be commercially successful abroad where no other group is allowed to use the term 'Kalamata olives' in that country. The EU therefore negotiates the inclusion of EU GIs[60] in FTAs and claw-back terms, that is the reclaiming of GIs protected in the EU but considered generic in the territory of

---

[56] Monique Bagal and others, *Manual for Geographical Indications in Africa* (2nd edn, European Union Intellectual Property Office 2023).

[57] EAC–EU EPA, art 89(d)(ii).

[58] Namkwahe John and Zephania Ubwani, 'Tanzania Backs Out of EAC Deal with EU over Brexit' (*International Trade Union Federation–AFRICA*, nd) <www.ituc-africa.org/Tanzania-backs-out-of-EAC-deal-with-EU-over-Brexit.html>.

[59] Sunner (n 56) 7.

[60] By way of illustration, in the bilateral Protocol (Protocol 3) on trade in wine and spirits between South Africa and the EU included in the SADC–EU EPA, South Africa protects 251 EU GIs while the EU protects 105 GIs from South Africa: Adebola (n 34) 19. In the EU–Vietnam FTA, Vietnam protects 169 EU GIs while the EU protects 39 GIs from Vietnam: OriGIn, 'Vietnam–EU: The FTA, Which Contains Important GIs Provisions, Has Been Approved by the INTA Committee of the EP' (*OriGIn*, 30 January 2020) <www.origin-gi.com/web_articles/vietnam-eu-the-fta-which-contains-important-gis-provisions-has-been-approved-by-the-inta-committee-of-the-ep>.

the other negotiating party. The EU wishes for EU GIs to be equally well protected abroad.

Of course, the EU is not the only player in town and must contend with countries of the 'New World'. To counter the EU strategy of an ever-increasing GI protection, GI-sceptic countries, in particular the United States, have also engaged in trade negotiations. The US *2022 Special 301 Report*, which reviews the situation of IPR in trading partners worldwide, highlighted the intensive work of the United States through 'bilateral and multilateral channels to advance U.S. market access interests in foreign markets and to ensure that geographical indications (GI)- related trade initiatives of the European Union (EU), its Member States, like-minded countries, and international organizations do not undercut such market access'.[61] The United States currently has FTAs in force with twenty countries but in Africa only with Morocco. Under its FTAs, the United States aims to ensure that any pre-existing trade marks take precedence over any later-in-time GI application, that the availability of common names is not diminished by GI protection, that opposition procedures remain available against GIs, that a GI with multiple terms does not impact any common name components, and that the protection offered to wine and spirits under TRIPS is not extended.[62] A good illustration is the US–Morocco FTA signed on 15 June 2004 and which entered into force on 1 January 2006. Under the FTA, Morocco and the United States must provide that the owner of a registered trade mark shall have the exclusive right to prevent all third parties not having the owner's consent from using, in the course of trade, identical or similar signs, including GIs, for goods or services that are related to those goods or services in respect of which the owner's trade mark is registered, where such use would result in a likelihood of confusion. In the case of the use of an identical sign, including a GI, for identical goods or services, a likelihood of confusion is presumed.[63] The FTA provides for the publication of a GI application for opposition and the possibility of cancelling a registration.[64] Under the FTA, a GI may be refused protection or recognition where it is likely to be confusingly similar to a trade mark that is the subject of a good-faith pending application or registration or where the GI is confusingly similar to a pre-existing trade mark, the rights to which have been acquired in the territory of the country through use in good faith.[65]

---

[61] Office of the United States Trade Representative, *2022 Special 301 Report* (Office of the United States Trade Representative 2022) 26.
[62] ibid 28.
[63] US–Morocco FTA, art 15.2(4).
[64] ibid art 15.3(1).
[65] ibid art 15.3(2).

3
Geographical Indications and Trade Marks

Article 22 of the World Trade Organization (WTO) Agreement on Trade-Related Aspects of Intellectual Property Rights (TRIPS) does not specify the legal means for the protection of geographical indications (GIs), and member states are free to determine the appropriate implementation mechanism, whether through *sui generis* laws, trade mark laws, unfair competition laws, or modalities focusing on business practices, including administrative product approval schemes. In practice, more and more states are adopting *sui generis* systems to protect GIs, that is 'a system that applies specifically and exclusively' to GIs.[1] As of 2017, thirty-three African states had adopted a *sui generis* protection for GIs, while eighteen African states protected GIs through trade mark law, whether through collective or certification marks.[2]

In countries having adopted a *sui generis* system for the protection of GIs, the *sui generis* system coexists with the trade mark system. Issues of overlap and conflicts between trade marks and GIs are potential problems. Some of the problematic situations include the registration of a sign first as a trade mark and, later in time, the registration of a GI reproducing or containing the said sign, whether for identical or dissimilar products. This conflict is unsurprising. Both a GI and a trade mark designate the origin of a product—in one case, the geographical origin of a product and, in the other, the commercial origin of a product. The name of a region could serve both functions. For example, KUGA is both a trade mark for a car registered by FORD and the name of a district in Japan. A similar example is RIO, registered as a trade mark for a car by KIA and which also refers to Rio de Janeiro in Brazil. If one adds in migrants wishing to name their brands after localities in their home towns and the fact that surnames and first names often coincide with geographical names, it is no wonder that trade marks and GIs may enter into conflict.[3] With the growing expansion of GIs, conflictual situations between GIs and trade marks will become increasingly common. It is therefore necessary to discuss how to resolve these differences.

---

[1] World Intellectual Property Organization (WIPO), *Geographical Indications: An Introduction* (WIPO 2021) 26.

[2] African Union Commission Department of Rural Economy and Agriculture, 'Continental Strategy for Geographical Indications in Africa 2018–2023' (African Union Commission Department of Rural Economy and Agriculture nd) 82–86.

[3] Burkhart Goebel and Manuela Groeschl, 'The Long Road to Resolving Conflicts between Trademarks and Geographical Indications' (2014) 104(4) *The Trademark Reporter* 829.

This chapter looks at the various solutions brought forward to solve conflicts between trade marks and GIs, between signs registered as GIs in one country but considered generic in others, and between homonymous GIs. As readers will find out, significant uncertainty still exists, and a unanimous solution satisfying both proponents of GIs and trade marks for all conflicting scenarios has yet to be found.

1. Conflict between Trade Marks and GIs

A conflict between a GI and a trade mark occurs when different parties wish to use an identical or similar sign for a trade mark and a GI. In this scenario, questions arise as to who is entitled to the sign, under which conditions use should be allowed, whether one right should prevail over the other, or whether there should be coexistence of the trade mark and the GI.

The first scenario where conflict might occur is when a person wishes to register a trade mark incorporating a prior registered GI for goods not originating in the relevant area, for example the sign '*Gorgonzola*' as part of a trade mark for goods not originating from the relevant provinces and municipalities in Italy. In conflict scenarios between a GI and a later-in-time trade mark, the beginning of a solution may be found in article 22(3) of the TRIPS Agreement, which applies to all WTO member states.[4] Under article 22(3) of the TRIPS Agreement, member states must refuse or invalidate the registration of a trade mark that contains or consists of a GI with respect to goods not originating in the territory indicated, where the trade mark is of such a nature as to mislead the public as to the true place of origin of the good. If the trade mark is still at the application stage, the application should be refused, generally by the Trade Mark Office of the country where the trade mark application has been filed. If the trade mark has been registered, it should be invalidated. These actions may, where provided in the domestic legislation, be taken *ex officio*, that is by the competent public authority on its own initiative or upon request by any interested party. An additional layer of protection exists for wines and spirits under article 23(2): either the Trade Mark Office *ex officio* or an interested party must have the legal means to prevent the registration of a trade mark for wines that contains or consists of a GI for wines or spirits and that does not come from the geographical area indicated. There is no requirement that the use of the trade mark misleads the public or constitutes

---

[4] Article 22(3) of the TRIPS Agreement cannot be used to resolve conflicts between a GI and prior trade marks that benefit from the exception under art 24(5) of the TRIPS Agreement: WT/DS174/R European Communities—Protection of Trademarks and Geographical Indications for Agricultural Products and Foodstuffs—Complaint by the United States—Report of the Panel (15 March 2005) (WT/DS174/R) para 7.622 and WT/DS290/R European Communities—Protection of Trademarks and Geographical Indications for Agricultural Products and Foodstuffs—Complaint by Australia—Report of the Panel (15 March 2005) (WT/DS290/R) para 7.622.

unfair competition. The only requirement is to establish the false origin of the wine or spirit.[5] This situation is one of the least controversial in the conflict between trade marks and GIs.

Another situation where a conflict might occur is when a person registers or uses a mark incorporating a prior registered GI for goods or services different from those for which the GI is registered. The TRIPS Agreement does not provide a clearcut answer. It could be argued that use of a mark incorporating a prior registered GI for goods or services different from those for which the GI is registered could come under the purview of article 22(2)(b) of the TRIPS Agreement: member states must 'provide the legal means for interested parties to prevent [. . .] any use which constitutes an act of unfair competition within the meaning of article 10bis of the Paris Convention (1967)'. Article 10*bis*(2) of the Paris Convention for the Protection of Industrial Property (as amended on 28 September 1979) defines an act of unfair competition as '[a]ny act of competition contrary to honest practices in industrial or commercial matters'. This is broad enough to comprise numerous dishonest practices in industrial or commercial matters.[6] Right owners may further rely on article 10bis(3)(iii) of the Paris Convention, which mentions as prohibited acts of unfair competition 'indications or allegations the use of which in the course of trade is liable to mislead the public as to the nature, the manufacturing process, the characteristics, the suitability for their purpose, or the quantity, of the goods'. An argument could be made that using a mark incorporating a prior registered GI for goods different from those for which the GI is registered is misleading as to the nature and characteristics of the goods.

Member states are thus free to legislate on situations when a person registers or uses a mark incorporating a prior registered GI for goods or services different from those for which the GI is registered. In many countries, GI owners may have recourse to the rules against unfair competition. To succeed in a case of unfair competition, the GI owner must, however, show that the use of the GI through the trade mark was misleading and that damages, or a likelihood of damages, may result from such a use. In practice, such actions are more likely to succeed where the relevant public closely associates the products sold under the GI to a distinct place

---

[5] Dwijen Rangnekar, 'Geographical Indications: A Review of Proposals at the TRIPS Council: Extending Article 23 to Products Other than Wines and Spirits' (International Centre for Trade and Sustainable Development & United Nations Conference on Trade and Development 2003) 22. Please note the exception under art 24(4) of the TRIPS Agreement limited to GIs for wines and spirits, which provides that a member state is not required to

> prevent continued and similar use of a particular geographical indication of another Member identifying wines or spirits in connection with goods or services by any of its nationals or domiciliaries who have used that geographical indication in a continuous manner with regard to the same or related goods or services in the territory of that Member either (a) for at least 10 years preceding 15 April 1994 or (b) in good faith preceding that date.

[6] WT/DS435/R; WT/DS441/R; WT/DS458/R; WT/DS467/R Australia—Certain Measures Concerning Trademarks, Geographical Indications and Other Plain Packaging Requirements Applicable to Tobacco Products and Packaging—Report of the Panels (28 June 2018) para 7.2847.

of origin and/or certain characteristics.[7] One country that has chosen to legislate specifically on the matter is the European Union. In the European Union (EU), under Regulation (EU) No 1151/2012, registered names (ie Protected Designation of Origin (PDO) and Protected Geographical Indication (PGI) for agricultural products and foodstuff) are protected against

> any direct or indirect commercial use of a registered name in respect of products not covered by the registration where those products are comparable to the products registered under that name or where using the name exploits the reputation of the protected name, including when those products are used as an ingredient.[8]

The use of a trade mark containing a GI or a term corresponding to that indication, even for products not covered under the specifications, in particular to take unfair advantage of that GI, is not permissible.[9] This provision applies where the mark in question uses the registered GI in an identical form or at least in a phonetically and/or visually highly similar form.[10]

Registered GI names in the EU are further protected under the concept of 'evocation': 'Evocation is a *sui generis* standard of protection within the EU's sui generis system for protection of geographical indications.'[11] The concept of 'evocation' covers situations when the consumer is confronted with the disputed sign, packaging, or appearance and the image triggered in its mind is that of the product whose indication or designation is protected. A sufficiently clear and direct link between the disputed sign, packaging, or appearance and the relevant GI must exist.[12] Evocation can occur where the disputed sign incorporates part of a PGI or a PDO due to conceptual proximity or visual and/or phonetic similarity or where the products covered are similar.[13] The likelihood of confusion between the products concerned is not required.[14] The similarity of the goods is not a condition for

---

[7] Standing Committee on the Law of Trademarks, Industrial Designs and Geographical Indications, 'Possible Solutions for Conflicts between Trademarks and Geographical Indications and for Conflicts between Homonymous Geographical Indications' (2000) Annex 2, para 44.

[8] Regulation (EU) No 1151/2012 of the European Parliament and of the Council of 21 November 2012 on quality schemes for agricultural products and foodstuffs [2012] OJ L 343, art 13(1)(a). A rather similar provision for is found at art 103(2)(a) of Regulation (EU) No 1308/2013 of the European Parliament and of the Council of 17 December 2013 establishing a common organisation of the markets in agricultural products which concern certain agricultural products and wine [2013] OJ L 347/671.

[9] Case C-44/17 *Scotch Whisky Association v Michael Klotz*, Judgment, ECLI:EU:C:2018:415, para 38.

[10] ibid para 39.

[11] Evocation does not exist under international law: Vicente Zafrilla Díaz-Marta and Anastasiia Kyrylenko, 'The Ever-Growing Scope of Geographical Indications' Evocation: From Gorgonzola to Morbier' (2021) 16(4–5) JIPLP 443.

[12] Manon Verbeeren and Olivier Vrins, 'The Protection of PDOs and PGIs against Evocation: A "Grand Cru" in the CJEU's Cellar?' (2021) 16(4–5) JIPLP 320–21.

[13] Case C-783/19 *Comité Interprofessionnel du Vin de Champagne v GB*, Judgment, ECLI:EU:C:2021:713, para 58.

[14] Case C-87/97 *Consorzio per la tutela del formaggio Gorgonzola v Käserei Champignon Hofmeister GmbH & Co KG and Eduard Bracharz GmbH*, Judgment, ECLI:EU:C:1999:115, para 26.

evocation to apply; evocation may even apply to services.[15] The critical test for a finding of 'evocation' under EU law is whether the public is likely to establish a direct and unequivocal link between the trade mark and the GI. Evocation is assessed globally, taking account of all the circumstances of the case.[16]

These situations concern the registration of a trade mark or the use of a sign incorporating a prior registered GI. What happens when a later-in-time GI incorporates or reproduces a prior mark? This can occur where a trade mark did not initially have a geographical signification but afterwards appears to correspond to a specific area. One example is Torres, a Spanish trade mark for wine, the winemakers' family name, and the Torres Vedras region in central Portugal renowned for its vineyards.

The TRIPS Agreement provides for exceptions to GI protection for prior trade mark rights under article 24(5). Where a trade mark, identical with or similar to a GI, has been applied for, registered, or the rights to that trade mark have been acquired either before the date of application of the TRIPS Agreement in the country concerned (including at the end of any relevant transition period) or before the GI became protected in its country of origin, members must ensure that, in implementing the TRIPS rules on GIs, they do not prejudice the prior trade mark rights. Member states shall not 'prejudice eligibility for or the validity of the registration of a trademark, or the right to use a trademark, on the basis that such a trademark is identical with, or similar to, a geographical indication'.[17] This only applies to trade marks that have been applied for or registered in good faith or where rights to a trade mark have been acquired through use in good faith.

The Panel Report brought more clarification on the issue of coexistence under the TRIPS Agreement in the disputes between the United States and the European Community (EC) [18] (nowadays the EU) and Australia and the EC.[19] The disputes concerned the compatibility of various aspects of the EC Regulation No 2081/92 on the protection of GIs and designations of origin for agricultural products and foodstuffs with the TRIPS Agreement and the General Agreement on Tariffs and Trade. Of interest to this chapter is the issue of coexistence between trade marks and GIs. Through Council Regulation No 2081/92, the EC established a Community-wide notification and registration system for its member states' GIs for agricultural products and foodstuffs. The Regulation under article 14(2) allowed the EC to register GIs even when they conflicted with a prior trade mark under certain conditions.

---

[15] ibid para 66.
[16] Olivier Vrins, 'No Champagne for "Champanillo": The Protection of PDOs and PGIs against Evocation for Services' (2021) 16(11) JIPLP 1173.
[17] TRIPS Agreement, art 24(5).
[18] WT/DS174/R (n 4).
[19] ibid. Australia and the United States started by requesting a single Panel to rule on the dispute. These disputes made similar but not identical claims as well as separate submissions. The Panel ended up submitting separate reports following an undisputed request by the EC: WT/DS174/R (n 4), paras 2.14 and 2.15.

Following the registration of a GI, only parties from the relevant regions whose goods met certain production criteria could use the registered denomination in marketing their goods within the EC. Other traders were prevented from using or evoking the registered term in respect of goods covered by the registration, even if no consumer confusion occurred. An exception was provided for under article 14(3) of the Regulation, which prevented the registration of a GI where, in light of an earlier trade mark's 'reputation and renown and the length of time it has been used', such registration would be liable to mislead consumers.

In the dispute between the United States and the EC, the United States claimed that the Regulation was inconsistent with article 16(1) of the TRIPS Agreement by denying a trade mark owner the right to prevent uses of GIs that would result in a likelihood of confusion with a prior trade mark.[20] Although couched as an exception, article 14(2) of EC Regulation 2081/92 allows for coexistence and thus constitutes, as argued by the United States, a limit to the right of the trade mark owner against the use of the GI.[21]

In reply, the EC argued that the prejudice to the trade mark owner's interest was avoided by article 14(3) of the Regulation. Regarding coexistence, the EC argued that article 24(5) of the TRIPS Agreement provides for the coexistence of later-in-time GIs with prior trade marks. Moreover, Regulation 2081/92 was grandfathered by article 24(3) of the TRIPS Agreement, which provides that the level of protection for GIs that existed in a member state immediately prior to the date of entry into force of the TRIPS Agreement shall not be diminished. In any event, article 14(2) of the Regulation is a permissible exception to the rights conferred by a trade mark under article 17 of TRIPS.[22]

The Panel rejected the argument that article 24(5) of the TRIPS Agreement provides for coexistence, finding that 'it is inappropriate to imply in article 24.5 either the right to prevent confusing uses or a limitation on the right to prevent confusing uses'.[23] On the issue of grandfathering under article 24(3) of the TRIPS Agreement, the Panel found that article 24(3) only applies to individual GIs but does not protect an entire legal regime.[24] No GIs had been registered under the Regulation before 1 January 1995, so the article was inapplicable in that case.[25] The Panel found that under article 16(1) of the TRIPS Agreement, members are required to make available to trade mark owners a right against certain uses, including use of a sign as a GI, subject to any applicable exception.[26] Article 17 expressly permits those

---

[20] ibid para 7.512.
[21] ibid para 7.555.
[22] ibid para 7.513. Article 17 of the TRIPS Agreement provides: 'Members may provide limited exceptions to the rights conferred by a trademark, such as fair use of descriptive terms, provided that such exceptions take account of the legitimate interests of the owner of the trademark and of third parties.'
[23] WT/DS174/R (n 4), para 7.619.
[24] ibid para 7.635.
[25] ibid para 7.636.
[26] ibid para 7.625.

limited exceptions. In the present case, the Panel found that article 14(3) of the EC Regulation No 2081/92, as written, was a justifiable exception under article 17 of the TRIPS Agreement.[27]

Regulation 2081/92 was subsequently replaced by Council Regulation (EC) No 510/2006 of 20 March 2006 on the protection of geographical indications and designations of origin for agricultural products and foodstuffs. While article 14(2) of EC Regulation 2081/92 allowed the coexistence of a later-in-time GI with a prior registered trade mark under certain conditions, article 14(2) of Regulation 510/2006 expands the exception to trade marks that have been applied for, registered, or established by use, if that possibility is provided for by the legislation concerned, in good faith within the territory of the EC, before either the date of protection of the designation of origin or GI in the country of origin or before 1 January 1996.

Although the TRIPS Agreement caters to certain conflicts that may arise between trade marks and GIs, not all situations are provided for, leaving the door open to debates on the correct approach.

The 'First in Time, First in Right' (FITFIR) principle has been suggested as a possible approach to resolving conflicts between trade marks and GIs. Put simply, the first registered or used right in a given territory is the winner, and there is no question as to coexistence between a GI and a trade mark. The FITFIR principle can be seen within the framework of the Lisbon Agreement for the Protection of Appellations of Origin and their International Registration (Lisbon Agreement) of 1958, under which a member state may refuse the registration of an appellation of origin of which it has been notified within a specific time limit and by providing indications of the ground thereof.[28] In practice, states have refused registration on the basis of prior rights, including earlier trade marks, and this has been deemed acceptable.

Unsurprisingly, the United States is a proponent of the FITFIR principle.[29] In the context of the US–Morocco free-trade agreement, which entered into force on 1 January 2006, article 15.3(2) provides that the grounds for refusing protection or recognition of a GI are that the GI is likely to be confusingly similar to a trade mark that is the subject of a good faith pending application or registration or that the GI is confusingly similar to a pre-existing trade mark, the rights to which have been acquired in the territory of the Party through use in good faith. The International Trademark Association (INTA) is also a proponent of the FITFIR principle, which is unsurprising given its focus on trade marks. The INTA 'supports the principle

---

[27] WT/DS290/R (n 4) para 7.685. A similar position was reached in the Australia–EC dispute: ibid para 8.1(m).

[28] Lisbon Agreement, art 5(3).

[29] See, eg document by the United States Patent and Trademark Office, 'Geographical Indication Protection in the United States', which states that 'a prior right holder has priority and exclusivity over any later users of the same or similar sign on the same, similar, related, or in some cases unrelated goods/services where consumers would likely be confused by the two uses', <www.uspto.gov/sites/defa ult/files/web/offices/dcom/olia/globalip/pdf/gi_system.pdf>.

of "first in time, first in right" priority when resolving conflicts between geographical indications and trademarks'. The support is so emphatic that INTA 'unequivocally states that coexistence between a later GI and a prior trademark is not an acceptable alternative'.[30] In 1994, the General Assembly of the intergovernmental International Vine and Wine Office (OIV)[31] adopted Resolution OIV/ECO 3/94 on the relationship between trade marks and GIs.[32] The Resolution provides for the necessity to avoid any prejudice, diminution, or weakening of a trade mark or GI and the prohibition of the use of an identical or similar designation as both a GI or trade mark.[33] Priority shall determine the protection of trade marks and GIs, although the reputation and distinctive character of a GI and of a trade mark must also be considered.[34]

Other organizations have been more nuanced in their approach, advocating for the coexistence of trade marks and GIs in appropriate cases. The International Association for the Protection of Intellectual Property, known as AIPPI, at its meeting in Rio de Janeiro in May 1998, rejected the superiority of GIs and considered that the FITFIR principle could be the guiding principle for the resolution of conflicts between GIs and trade marks. The AIPPI, at the same time, however,

> recommends in principle coexistence, unless the mark has acquired reputation or renown prior to the date the indication of source or appellation of origin has been established or recognized as such. In this case, protection of the indication or appellation should be denied, and registration refused or canceled. This, however, does not preclude the use of the indication or appellation to identify the geographical origin of the goods or services under the conditions specified in Paragraph 3.1 of this Resolution.[35]

As mentioned before, in most countries, GIs are latecomers to the party. The FITFIR principle will therefore, more often than not, lead to priority being given to trade marks. The EU, however, as a major proponent of GIs, advocates either the primacy of GIs regardless of priority dates or coexistence as the next best

---

[30] Dev Gangjee, 'Quibbling Siblings: Conflicts between Trademarks and Geographical Indications' (2007) 82(3) Chi-Kent L Rev 1265.
[31] The OIV provides information on regulations to grape and wine producing and consuming countries. With forty-nine member states and eighteen observers as of July 2023, the OIV regroups 87 per cent of the global wine production and 71 per cent of the global wine consumption: OIV, 'Presentation' (*OIV*, nd) <www.oiv.int/who-we-are/presentation>.
[32] The Resolution refers not to GIs as such but to recognized appellations of origin, recognized geographical indications, and recognized traditional denominations.
[33] International Bureau of WIPO, 'Geographical Indications: Historical Background, Nature of Rights, Existing Systems for Protection and Obtaining Protection in Other Countries' (WIPO 2003) Annex II 35.
[34] Standing Committee on the Law of Trademarks (n 7) Annex 2.
[35] AIPPI Resolution, 'Question Q 62: Appellations of Origin, Indications of Source and Geographical Indications' (1999) VIII AIPPI Yrbk 1998, 390.

alternative. Under EU law, a trade mark applied for, registered, or established by use in good faith before the date of application to register a GI at EU level should coexist with the registered GI.[36] The registration of a GI should prevent registration of a later-in-time trade mark where this would conflict with the protection granted to the GI. Such applications should be refused *ex officio*.[37] A pre-existing trade mark with reputation may prevent a GI from being registered only where this registration may mislead consumers as to the product's true identity.[38] The current EU position is itself a softening of the position under repealed Regulation Nos 1493/1999 and 2392/89, which provided, until 2008, for prior marks conflicting with a later GI for wine to be abolished unless the trade mark was well known, had been registered for more than twenty-five years before the official recognition of the GI, and had been in continuous use. Where a trade mark fulfilled all these conditions, the trade mark was allowed to coexist with the later-in-time GI.[39]

The FITFIR principle is often appealing for its clarity, predictability, and even-handedness: no more surprises! At the same time, the FITFIR principle glosses over real-life complications. The principle works best when assessing a trade mark and a GI within a single jurisdiction but ignores developments in other jurisdictions. Simply because a GI was not registered and protected in a foreign territory does not mean that the GI was unknown in that foreign country. Information and knowledge on products today circulate faster than registration is achieved, and the FITFIR principle disregards a world where markets are merging and the territorial reach of a name is amplified by the internet.[40] At the same time, neither coexistence nor superiority of the GI is more satisfactory. Why should a trade mark right owner have its rights curtailed by the existence of a later-in-time GI: where the trade mark owner once enjoyed a monopoly over the mark, as a GI, the sign becomes available to all producers in the region provided they comply with the specifications. The distinctiveness of a trade mark is diluted, and the owner's goodwill is diminished.[41] The deprivation of the property right of a trade mark owner is felt even more acutely in the case of a well-known trade mark to which an enhanced reputation is attached.

There is no easy answer to the question of the conflict between trade marks and GIs, and as more and more countries provide for *sui generis* systems for the registration of GIs, we can expect an ever-growing body of jurisprudence on the matter.

---

[36] Regulation (EU) No 1151/2012 (n 8), art 14(2) and Regulation (EU) 2019/787 of the European Parliament and of the Council of 17 April 2019 on the definition, description, presentation, and labelling of spirit drinks, the use of the names of spirit drinks in the presentation and labelling of other foodstuffs, the protection of geographical indications for spirit drinks, the use of ethyl alcohol and distillates of agricultural origin in alcoholic beverages, and repealing Regulation (EC) No 110/2008, art 36(2).
[37] Regulation (EU) No 1151/2012 (n 8), art 14(1) and Regulation (EU) 2019/787 (n 36) art 36(1).
[38] Regulation (EU) No 1151/2012 (n 8), art 6(4) and Regulation (EU) 2019/787 (n 36) art 35(2).
[39] Goebel and Groeschl (n 3) 846.
[40] Gangjee, 'Quibbling Siblings' (n 30) 1269–70.
[41] Stephen Stern, 'The Overlap between Geographical Indications and Trade Marks in Australia' (2001) 2(1) Melb J Int Law 226.

2. GIs Considered as Generic in Other Countries

As a direct consequence of the principle of territoriality, a GI may be protected in one country where, however, the term is considered as generic or a common term in another country. The names of regional products are particularly vulnerable to genericity as they are used by a group of regional producers to begin with. As they designate a type of product rather than a particular producer, migrants from a particular region are often tempted to reproduce the techniques and names in their new country. This is how numerous designations made their way from Europe to the United States, Australia, and South Africa. As the link between the designation and the product diminishes, other producers in the country of migration start using the same terms for the same kind of products. Examples of such occurrences include Havarti cheese and the much-disputed Feta cheese. Unsurprisingly, determining whether a designation constitutes a GI or a generic name is one of the most controversial aspects of GI protection and impacts international relations. South Africa, for example, complained, at the TRIPS Council, that South African producers and exporters of Feta, a product considered generic in its country, were receiving threatening letters from the EU and being blocked from exporting into the EU.[42]

As explained in Chapter 2, under article 24(6) of the TRIPS Agreement, a member state need not protect the GI of another member state where the term is considered generic for the goods or services domestically.

How does one determine the generic status of the name of a particular good? In theory, it is a simple task based on linguistic usage in the country: is the term commonly used for the type of product by consumers, traders, marketers, in advertising, or in the media? This, however, does not reflect the fluidity of human language: at what point can one exactly say that the shift in meaning from an indication of the product's geographical origin to an indication of a certain type of product has occurred? Must the GI have been adopted as a generic term by the whole country, or does a region-specific use suffice? Must the use be constant, or does frequent use suffice? Neither the Paris Convention for the Protection of Industrial Property of 1883 (Paris Convention), the Madrid Agreement for the Repression of False or Deceptive Indications of Source on Goods of 1891 (Madrid Agreement), the Lisbon Agreement, nor the TRIPS Agreement provides a formula for determining genericness. Domestic courts remain sovereign in determining whether a name for a product is now generic based on a detailed analysis of the

---

[42] Council for Trade-Related Aspects of Intellectual Property Rights, Special Session Minutes of Meeting held on 16–17 March 2006, para 100. The Feta issue is now provided for under the bilateral protocol between the EU and South Africa, which was later integrated into domestic laws. Producers with prior trade marks established through registration, prior use, or under common law may continue using Feta on their label indefinitely. New entrants in the market must use South African feta, or feta-style, or feta-type: South Africa Government Gazette (21 October 2016) 3978 No 40356.

facts presented by the parties. The EU, for example, in determining genericness for an agricultural product or a foodstuff, considers all relevant factors, particularly the existing situation in areas of consumption and the relevant national or Union legal acts.[43] The term 'areas of consumption' has been clarified as referring to consumers, as consumers act as the ultimate interpreters of the meaning a name has on the market.[44] Even then, determination of genericity is far from easy, as may be seen from the fifteen-year battle for the protection of Feta as a PDO, with legal claims brought by Denmark, France, and Germany.[45]

At the same time, one must be cognizant that international or bilateral trade agreements may influence the determination of genericity. A claw-back clause is relevant for that purpose. In a claw-back, country A will request country B to protect as a GI a term considered generic in country B but protected as a GI in country A. During the agriculture negotiations within the Doha Development Agenda, also known as the Doha Round, of the WTO, the EU put forward a list of forty-one EU product names that the EU wanted to recuperate such as *Roquefort cheese*, *Parma ham*, or *Rioja wine*. Those product names, which were registered as GIs in the EU, were claimed as generic or registered as trade marks in third countries. The EU viewed the recuperation of those names as an issue of 'fairness'[46] since 'abuses in third countries undermine the reputation of EU products and create confusion for consumers'.[47] Although the EU characterized the list of product names as recuperation, the list quickly became known informally as the claw-back list. The move met with much resistance, including from the United States, and was inconclusive. The EU has since focused its efforts on bilateral and plurilateral negotiations, such as in the wine agreements with Australia, Chile, and South Africa. Under the now-terminated European Community–South Africa Agreement on trade in wine supplementing the Trade, Development and Cooperation Agreement, which came into force on 28 January 2002, South Africa had to phase out *Port* and *Sherry* within eight years of the signature of the agreement for non-South African Customs Union (SACU) South African Development Community (SADC) countries,[48] five years on all export markets, and twelve years for the South African

---

[43] Regulation (EU) No 1151/2012 (n 8) art 41(2).

[44] Joined cases C-465/02 and C-466/02 *Federal Republic of Germany, Kingdom of Denmark v Commission of the European Communities ('Feta II')*, Opinion of Advocate General Ruiz-Jarabo Colomer [2005] (Unreported) para 152.

[45] It is now settled that Feta is not generic and is a PDO from Greece: Joined cases C-465/02 and C-466/02 *Federal Republic of Germany, Kingdom of Denmark v Commission of the European Communities ('Feta II')*, Judgment [2005] ECLI:EU:C:2005:636.

[46] Quote by EU Farm Commissioner Franz Fischler, 'WTO Talks: EU Steps Up Bid for Better Protection of Regional Quality Products' (*European Commission*, 28 August 2003) <https://ec.europa.eu/commission/presscorner/detail/en/IP_03_1178>.

[47] Quote by EU Trade Commissioner Pascal Lamy, ibid.

[48] The non-SACU SADC countries are Angola, Comoros, Democratic Republic of Congo, Madagascar, Malawi, Mauritius, Mozambique, Seychelles, United Republic of Tanzania, Zambia, and Zimbabwe.

domestic market.[49] It is doubtful whether South Africa would have accepted such conditions if they were not coupled with the grant of a larger quota for its export of duty-free wine to Europe and the grant of 15 million euro for the restructuring of the South African wines and spirits sector and the marketing and distribution of South African wines and spirits products.[50]

Once the generic status of an indication has been agreed upon, what should be done? Article 4 of the Madrid Agreement on Indications of Source specifies that 'the courts of each country shall decide what appellations, on account of their generic character, do not fall within the provisions of [the] Agreement, regional appellations concerning the source of products of the vine being, however, excluded from the reservation specified by this Article'. A geographical identifier that the court recognizes as generic is thus excluded from the protection of the Madrid Agreement. However, this does not apply to terms of viniculture, which benefit from enhanced protection against genericity. Given the low level of ratification of the Madrid Agreement, the article's impact is limited. According to article 24(6) of the TRIPS Agreement, member states are not required to apply TRIPS provisions to a GI of any other member with respect to goods or services for which the relevant indication is identical with the term customary in common language as the common name for such goods or services in the territory of that member. For products of the vine, member states may exclude a GI where the relevant indication is identical with the customary name of a grape variety existing in the territory of that member as of the date of entry into force of the WTO Agreement. Although article 24(6) of the TRIPS Agreement does not use the word 'generic', it is commonly viewed as providing for an exception for generic terms.

One feature that must be discussed due to its controversial nature is the freezing of protected terms whereby a protected GI is shielded from genericide. This is provided for at article 6 of the Lisbon Agreement of 1958: 'An appellation which has been granted protection in one of the countries of the Special Union [. . .] cannot, in that country, be deemed to have become generic, as long as it is protected as an appellation of origin in the country of origin.' In the EU, once protected, a GI cannot become generic in the Union.[51] While the shielding of GIs may bring peace of mind to producers, allowing them to invest further in the quality of their

---

[49] For the purpose of the Wines and Spirits Agreement, the South African domestic market is defined to cover SACU (Botswana, eSwatini, Lesotho, Namibia, and South Africa): Agreement between the European community and the Republic of South Africa on Trade in wine referring to ANNEX X of the Agreement on Trade, Development and Cooperation between the European Community and its Member States, of the one part, and the Republic of South Africa, of the other part—Protocol 1 concerning the definition of the concept of 'originating products' and methods of administrative cooperation—Protocol 2 on mutual administrative assistance in customs matters—Final Act—Declarations, art 9.

[50] Andries van der Merwe, 'Geographical Indication Protection in South Africa with Particular Reference to Wines and the EU Connection' (2008) 33(1) JJS 116.

[51] See, eg Regulation (EU) 2019/787 (n 36) art 21(3) and Regulation (EU) No 1151/2012 (n 8) art 13(2).

product, some argue that the insulation of certain names against genericide interferes with the natural evolution of language and imposes an artificial barrier between reality and the law. These criticisms were, in fact, raised during revisions to the Lisbon Agreement. Delegations raised concerns on the artificial constraint against genericism, which undermines trade mark system principles, and criticized article 6 for operating in perpetuity and extraterritorially without an opportunity for review at the national level. [52]

3. Homonymous GIs

A homonym is two or more words spelled and/or pronounced alike but different in meaning. Conflicts may arise between homonymous GIs, such as when the same designation is used for similar products from different countries. This could occur where the name of the locality is found in different countries. An often-cited example is Rioja wine for wines produced in Spain and Argentina in the regions of Rioja. Under article 22(4) of the TRIPS Agreement, even if literally true, the use of a homonymous designation is not permitted if such use would falsely represent to the public that the product originates in the reputed region. Conversely, the honest use of homonymous GIs is permissible where the true origin of the GI is indicated.[53]

As to homonymous indications for wine, they may coexist subject to there being no false representation to the public that a wine from a place identified by one of the GIs comes from the place identified by the other denomination. Member states must determine the practicalities related to such coexistence to ensure equitable treatment of the producers concerned and that consumers are not misled.[54] Additional information as to the origin of the product may be required.

In practice, member states have adopted means to regulate conflicts between homonymous GIs, the common thread being that concurrent use is not permitted where it would mislead the public as to the nature or certain qualities of the product.[55] The OIV, in its Resolution ECO/3/99, proposed the following considerations to be applied by states for differentiating homonymous names: 'the official recognition used in the country of origin; the length of time the name has been in use; whether the usage is in good faith; the importance of presenting the homonymous labels to marketing; and encourage mentioning sufficient distinguishing information to avoid confusion of consumers'.[56]

---

[52] Dev Gangjee, 'Genericide: The Death of a Geographical Indication? in Dev Gangjee (ed), *Research Handbook on Intellectual Property and Geographical Indications* (Edward Elgar 2016) 39.
[53] Matija Damjan, 'Homonymous Names of Wines and Grape Varieties: The Case of Teran' in Carlos Torres and others (eds), *Wine Law* (Estoril Higher Institute for Tourism and Hotel Studies 2021) 88.
[54] TRIPS Agreement, art 23(3).
[55] Standing Committee on the Law of Trademarks (n 7) para 85.
[56] Cited in Damjan (n 53) 89.

4. Concluding Remarks

The conflict between trade marks and GIs has been discussed and deliberated on the international and national levels. However, the controversy has not yet been resolved to the satisfaction of all parties. The TRIPS Agreement only caters for a limited number of conflictual situations between trade marks and GIs. Even the available articles do not provide a clear-cut and straightforward answer, as evidenced by the complex and extended disputes between the United States and the EC (nowadays the EU) and Australia and the EC before the WTO Panel. The WIPO, through the Standing Committee on the Law of Trademark, Industrial Designs and Geographical Indications, has also focused extensively on the matter in an effort to provide a proper solution.

Both trade marks and GIs operate in the brand market. The two main solutions to conflicts between trade marks and GIs are the FITFIR, which will exclude either certain trade marks or GIs, or the coexistence approach, where the scope of operation is demarcated to allow both to operate without friction. Both solutions are unsatisfactory to their opponents. For the GI proponents, a GI should be granted priority, or at least coexistence, with trade marks. A GI representing any group or community should be preferred to trade marks.[57] On the other hand, proponents of the trade mark system would prefer that GIs impact no rights created under trade mark law. Coexistence is seen as potentially causing confusion in the consumers' minds.[58]

---

[57] Oindrila Roy Muhuri, 'An Analysis on Overlapping of Geographical Indication and Trademark' (2002) 5(1) *International Journal of Rural Management & Humanities* 201.
[58] ibid 202.

4
The African Regional Intellectual Property Organization*

The African Regional Intellectual Property Organization (ARIPO) is one of the two regional intellectual property organizations in Africa. Membership is open to member states of the African Union or the United Nations Economic Commission for Africa.[1] In February 2024, there were twenty-two member states of ARIPO: Botswana, Cape Verde, Kingdom of Eswatini, the Gambia, Ghana, Kenya, Kingdom of Lesotho, Liberia, Malawi, Mauritius, Mozambique, Namibia, Rwanda, Sao Tome and Principe, Seychelles, Sierra Leone, Somalia, Sudan, Uganda, United Republic of Tanzania, Zambia, and Zimbabwe. Most of these countries are anglophone countries found in Eastern and Southern Africa.

ARIPO was first established under the denomination of the Industrial Property Organization for English-Speaking Africa (ESARIPO) through the 'Agreement on the Creation of the Industrial Property Organization for English-Speaking Africa' (Lusaka Agreement), adopted on 9 December 1976. The original signatories were Ghana, Kenya, Mauritius, Somalia, Uganda, and Zambia. The aim was to pool resources of member countries to avoid duplication of financial and human resources in intellectual property (IP) matters. This included the joint development of national IP laws.[2] At that time, some of the founding member states did not grant IP rights but only extended the effect of IP rights granted in another foreign state (mainly the United Kingdom) to their territories. ARIPO (at that time ESARIPO) aimed to maximize member states' economic and industrial development through the effective and continuous sharing of information and the harmonization and coordination of IP laws and activities. Today, the central tenet of ARIPO remains cooperation amongst the member states.

Under the ARIPO system, countries may join the organization by ratifying or acceding to the Lusaka Agreement. Once an ARIPO member, the state may elect to become a member of one protocol, more than one, or none. There are currently four protocols, with each protocol governing a specific IP right: the Harare Protocol on Patents and Industrial Designs, the Banjul Protocol on Marks (Banjul

---

* The authors would like to thank Monique Bagal for sharing valuable information for this chapter.
[1] All fifty-four member states of the United Nations Economic Commission for Africa are members of the African Union. The Sahrawi Arab Democratic Republic is part of the African Union but not of the United Nations Economic Commission for Africa.
[2] ARIPO, 'Our History' (*ARIPO*, nd) < https://www.aripo.org/browse/about-us/our-history>.

Protocol), the Swakopmund Protocol on Protection of Traditional Knowledge and Expressions of Folklore, and the Arusha Protocol for the Protection of New Varieties of Plants. For example, Mauritius is a member of ARIPO but is not party to any protocol. Thus, it is impossible to designate Mauritius to protect IP rights under the ARIPO system.

There is currently no protocol related to geographical indications (GIs) at ARIPO. There is, however, a recognition that a regional GI system could serve as a model for member states, increase the value of origin-based goods and products, and enable ARIPO to address transboundary GIs.[3] During its thirteenth session, held in Accra, Ghana in 2011, the ARIPO Council of Ministers approved the inclusion of GIs in the overall mandate on IP. Other linked proposals included the creation of awareness on the importance of GI protection for economic development and linking ARIPO initiatives on GIs with that of the World Intellectual Property Organization (WIPO), the World Trade Organization, and the European Union (EU). The ARIPO Council of Ministers tasked the Secretariat to work towards the adoption of an appropriate regional legal framework on GIs and to assist member states in adopting appropriate national legislation on GIs. In 2012, at the thirty-sixth session of the ARIPO Administrative Council, a Memorandum of Understanding was signed between ARIPO and the Directorate General for Agriculture and Rural Development of the European Commission. As part of the implementation of the said memorandum, a series of workshops on GIs were held in Kenya, Uganda, Zambia, and Zimbabwe. In 2014, workshops were jointly organized by ARIPO and the EU in Botswana and Mozambique under the theme: 'GIs in Africa: from Theory to Practice'.[4]

A draft policy and legal framework were prepared in 2014 by the ARIPO Secretariat following broad consultations with various stakeholders, such as member states, the EU, and WIPO. A road map for the adoption of the draft legal framework was designed. A timeline was drawn up: from the circulation of the draft policy and legal framework to member states through their national IP offices and to regional economic blocs in Africa for their comments and suggestions by the end of March 2014, up until the convening of the diplomatic conference in 2016 for the adoption of the protocol.[5] For several reasons, it was impossible to implement this road map, although, by 2014, a draft ARIPO protocol on GIs had been achieved.

Though its title refers only to GIs, the draft protocol also provides for the protection of appellations of origin. A GI is thus defined as an 'indication which identifies

---

[3] Emmanuel Sackey, 'ARIPO as a Regional Development Ocean of Intellectual Property System in Africa' (*Slide Share*, 22–25 November 2016) <www.slideshare.net/ExternalEvents/aripo-presentation-and-activities>.

[4] Intellectual Property Rights and Innovation in Africa (AfrIPI), *Manual for Geographical Indications in Africa* (European Union Intellectual Property Office 2022) 15, 17.

[5] ARIPO Secretariat, 'ARIPO: Who We Are & What We Do' (ARIPO 2016) 32.

a good as originating in the territory of a state, or a region or locality in that territory where a given quality reputation or other characteristic of the good is essentially attributable to its geographical origin', while an appellation of origin is defined as 'a type of geographical indication that identifies a good wholly produced within its defined geographical area and which refers to a territory lesser in extent than a state'.[6] The registration process and the protective and enforcement mechanisms are similar for both. Under the draft protocol, applications for the registration of a GI would be lodged at the national competent authority in the territory where the good is produced or, in the case of goods produced outside the territory of Contracting States, in the territory where the applicant is established. The national authority checks the completeness of the application and notifies the ARIPO Office. The ARIPO Office publishes the application. It invites comments and statements of opposition for a period of four months. Within six months of receiving the complete application, the national authority assesses the application to verify whether it meets the requirements laid down in the protocol.[7] Once the assessment is completed, the national authority either lodges the application with the ARIPO Office stating that the application is complete and accurate or, in the contrary case, returns the application to the applicant. The ARIPO Office assesses the application lodged by the national authority in the light of any comments and statements of opposition pursuant to the publication. Within twelve months of receipt of the complete application by the national authority, the ARIPO Office must finalize its assessment of the application. Where the application meets the requirements under the protocol and the national procedure has been satisfactorily completed, ARIPO enters the GI in the Register of GIs. If not, ARIPO publishes a notice in the Official Gazette that the application is withdrawn.

The draft protocol also provides for a Register of GIs to be maintained at the seat of ARIPO. The Register of GIs would contain every GI, its product category, the country or countries of production, information as to whether all steps of production of the goods take place in the geographical area, and whether the GI also qualifies as an appellation of origin, as well as the date of application.[8]

The draft protocol was never adopted. Far from being deterred by the failure to adopt the draft protocol, at its seventh session, held in Harare in 2017, the technical committee of the ARIPO Administrative Council adopted a recommendation for the Secretariat to conduct a comprehensive study on the best approach to implement the mandate on GIs in the region. The Administrative Council endorsed the recommendation at its forty-sixth session held in Lilongwe, Malawi, in November 2017.[9]

---

[6] ARIPO Secretariat, 'The Draft Policy and Legal Framework for the Protection of Geographical Indications' (ARIPO 2014), s 2.
[7] ibid s 7.1.
[8] ibid s 10.
[9] AfrIPI, *Manual* (n 4) 15.

Over the years, numerous conferences have been organized on GIs, such as the November 2021 regional conference on GIs organized by ARIPO in collaboration with AfrIPI. The conference aimed to define a strategy amongst the ARIPO member states with regard to setting up a GI legal framework on a regional or national level.[10] One of the conclusions adopted at the conference and which was later endorsed by the ARIPO Administrative Council was the creation of an ad hoc working group on GIs to reflect on the legal framework and on the convergence of efforts that ARIPO member states must implement for GIs in the region. The working group first met in March 2022 to discuss the most suitable legal framework in the region and to draw up a road map of priorities. The working group further agreed to create an ad hoc sub-working group on GIs with volunteer delegates from Ghana, Kenya, Liberia, Malawi, Mozambique, and Zambia.[11] The first meeting took place in June 2022. The sub-group of the ad hoc working group decided to update the existing draft protocol. To assist them in their task and ensure that a model law be adopted that reflects the needs of the member states, a consultant was recruited to work on a GI needs assessment. By August 2023, the ad hoc sub-working group on GIs had met three times. A questionnaire had also been circulated to member states. The content of the questionnaire will inform the need assessment and the provisions of model law.

Still, there is no denying that ARIPO has been slow on the GI front, in particular, compared to the African Intellectual Property Organization (OAPI). It is only in November 2020 that Mozambique registered the *Cabrito de Tete Goat*, the first and only GI by an ARIPO member state through its domestic *sui generis* system, with much support from the EU. Following a screening by the European Union Intellectual Property Office (EUIPO) in 2019, ten products were identified as potential GIs amongst the member states of the organization, with the first five being highlighted as particularly interesting: Anlo Shallots from Ghana, Kisii Soapstone from Kenya, Gisovu Tea from Rwanda, Kenema Kola Nuts from Sierra Leone, and Cabrito de Tete from Mozambique.[12]

1. Legislation on GIs

There is no specific protocol for registering GIs at ARIPO's level. There is, however, the Banjul Protocol governing the registration of trade marks, to which thirteen member states were parties in February 2024: Botswana, Cape Verde, Eswatini, the

---

[10] AfrIPI, 'Conference on Geographical Indications for ARIPO Countries' (*AfrIPI*, nd) <https://afripi.org/activities/conference-geographical-indications-aripo-countries>.

[11] AfrIPI, 'First Meeting of the ARIPO Sub-Group of the Ad Hoc Working Group on GIs' (*AfrIPI*, 17 June 2022) <https://internationalipcooperation.eu/en/afripi/news/first-meeting-aripo-sub-group-ad-hoc-working-group-gis>.

[12] AfrIPI, *Manual* (n 4) 33.

Gambia Lesotho, Liberia, Malawi, Mozambique, Namibia, Sao Tomé and Principe, Tanzania, Uganda, and Zimbabwe. The Banjul Protocol offers a simplified application system whereby applicants can pick and choose countries where they wish to obtain protection for their trade mark (an African mini-Madrid of sorts). It is important to note that state parties to any protocol under ARIPO retain their national IP legislation and have national IP offices that concurrently issue and register IP titles valid domestically. Thus, right holders may choose for each of the thirteen state parties to the Banjul Protocol to file an application either through the ARIPO Secretariat in Harare, Zimbabwe or domestically.

As of July 2023, amongst the ARIPO member states, Botswana, Cape Verde, Ghana, Mauritius, Mozambique, Rwanda, Sao Tome and Principe, Seychelles, Uganda, Zanzibar, and Zimbabwe had adopted *sui generis* legislation to protect GIs at the national level.

The Gambia, Kenya, Liberia, Malawi, Namibia, Sierra Leone, the United Republic of Tanzania (except for Zanzibar), and Zambia are considering the registration of GIs as *sui generis* right. Eswatini, Lesotho, Somalia, and Sudan neither have a system in place for the registration of GIs nor are considering doing so.

2. Registration of GIs Domestically

There are three ways to register GIs in ARIPO member states. At the national level, in Botswana, Cape Verde, Ghana, Mauritius, Mozambique, Rwanda, Sao Tome and Principe, Seychelles, Uganda, Zanzibar, and Zimbabwe, right holders may apply for the *sui generis* registration of their GI. In all of these countries except Uganda, right holders may also choose to register the GI as a collective mark. In all of the countries except Botswana, right holders may choose to register a GI as a certification mark.

In states that do not offer the possibility of *sui generis* registration, right holders may turn to either certification or collective marks. Collective marks are available in the Gambia, Kenya, Lesotho, Liberia, Namibia, Malawi, Tanzania, Somalia, and Sudan. Certification marks are an option in Kenya, Malawi, Namibia, Sierra Leone, Tanzania, and Zambia.

It is finally possible to go through the Banjul Protocol for states that are party to the Protocol and which provide for either collective or certification marks in their domestic laws. As such, right owners may apply for a collective mark through a single application at ARIPO for Botswana, Cape Verde, the Gambia, Lesotho, Liberia, Malawi, Mozambique, Namibia, Sao Tome and Principe, Seychelles, and Tanzania. The right owner may apply for a certification mark through a single application at ARIPO for Cape Verde, Malawi, Namibia, Sao Tome and Principe, Seychelles, and Tanzania. Right holders can file a single application in one language (English) indicating all or part of these states. The single application is filed either in the national IP office of the contracting state or directly with the ARIPO Office in Harare, Zimbabwe. For applicants whose ordinary place of business is not in any of the Banjul Protocol contracting states, an authorized representative (trade mark agent or legal practitioner) must be appointed. The ARIPO Office formally examines each application in accordance with the Protocol. If all formal requirements are complied with, ARIPO gives notice of the intended registration to the national office of each designated state. The applicant may request the ARIPO Office to review its refusal of a trade mark.[13]

The national office will conduct the substantive examination in accordance with its national laws. Within nine months, the national office must notify ARIPO of its decision in writing. The national office may notify ARIPO that the registration shall have no effect on its territory on the basis of both absolute and relative grounds, including the existence of third-party rights.[14] Any refusal must be motivated and communicated to ARIPO. The refusal may be appealed or reviewed. The appeal or review is filed with ARIPO but considered under domestic laws. In the absence of any notification in that regard, the application is accepted. The application is then published in the ARIPO *Journal*. Any interested person may oppose the mark within three months of publication date. The notice of opposition is filed at ARIPO but reviewed in accordance with the national laws of the country it concerns.[15] The Registry of the member state examines the opposition and renders a decision. This decision is subject to appeal or review as per domestic laws. If an appeal or review is filed, the national office must inform the ARIPO Office and both the opponent and applicant of the outcome of such appeal without delay. The ARIPO Office will then record the decision in the Register and publish it in the ARIPO *Journal*. A trade mark registered through ARIPO has the effect of a regular national filing in the states designated in the application.[16]

Once registered, a mark is valid for ten years from the filing date, renewable indefinitely for a ten-year period. National laws determine issues related to enforcement and other administrative aspects.[17]

---

[13] Banjul Protocol on Marks, s 5*bis*(1).
[14] ibid s 6(2).
[15] ibid s 6*bis*(4).
[16] ibid s 8(1).
[17] The validity and enforceability of ARIPO trade marks is a recurring question with no easy answer. Some countries, such as Botswana, Malawi, Mozambique, Namibia, Sao Tomé and Principe, and Zimbabwe, have domesticated the Banjul Protocol, and enforceability is not in doubt. In other countries, there is more of a grey zone where, although there has been no explicit domestication, there are other aspects, such as legal provisions and court cases, that lead the authors to believe that ARIPO registrations will be held valid and enforceable. These include Lesotho, Liberia, and Uganda. In Eswatini, the Gambia, and Tanzania, the Banjul Protocol has not been domesticated, and either the practice or the law indicates that a treaty must be incorporated into domestic law to become applicable. In practice, it is unlikely that ARIPO will allow a decision holding its trade marks to be invalid to stand. The authors expect an appeal or thorough lobbying from ARIPO to the authorities if this is the case.

3. Looking Forwards

As mentioned earlier, ARIPO now has an ad hoc sub-working group on GIs. Consultants have been recruited to assist the working group, with the ultimate aim of working out the most suitable legal framework for protecting GIs. This will occur through a legal gap analysis and review of the draft 2014 protocol on GIs and by assessing the needs of the member states.[18]

Hopefully, this will lead to a system that will benefit member states. Currently, on the topic of GIs, ARIPO member states work in isolation instead of combining their forces. A regional protocol would lead to a more straightforward and more effective registration process, benefiting both African and foreign GIs. There is no doubt that with the combined membership of ARIPO and the OAPI (thirty-seven countries), the adoption of any protocol on GIs by ARIPO would strongly influence and shape GI development in Africa.[19]

---

[18] AfrIPI, 'Second Meeting of the ARIPO Sub-Group of the Ad Hoc Working Group on GIs' (*AfrIPI*, 27 July 2022) <https://internationalipcooperation.eu/en/afripi/news/second-meeting-aripo-sub-group-ad-hoc-working-group-gis>.

[19] Adebola Titilayo, 'The Legal Construction of Geographical Indications in Africa' (2023) 26(3) J World Intellect Prop 12.

5
The African Intellectual Property Organization

The African Intellectual Property Organization (OAPI, an acronym of *Organisation Africaine de la Propriété Intellectuelle*) is one of the two regional intellectual property organizations in Africa. Membership is open to all African states who become party to the Agreement of Bangui. There are currently seventeen member states: Benin, Burkina Faso, Cameroon, Central African Republic, Chad, Comoros, Congo, Côte d'Ivoire, Equatorial Guinea, Gabon, Guinea, Guinea-Bissau, Mali, Mauritania, Niger, Senegal, and Togo. Most of these countries are West African francophone countries.

First created in September 1962 as the African and Malagasy Office of Industrial Property (OMAPI), the organization was revamped following the departure of Madagascar, the attribution of new responsibilities in the area of copyright, and the interlink of intellectual property with development. This led to the adoption of the Agreement of Bangui in March 1977 and the creation of the OAPI. A new revision of the Agreement of Bangui took place on 24 February 1999 to ensure the conformity of the Agreement to the World Trade Organization (WTO) Agreement on Trade-Related Aspects of Intellectual Property Rights (TRIPS), to which all OAPI member states are party. This revision entered into force on 28 February 2002. The latest revision dates back to 14 December 2015 through the Acte de Bamako. The 2015 version of the Agreement of Bangui came into force on 14 November 2020, together with Annex VI on Geographical Indications (GIs), Annex VII on literary and artistic rights, Annex VIII on unfair competition, and Annex X on plant variety rights. Annexes III (marks), Annex IV (industrial designs), and Annex V (commercial names) as amended by the Acte de Bamako entered into force on 1 January 2022. Annex I (patents), Annex II (utility models), and Annex IX (layout designs of integrated circuits) have yet to come into force.

GIs can be protected in the OAPI either through the *sui generis* system or as collective marks or certification marks. Far from being a new topic, the *sui generis* protection of GIs has been possible at the OAPI since 1977, as appellations of origin inspired by the definition in the Lisbon Agreement for the Protection of Appellations of Origin and their International Registration (Lisbon Agreement) of 1958, and since 1999 as a GI. Still, no GI was registered in the region for a long time; the first GI registered in 2006 was *Champagne*. Today, other foreign GIs for spirits include *Scotch Whisky* and *Cognac*.

The first promotional activities to develop GIs in the region occurred in the early 2000s, with the OAPI relying on French technical assistance. French experts trained national officials to identify products potentially suitable for GI protection. One of the aims of the training was to support the OAPI in anticipation of the OAPI Ministerial Conference on GIs scheduled in Ouagadougou, Burkina Faso on 7 December 2005.[1] The Ministerial Conference gathered Ministers responsible for intellectual property and Ministers of Agriculture of OAPI member countries. The declaration and action plan on GIs adopted at this conference provided for the establishment of National Committees on GI in each country and GI focal points in every Ministry of Agriculture, as well as the selection of pilot products. Member states urged the OAPI to intensify its effort to promote GIs by seeking funding and by mobilizing technical assistance.[2] Its member states further mandated the OAPI to formulate the means of implementation of the action plan.[3]

In 2006, the OAPI reached out to the *Agence française de développement* (AFD) for further support on this matter, leading to the coming into operation of the *Projet d'Appui à la Mise en Place des IG dans les Etats Membres* (PAMPIG) in 2010. Set up by the OAPI and financed by the AFD, PAMPIG aimed to accompany countries in identifying potential GIs and reinforcing the capacities of the OAPI and national public and private partners to promote and protect GIs. Training and communication activities were also conducted under the aegis of PAMPIG to popularize opportunities offered by GIs. Four products from three different OAPI member states were identified: *Oku White Honey* and *Penja Pepper* from Cameroon, Korhogo cloths from the Ivory Coast, and *Coffee of Ziama* from Guinea. PAMPIG helped identify and organize the relevant actors and draft the specifications chart and control mechanisms. Through PAMPIG, the OAPI became closely involved in identifying and developing GIs from the member states. For an intellectual property (IP) office, the OAPI is in the unlikely situation of being both judge and party at the same time. The OAPI has, however, publicly claimed this role as a development agency, actively promoting local GIs.[4] Only three of the identified products under PAMPIG were registered as GIs, with *Penja Pepper*, published on 18 April 2013, being the first GI. *Penja Pepper* is also the second GI from Africa registered as a protected GI in the EU.[5] Korhogo cloths could not be registered due to insecurity in the region.

---

[1] Intellectual Property Rights and Innovation in Africa (AfrIPI), *Manual for Geographical Indications in Africa* (European Union Intellectual Property Office 2022) 13.
[2] ibid 14.
[3] African Union Commission Department of Rural Economy and Agriculture, 'Continental Strategy for Geographical Indications In Africa 2018–2023' (African Union Commission Department of Rural Economy and Agriculture, nd) 2.
[4] International Trademark Association, 'OAPI Advances IP in French-Speaking Africa' (*International Trademark Association*, 15 March 2023) <www.inta.org/perspectives/interviews/oapi-advances-ip-in-french-speaking-africa>.
[5] *Rooibos/Red Bush* was the first protected designation of origin in Europe from Africa.

The OAPI has created a logo, unveiled in May 2018, to be affixed to labels and packages of products protected as GIs by the OAPI. The first beneficiaries of the logo were the producer associations of *Penja Pepper* and *Oku White Honey*.[6] As the logo must be applied by the representative grouping of the GI (ie the producers' association owner of the GI at the OAPI), in practice, the logo is used only for GIs originating from, and protected in, the OAPI. The regulations on the reproduction, use, and management of the PGI logo of the OAPI at article 2 further provide that the use of the logo for products repackaged outside of the OAPI territory and destined to their markets may be considered under certain conditions and subject to the signature of a contract.

A follow-up to PAMPIG, PAMPIG II, runs from 2017 to 2024. PAMPIG II aims to consolidate the three GIs registered under PAMPIG, identify and support six new potential GIs from Benin, Cameroon, Guinea, and the Ivory Coast, and reinforce capacities at the national and regional levels. As of February 2024, ten GIs from the region have been registered at the OAPI, including *Ananas Pain de Sucre du Plateau d'Allada* (Benin), *Hat of Saponé* (Burkina Faso), *Kilichi du Niger* (Niger); *Pagne Baoulé*, Attiéké des Lagunes(both from Ivory Coast), and *Échalote de Bandiagara* (Mali). The *Hat of Saponé* is the first GI for handicrafts registered at the OAPI. Other products that will likely be registered as GIs following training and advice by the OAPI and other development actors include 'Baronne de Guinée', 'Gari Sohui of Savalou', and 'Cacao Rouge of Cameroun'. Today, following amendments bought about by the Acte de Bamako, the promotion of GIs is one of the objectives of the OAPI.[7]

The OAPI also allows for the registration of collective marks. Quality products originating from the OAPI and registered as collective marks include Faso Danfani (Burkina Faso) and tchoukou cheese, and the skin of the red head goat (both of Niger).

1. Legal Framework

Under the OAPI, all member states apply a uniform law, the Bangui Agreement and its ten annexes, with a common administrative procedure giving rise to unitary IP rights. The annexes have the status of domestic laws in each member state.[8]

---

[6] OAPI, 'Commerce international: Le poivre de Penja et le miel blanc d'Oku ont désormais leur label de qualité' (*OAPI*, nd) <http://oapi.int/index.php/fr/services/marque-de-produits-de-services/taxes/item/285-commerce-international-le-poivre-de-penja-et-le-miel-blanc-d-oku-ont-desormais-leur-label-de-qualite>.

[7] Agreement of Bangui instituting the African Intellectual Property Organization, Act of 14 December 2015 (Agreement of Bangui), art 2(i).

[8] World Trade Organization, 'Trade Policy Review: Members of the West African Economic and Monetary Union (WAEMU)' (Trade Policy Review Body 2017) 55.

There is no coexistence of a national protection system with the regional system as all countries, upon joining the OAPI, waive their right to national filing. The OAPI, headquartered in Yaoundé, Cameroun, is the common bureau of industrial property and serves as the supra-national IP rights protection office for each member state.[9] The Organization deals with the administrative matters pertaining to the registration, maintenance, and upkeep of unitary IP rights, such as patents, trade marks, trade names, and designs. Procedures are centralized such that an application at the OAPI or at the national liaison office/ministry in charge of IP, which shall then transfer it to the OAPI, is equivalent to a filing in every member state. The OAPI's titles are unitary and valid in all member states. The designation of specific countries in the application is not required and, in fact, impossible. There is a single registration procedure for GIs in OAPI countries and a specific register that exists at the level of the OAPI. The only exception to this unitary system relates to copyright. OAPI member states must adopt the provision in the annex on copyright as the minimum level of protection. Member states may, however, adopt laws that provide additional protection for copyright.

Contentious matters are handled by the domestic courts of the member states in which the matter arises. There is no 'OAPI community court', and no member state has specialized IP courts. Disputes are therefore usually heard before the commercial courts or, where there is none, in lower courts.[10] Penalties for the infringement of IP rights are a matter for domestic laws. A final judgment on the validity of titles in one member state is, however, authoritative in all member states, except where it concerns decisions based on public order and morality.[11] A final judgment related to the infringement of an IP right in one member state is valid exclusively in that state. It may not be relied upon before the authorities of another member state.[12] The latest amendment through the Acte de Bamako introduced the possibility of arbitration, although implementing regulations were still pending as of July 2023.

2. Regional Legislation on GIs

Under the Bangui Agreement, member states also agree to adhere to the Paris Convention for the Protection of Industrial Property of 1883 and the Lisbon Agreement for the Protection of Appellations of Origin and Their International Registration (Lisbon System) of 1958. The OAPI is itself a member of the Lisbon System, having acceded to the Geneva Act of the Lisbon Agreement on

---

[9] Bangui Agreement, art 2(4).
[10] World Trade Organization (n 8) 55.
[11] Bangui Agreement, art 18.
[12] OAPI, *Le contentieux de la propriété intellectuelle dans l'espace OAPI: Guide du Magistrat et des auxiliaires de justice* (1st edn, OAPI 2009) 77.

15 December 2022. The OAPI joined the Madrid Protocol for the International Registration of Trade Marks (Madrid System) in 2014. It is thus possible to designate the OAPI in an international trade mark application. OAPI member states fully comply with the TRIPS Agreement's provisions following the revision of the Bangui Agreement in 1999. In fact, some of the provisions are TRIPS-plus.

3. Registration of GIs

3.1 GIs

Annex VI of the Bangui Agreement provides for the *sui generis* registration of GIs in the OAPI. GIs are defined as an indication identifying a product as originating in an area, a region, or a country where the quality, reputation, or other determining characteristic of the product can be attributed essentially to that geographical origin.[13] This definition is in line with article 22(1) of the TRIPS Agreement. The definition is wide-ranging, extending to natural, agricultural, artisanal, or industrial products. Interestingly, a GI may concern two or more states.[14] This recognizes that in Africa, a community with a shared history may live across different countries.

Any signs that do not conform to the definition of a GI; are contrary to public order or public morals; or which could mislead the public, namely as to the nature, origin, mode of fabrication, qualities, characteristics, or fitness for use of the product or which are not protected or are no longer protected in the country of origin cannot be registered.

It is possible to register at the OAPI a GI originating from member states and from a third country. A foreign GI is protected in the OAPI where it has been registered either by the OAPI or through an international agreement to which member states of the OAPI or the OAPI itself are party to.[15] This refers to appellations of origin registered under the Lisbon Agreement.

3.2 Collective and certification marks

It is also possible to register either a collective or certification mark at the OAPI under Annex III of the Bangui Agreement. A collective mark is defined as a mark for goods or services whose conditions of use are laid down in a regulation approved by the competent authority and which may only be used by publicly

---

[13] Bangui Agreement, Annex VI, art 1.
[14] ibid Annex VI, art 2.
[15] ibid Annex VI, art 4.

recognized groups, trade unions, or a grouping of trade unions, associations, groups of producers, industrialists, craftsmen, or traders, provided that they are officially recognized and have legal capacity.[16] A certification mark is defined as a mark applied to a product or service presenting in its nature, properties, qualities, or characteristics specified in its regulations.[17]

The rules applicable for a GI, a collective, or certification mark apply to all goods and services. No specific rules and/or additional protection apply to wines and spirits.

4. Registrability of Names

4.1 GIs

One single provision governs acceptable names for a GI: a GI, which, although correct as to the territory, the area, or locality from which the products originate, leads the public to think that the products originate from another territory will be refused or invalidated.[18] There is no express provision regarding coexistence of GIs as per article 24(5) of the TRIPS Agreement.

4.2 Collective and certification marks

Rules governing marks are more extensive. A trade mark that contains, imitates, or is constituted by a GI, or the imitation of a GI, may be refused or invalidated if the use of this indication for such products is likely to mislead the public as to the genuine origin of the product.[19] An *a contrario* interpretation would allow the registration of a trade mark containing, imitating, or constituted by a GI where use is unlikely to mislead the public. A mark may further not be validly registered where it lacks distinctiveness; is identical or confusingly similar to a previously registered mark for similar or identical products; is contrary to public order, good morals, or illegal; is likely to mislead the public or the commercial community in particular as to the geographical origin, nature, or characteristics of the goods or services concerned; and without authorization reproduces, imitates, or contains among its elements coats of arms, flags or other emblems, abbreviations, sign or official stamp of a country or an international organization created by international convention.[20]

---

[16] ibid Annex III, art 2(2).
[17] ibid Annex III, art 2(3). The OAPI has chosen a somewhat surprising and slightly confusing appellation for certification mark, labelling them as collective marks of certification.
[18] Bangui Agreement, Annex VI, art 3(2).
[19] ibid Annex VI, art 3(1).
[20] ibid Annex III, art 3.

5. Procedure and Requirements for Registration

5.1 GIs

At the OAPI, there is a three-actor system for registering a GI originating from the OAPI member states: the grouping of producers, the National Committee on GIs, and the OAPI. The grouping of producers drafts the specification chart of the proposed GI and forwards it to the National Committee on GIs. The National Committee on GIs is a technical advisory committee in charge of coordinating activities of identifying, valorizing, controlling, defending, and evaluating the process of GIs domestically. The National Committee validates the product specifications chart and gives its opinion on the link between the product's characteristics and its geographical origin. It develops the legal and institutional framework protecting GIs. The National Committees also have a coordination and monitoring mission once the GI is registered. Once the product specifications have been validated, the National Committee transmits the specification chart to the OAPI through the National Liaison Structure for registration. The OAPI receives the application and acts as the IP Office.[21] In June 2022, ten out of seventeen National Committees had been created, although ultimately, every member state should have a national committee. For a foreign GI, the application is made to the OAPI by the relevant legal entity.

The applicants for a GI registration are either legal entities carrying out the activity of producers in the relevant geographical region, any groupings of such persons, or any competent authority. In exceptional cases, the application may be filed by a physical person. What constitutes an exceptional case has yet to be defined. A producer is defined in article 1 of Annex VI as a grower or farmer of natural products, manufacturer of handicrafts or industrial products, or a processor of natural or agricultural products. Interestingly, alongside this classic definition, article 1 includes anyone who trades in natural, agricultural, industrial, and handicrafts products as a producer. Associations of retailers and distributors are therefore included in the definition of producers.

The application for registration is filed with the OAPI (foreign GIs) or the National Liaison Structure (regional GIs). The application is made through the prescribed form IG 60. The following information must be provided:

a) Name, contact details, nationality, and date of constituent act of the applicant. The applicant must be formally constituted in a grouping. Copies of this formal constitution must be provided;
b) Name and contact details of agent (if applicable). The registration of foreign GIs must be applied for through an agent and a power of attorney is required;

---

[21] AfrIPI (n 1) 30.

c) a representation of the GI;
d) specification chart of the GI. The specification chart contains the name of the applicant, the name of the product; the type of product; a description of the product highlighting the quality, reputation, or other characteristic of the products for which the indication will be used; exact delimitation of the geographical area; production method; link with the place of origin; control plan and labeling.
e) name of the control authority;
f) date and registration number of the GI in the country of origin for foreign GI; and
g) a presentation note showing clearly the reasons behind the choice of a GI, the production sector of the GI, the representativeness of the group requesting the registration of a GI and the strategic reflection on how the GI will be implemented and developed;
h) reasoned opinion validating the request for GI registration by the National Committee on GIs for regional GIs; and
i) proof of payment of prescribed taxes.[22]

For regional GIs, the application is forwarded to the National Liaison Structure. The National Liaison Structure receives the application and examines its admissibility, that is whether all the required information has been provided and the taxes paid. If found complete, the application is then forwarded by mail or post to the OAPI for examination within five working days. For foreign GIs, the application is referred directly to the OAPI.

In case of a transnational GI covering one or more member states of the OAPI, any of the concerned members may file the application, or all the states concerned may file a common application. In case of a transnational application concerning one or more member states of the OAPI and one or more third-party states that are also party to the Lisbon Agreement of 2015, all the concerned states may file a single application. In case of a common application, the application request must also contain an authorization to file by the competent administrative authority of all parties concerned.

Every applicant obtains an acknowledgment of receipt with the date and time of the application. The OAPI formally examines the application. If taxes have not been paid or the applicant does not have the capacity to request registration, the application is rejected. If the application lacks other requirements, it is considered irregular. The applicant of an irregular application will be invited to correct any irregularities by the OAPI.

---

[22] Bangui Agreement, Annex VI, art 8.

The OAPI publishes every application for registration, and any interested person may oppose the registration within three months from the publication, setting out in writing to the OAPI the reasons for the opposition. An opposition is possible where

a) the application goes against the definition of a GI, a product, or producers;
b) the application infringes the provisions regarding marks containing a GI or is a misleading sign as to the origin of the product;
c) is contrary to public order or public moral;
d) the applied indication is not protected or no longer protected in the country of origin;
e) the application has not been filed by the appropriate body/person, or
f) infringes a prior registered right belonging to the opponent.[23]

The OAPI will share with the applicant a copy of the opposition. The applicant may forward a motivated response within three months, renewable once. The response is communicated to the opponent. The OAPI may hear the parties if the parties so request. The OAPI may either accept or reject the application. The OAPI's decision may be appealed to the *Commission Supérieure de Recours* within 60 days from notification of the decision to the parties. After registration of a GI, the applicant is granted a certificate. The OAPI publishes details as to the GI.

Upon payment of a fee, any GI application may be modified until a decision has been reached regarding its registration, during the opposition procedure, or during the appeal process. The modification may only concern the beneficiaries and the delimitation of the geographical area.

5.2 Collective and certification marks

Collective and certification marks have similar requirements and follow the same registration process as a trade mark. The application must contain a reproduction of the mark, the requested class(es), priority document (if applicable), and a signed power of attorney. Applicants whose place of business is outside of the OAPI must act through a representative domiciled in one of the member states. The only additional requirement for both collective and certification marks is the submission of regulations. The regulations for a collective mark must set out the conditions of use of the mark (persons authorized to use the mark and membership requirements), the common characteristics of the intended goods and services, and the control rules as to the specifications of the product or services, as well as any sanctions for

[23] ibid, Annex VI, art 12(1)

the wrongful use of the mark by its members. Foreign collective marks must further show that the regulations have been duly registered in the country of origin. The rules for a certification mark must indicate precisely the norm established by the owner of the mark, including a description of the specific characteristics to be possessed by the goods or services, the control mechanisms put into place and exercised by the owner of the mark, and the conditions to be fulfilled to be granted the right to use the mark. Upon submission of the filing request, the OAPI or the ministry in charge of IP will issue a filing receipt (*procès-verbal de dépôt*). The file will be deemed to be properly constituted where it contains all the required information. The applicant of an irregular application will be invited to correct any irregularities by the OAPI. The OAPI then carries out a preliminary admissibility examination verifying whether the application complies with the technical requirements necessary for publication; that is, it is readable and does not offend public policy and morality. An applicant will be invited to provide a readable sign. Where the sign goes against public policy or morality, the OAPI will provisionally refuse the publication. Still, the OAPI will proceed to a formal and substantive examination. If the sign passes the examination, it will be published for opposition. The opposition period is of six months' duration. If no notification of irregularity has been made, publication for opposition takes place within two months of the filing of the application. Within three months of the publication of the application, the OAPI starts the examination. It is during this examination that an opposition can be initiated. An opposition is initiated in writing on the prescribed form. It must set out the grounds for the opposition, which must be based on

a) a violation of article 2 (signs admissible as marks) and 3 (marks which cannot be registered) of Annex III;
b) a prior registered right belonging to the opponent; or
c) a prior filing or a filing with a prior anteriority date.[24]

The opposition is heard before the Commission of Oppositions. The result of the opposition will determine whether the mark should be registered. An appeal is possible to the *Commission Supérieure de Recours*.

6. Term of Protection

6.1 GIs

Subject to the provisions in the specification brief, the protection afforded to a GI is unlimited in time. There is no provision for the renewal of a GI.

---

[24] ibid., Annex III, art 15(1).

Once a GI has been registered, the relevant national authority must set out, through regulations, a protective mechanism. A GI representative group must be set up to ensure that the products comply with quality standards and all the specifications of the GI. The GI must also have a guarantee scheme to ensure that all stakeholders using the GI to market their products meet the requirements defined in the specification chart to prevent consumer deception and protect honest producers against unfair competition.

The description of the product, the restriction or extension of the area of origin, or producers of the product may be modified during the lifetime of the GI. Any modification that dilutes the link between the product and its region of origin will be rejected. A request for modification must describe and justify the desired modifications. The modification can consist either in removing or adding to the specification brief.

The owner of a previously registered trade mark that is identical or similar to a GI may continue using its trade mark except in cases where the mark is applied on agricultural, natural, or artisanal products.[25] This provision is stricter than articles 23(4) and 24(5) of the TRIPS Agreement, with marks applied on agricultural, natural, or artisanal products excluded independently of the time of their registration. There is no specific provision for homonymous GIs.

Any interested person or competent authority may request the court to nullify the registration of a GI where the GI does not obey the absolute grounds laid out at article 5 of Annex VI. Any interested person or competent authority may request the court to modify the registration of a GI on the basis that the geographical region mentioned in the registration does not correspond to the GI or that the products, quality, reputation, or other characteristic of the products for which the GI is used is missing or is not justified. Any interested person or competent authority may request the competent jurisdiction of a member state to modify the specification chart.[26] These requests are notified to the GI owner and to every person having the right to use the GI. Together with any interested person, they may present a request for intervention before the court. Any nullified registration is considered void from the date of its registration.

6.2 Collective and certification marks

Both collective and certification marks are valid for ten years, renewable indefinitely. A certification mark may be declared invalid by the competent national jurisdiction where the owner of the mark is no longer in existence, the regulations setting out use are contrary to public order or morals, the mark does not obey the

---

[25] ibid Annex VI, art 6(5).
[26] ibid Annex VI, art 21(1).

conditions laid out under the law, or the owner of the mark has allowed use of the mark in conditions other than those set out by the regulations.[27] A nullified mark is considered void as of its registration date.[28]

7. Rights of the Owner and Enforcement Mechanisms against Infringers

7.1 GIs

The registration of a GI grants producers undertaking their activity in the area of origin indicated in the Register the right to use the GI commercially for the products indicated on the Register, so long as these products have the qualities or essential characteristics indicated on the Register. Once the products have been put on the market, every person has the right to use the GI for these products.[29] Apart from those two cases, any commercial use either for products indicated or similar to those indicated on the Register or a similar denomination, even if the true origin of the products is indicated or the GI is translated or accompanied by expressions such as 'style', 'type', 'method', 'as produced in', 'imitation' or similar expressions, is illegal.[30] The use in the designation or representation of a product of any means that indicate or suggest that the products in question originate from a geographical region other than the true region of origin, in a manner that misleads the public as to the geographical origin of the product, is illegal. The protection afforded to GI is therefore quite extensive. Under the TRIPS Agreement, protection against translation and expressions such as 'style', 'type', 'method', 'as produced in', 'imitation', or similar expressions is reserved for wine and spirits.

The defence of a GI, as part of the country's national heritage, against fraudulent use in domestic, regional, and international markets is incumbent on the national authorities. Thus, prohibition of the use of a GI is governed through regulations drafted by the relevant national authority.[31] The relevant representative group must also aid in defending the GI. The GI representative group is qualified to inform the national fraud services and take legal action per the Bangui Agreement's provisions. The OAPI is informed where the infringement, misuse, or fraudulent use of the designations, with or without the OAPI PGI logo, is recorded and investigated by the national authorities.[32]

---

[27] ibid Annex III, art 45(1).
[28] ibid Annex III, art 41.
[29] ibid Annex VI, art 6(2).
[30] ibid Annex VI, art 6(3).
[31] ibid Annex VI, art 20(1).
[32] Regulation relating to use and management of PGI logo of OAPI (adopted in December 2015), arts 3 and 21.

Any interested person, relevant producer group, and group of consumers may lodge a civil action against any person illegally using a GI or contributing to the illegal use of GI. Civil actions may aim to stop the illegal use; to forbid imminent illegal use; or to destroy labels and other documents used, or likely to be used, for an illegal purpose.[33] Such illegal use further constitutes a criminal infringement punishable by between three months and one year's imprisonment and/or a fine of 5–30 million FCFA (Central African francs).[34] These penalties will double in case of recidivism or where the infringer is a member or a salaried employee of the GI grouping. Recidivism occurs when a condemnation has been pronounced five years prior to the offences in Annex VI against the infringer.

Any person having suffered a prejudice following the illicit use of a registered GI may request reparation from the infringer and those having contributed to the illegal use. The quantum of damages will be determined by the court taking into account the negative economic consequences, including loss of earnings by the infringed party, profits gained by the counterfeiter, and the moral prejudice caused to the right owner.[35]

7.2 Collective and certification marks

The registration of a collective or certification mark grants exclusive rights to its owner. The reproduction, use, or affixing of a trade mark, even with the addition of words such as 'formula, manner, system, imitation, kind, method', the use of a reproduced trade mark for goods or services identical to those designated in the registration, or the removal or alteration of a duly affixed mark, are prohibited without the owner's consent. It is further prohibited, without the authorization of the owner where it might result in a risk of confusion among the public, to reproduce, use, use a reproduced trade mark, or affix a trade mark for goods and services similar to the ones designated in the registration or to imitate or use an imitated mark for identical or similar goods and services to those designated in the registration.[36] Any infringement of the rights of the owner of a mark constitutes counterfeiting. Counterfeiting engages its author's civil and criminal liability and may be proved by all means.[37] The civil action is brought before the competent national jurisdiction and is tried in summary proceedings.[38]

Annex III of the Bangui Agreement offers the court a variety of measures to prevent the commission of counterfeiting acts. It is possible to request an interim

---

[33] Bangui Agreement, Annex VI, art 22(2).
[34] ibid Annex VI, art 23.
[35] ibid Annex VI, art 22(4).
[36] ibid Annex III, art 6.
[37] ibid Annex III, art 49 I.
[38] ibid Annex III, art 46(1).

injunction against the alleged infringer or the intermediaries whose services are used, if necessary, under threat of penalty, to prevent an imminent infringement or the continuation of allegedly infringing acts.[39] The court may order *ex parte* any urgent measures where the circumstances so require, in particular where any delay would likely cause irreparable damage to the applicant. Whether requested *ex parte* or in the presence of both parties, the court will only order the requested measures if the evidence, reasonably available to the claimant, makes it probable that its rights are being infringed or that such an infringement is imminent.[40] The court may prohibit the continuation of alleged infringing acts, make them subject to the furnishing of guarantees to ensure the possible compensation of the plaintiff, or order the seizure or delivery into the hands of a third party of the suspected products in order to prevent their introduction or circulation in the commercial circuits. The court may further request guarantees by the plaintiff to ensure the possible compensation of the defendant if the infringement action is subsequently found to be unfounded or the measures annulled. When the measures taken to stop an infringement are ordered before the introduction of an action on the merits, the plaintiff must take civil or criminal action within ten working days from the day following the day on which the measure is taken. Failing this, at the request of the defendant and without the latter having to state the reasons for its claim, the measures ordered shall be annulled, without prejudice to any damages that may be claimed.[41]

Where the act of counterfeiting has been, or is being, committed, the owner, through a bailiff and (if necessary) the assistance of an expert, may undertake a seizure against the suspected goods. The suspected goods may be detained or simply be described by the bailiff. The owner must request an order from the court prior to the seizure, providing the court with a copy of its certificate of registration. Foreign plaintiffs must provide security.[42] Within ten days of the seizure, the owner must initiate an action on the merits. Otherwise, the seizure is considered null, and damages may be requested.[43] Mark owners may also apply for information/discovery proceedings to determine the origin and distribution networks of the counterfeited goods and to obtain the production of documents or information detained by the defendant or any other person found in possession of these goods, using infringing processes or providing services used in infringing activities.[44]

A mark owner may request damages from the counterfeiter. The quantum of damages will be determined by the court taking into account the negative

---

[39] ibid Annex III, art 50(1).
[40] ibid Annex III, art 50(2).
[41] ibid Annex III, art 50(5).
[42] ibid Annex III, art 51.
[43] ibid Annex III, art 52.
[44] ibid Annex III, art 53.

economic consequences, including loss of profit suffered by the injured party, the profits made by the infringer, and the moral prejudice caused to the right holder as a result of the infringement.[45] Other sanctions include an order by the court, at the request of the injured party, that the infringing products, materials, and implements used mainly for their creation or manufacture be recalled or permanently removed from the channels of commerce, destroyed or confiscated, and/or that the judgment in whole or in extracts is published or displayed in newspapers or online. Both sanctions are ordered at the expense of the infringer.[46]

Any civil counterfeiting case must be initiated within five years from the date of the infringing acts, under penalty of prescription.[47]

Criminal sanctions are provided against those who

(a) fraudulently reproduce, use, or affix a mark, even with the addition of words such as: 'formula, manner, system, imitation, type, method' or fraudulently use a reproduced mark for goods or services identical to those designated in the registration;
(b) knowingly sell or offer for sale, supply, or offer to supply goods or services bearing an infringing or fraudulently affixed mark;
(c) fraudulently remove or alter a properly affixed mark;
(d) fraudulently remove or alter a properly affixed mark in such a way as to create a likelihood of confusion on the part of the public, reproduce, use or affix a mark, use a reproduced mark, for goods or services similar to those designated in a registration; those who, under the same conditions, imitate a mark, use an imitated mark, for goods or services identical or similar to those designated in a registration;
(e) knowingly sell, offer for sale, supply, or offer to supply goods or services bearing a fraudulently imitated mark or bearing such indications as to deceive the purchaser as to the nature of the goods, or services;
(f) fraudulently use a mark for goods put on the market by the owner of the mark, but whose condition has subsequently been changed or altered;
(g) those who knowingly supply a product or service other than that requested under a registered mark;
(h) use a mark bearing indications likely to mislead the buyer as to the nature of the product;
(i) knowingly make any use of a collective or a certification mark under conditions other than those laid down in the regulation laying down the conditions of use;[48]

---

[45] ibid Annex III, art 54.
[46] ibid Annex III, art 55.
[47] ibid Annex III, art 56.
[48] ibid, Annex III, art 58.

(j) sell or offer for sale one or more goods bearing a collective or certification mark, that is used improperly with respect to the regulations; or

(k) within a period of ten years from the date of cancellation of a collective or a certification mark, knowingly make any use whatsoever, sell or offer for sale, supply or offer to supply goods or services under mark reproducing or imitating the said collective or certification mark.[49]

The infringer may be punished by a fine of 5–30 million FCFA and/or imprisonment of three months to two years.[50] Where the infringer is condemned within five years of a past conviction under Annex III, the penalties are doubled.[51] Persons convicted of the unlawful exploitation of a mark may, in addition, be deprived of the right to participate, for a period not exceeding ten years, in elections to professional groups, in particular to chambers of commerce and industry and chambers of agriculture. The national court may order the posting of the judgment in such places as it may determine and its publication in full or in extracts in such newspapers as it may designate, all at the expense of the convicted person.[52]

Interestingly, even where a condemnation is not pronounced against an infringer, the court may confiscate and destroy counterfeit goods and order the confiscation of objects used specially for the commission of the counterfeiting offence.[53]

8. Customs Enforcement

Following changes brought by the Acte de Bamako to the Bangui Agreement, customs enforcement with regard to collective and certification marks is now possible. There is currently no provision allowing customs to act with regard to GIs. The owner or beneficiary of an exclusive right of exploitation may request customs to detain suspected counterfeit goods. The request shall be in writing and accompanied by proof of ownership of the highlighted right, that is the registration certificate. In case of detention, the public prosecutor, the requestor, and the importer of the detained goods are immediately informed by customs. Customs share the nature and quantities of the detained goods. The requestor must, within ten working days (or three working days for perishable goods), inform customs of either precautionary measures decided by the national court or of having taken civil

---

[49] ibid, Annex III, art 65.
[50] ibid Annex III, art 57 I.
[51] ibid Annex III, art 60.
[52] ibid Annex III, art 62 I.
[53] ibid Annex III, art 63. Article 63, however, refers to art 59 (Non-cumulation of penalties), which seems erroneous to the authors.

or criminal proceedings and furnishing guarantees for possible compensation of the holder of the goods in the event that the infringement is not subsequently recognized. The goods will otherwise be released. There is no provision for an extension to those delays. To aid in the introduction of a court case, the requestor may obtain from customs, the name and address of the sender, importer, and recipient of the goods as well as their quantities. In practice, member states have not yet implemented these provisions related to customs recordal. This would likely require each state to adopt detailed implementing regulations to aid customs in its task.

9. Bilateral Agreements

As mentioned in section 1 of this chapter, the OAPI is increasingly becoming an independent actor on the world stage. The OAPI is now a member of both the Madrid and Lisbon Systems. This has not been without challenges. When the OAPI joined the Madrid Protocol in 2014, there were debates about whether the OAPI could validly join the Madrid System without amending the Bangui Agreement. The OAPI believed it could and even went as far as provisionally suspending two trade mark agents for their involvement in a grouping waging a public campaign against OAPI joining the Madrid System.[54] The OAPI further published an Information Note clarifying issues regarding the Madrid Protocol. Likely due to the commotion caused, the Acte de Bamako amended the Bangui Agreement to provide, at article 3(3), that the Organization is the office of origin and designated office of its member states for the purposes of the Madrid System. There was no equivalent commotion when the OAPI joined the Geneva Act of the Lisbon System, which came into force on 15 March 2023.

The OAPI has not signed any agreement with the European Commission and the United States regarding the protection of GIs.

---

[54] Victor Nzomo, 'OAPI Suspends Agents: IP Community across Africa Is Watching' (*IP Kenya*, 4 February 2016) <https://ipkenya.wordpress.com/2016/02/04/oapi-suspends-agents-ip-community-across-africa-is-watching>.

6
Algeria

Algeria is located in the Maghreb region in northwest Africa. It borders the Mediterranean Sea, Tunisia, Libya, Morocco, Mauritania, Mali, Niger, and Western Sahara. It has an area of 2,381,741 km², making it the tenth largest country in the world and the largest in Africa. More than four-fifths of the country is desert. Algeria has a population of 44.17 million inhabitants. Since the constitutional review of 2016, the two official languages are Modern Standard Arabic and Tamazight (Berber). Ninety-nine per cent of the population speaks Arabic, Berber, or both. The Arabic dialectal, Darja, is the main lingua franca used by the population. All official documents are printed in Arabic. French was introduced in the country during the French occupation and is still widely used, though it has no official status. In court, all exchanges take place in Arabic. However, most magistrates and lawyers speak French as well. Since 2009, the weekend has comprised Friday and Saturday. The dinar is the monetary currency of Algeria (DZD). The currency is not convertible to foreign currency; exceptions are made for international trade, subject to regulation conditions and clearances.

Algeria is the fourth largest economy in Africa. Algeria's economy heavily relies on the hydrocarbon (oil and gas) industry, which accounted for 20 per cent of its gross domestic product, 41 per cent of its fiscal revenues, and 94 per cent of its export earnings in 2019.[1] Algeria is among the top five gas exporters in the world. Although the industry is currently experiencing structural decline, the hydrocarbon boom in the past two decades allowed Algeria to make significant advances in economic and human development. The gross national income per capita increased by about 30 per cent between 1990 and 2019.[2] Today, most of the workforce is employed in the tertiary sector.[3] Algeria has further made great strides in its domestic agricultural output, aiming for self-sufficiency in key crops such as cereals. Still, food imports accounted for roughly 18 per cent of all imports in 2016 and 2017. Algeria is the second most important food importer on the continent.[4]

---

[1] World Bank, 'The World Bank in Algeria' (*World Bank*, 20 October 2022) <www.worldbank.org/en/country/algeria/overview#1>.

[2] United Nation Development Programme (UNDP), 'Algeria' (*UNDP Human Development Reports*, 8 September 2022) <https://hdr.undp.org/data-center/specific-country-data#/countries/DZA>.

[3] Lloyds Bank, 'The Economic Context of Algeria' (*Lloyds Bank*, April 2023) <www.lloydsbanktrade.com/en/market-potential/algeria/economical-context>.

[4] Taku Fundira 'Africa's Food Trade: Overview' (*tralac*, September 2017) 2. <www.tralac.org/documents/publications/trade-data-analysis/962-africa-food-trade-overview-september-2017/file.html>.

Cereals, coffee and tea, dried vegetables, and meat altogether amounted to 75 per cent of all food imports.[5] Brazil is the leading food supplier.

Though the hydrocarbon boom has raised the standard of living in the country in the past decades, following difficulties faced by lower oil prices and the COVID-19 pandemic, Algeria was downgraded from an upper-middle-income to a lower-middle-income country in 2020 by the World Bank.[6] Unemployment is high at 14.7 per cent in 2022, particularly among the youth, women, and graduates.[7] Still, it is estimated that the total assets in the hands of affluent individuals, high net worth individuals, and ultra-high net worth individuals amount to USD 47 billion in Algeria.[8] Algeria is the seventh African country by number of millionaires in dollars.[9]

E-commerce is growing in Algeria. The COVID-19 pandemic and the resulting confinements have accelerated the adoption of e-commerce by the local population. However, numerous challenges still lie ahead. Tobacco, alcohol, and pharmaceutical products may not be purchased online. Foreign e-commerce websites must register in the country's commercial register and host their websites from a data centre in Algeria. In practice, this effectively excludes foreign websites from operating in Algeria. However, intermediary companies offer trans-shipment services for orders from foreign websites. Finally, few Algerians have access to international credit cards, which would allow them to pay for purchases online. Even where international credit cards are available, Algeria imposes a maximum value per transaction of 100,000 DZD (approximately USD 720) on citizens' purchases of goods outside the country.[10] In Algeria, the majority of transactions are made on the basis of cash on delivery.[11]

Algeria's history is intertwined with the current European wine policy of Protected designation of origin, which is closely linked to the French *Appellation d'origine contrôlée (AOC)*.[12] In the late nineteenth century, the phylloxera epidemic caused by an insect devastated vineyards in Europe. French wine producers

---

[5] Oxford Business Group, 'Algeria Aims to Lower Food Import Bill and Attain Self-Sufficiency in Key Crops' (*Oxford Business Group*, nd) <https://oxfordbusinessgroup.com/reports/algeria/2018-report/economy/national-priority-the-authorities-work-to-lower-the-food-import-bill-and-attain-self-sufficiency-in-key-crops>.

[6] Morgan Hekking, 'World Bank Downgrades Algeria to Lower-Middle-Income Country' (*Morocco World News*, 6 July 2020) <www.moroccoworldnews.com/2020/07/308022/world-bank-downgrades-algeria-to-lower-middle-income-country>.

[7] Standard Bank, 'Algeria: Economic and Political Overview' (*Standard Bank*, April 2023) <www.tradeclub.standardbank.com/portal/en/market-potential/algeria/economical-context>.

[8] Michael Bryane and Nenad Apostoloski, 'The Middle Eastern Wealth Management Industry: Boon or Bust?' (Middle East Institute Working Paper, 2012) <https://dx.doi.org/10.2139/ssrn.2128213>.

[9] Echorouk Online, 'Report: Algeria Has 4,700 Millionaires in Dollars' (*Echorouk Online*, 10 August 2015) <www.echoroukonline.com/report-algeria-has-4700-millionaires-in-dollars>.

[10] United States Trade Representative, '2023 National Trade Estimate Report on Foreign Trade Barriers' (nd) 8, <https://ustr.gov/sites/default/files/2023-03/2023%20NTE%20Report.pdf>.

[11] International Trade Administration, 'Algeria—Country Commercial Guide' (*Official Website of the International Trade Administration*, 31 January 2023) <www.trade.gov/country-commercial-guides/algeria-ecommerce>.

[12] Julian Alston and Davide Gaeta, 'Reflections on the Political Economy of European Wine Appellations' (2021) 7 ItEJ <https://doi.org/10.1007/s40797-021-00145-4>.

responded by developing the wine industry in Algeria, the latter being a French colony at that time. By the 1930s, Algeria was the world's largest exporter of wine, a title it held onto until 1962. This, however, led to dissatisfaction and resentment when vineyards in France recovered and felt that they were experiencing unfair competition from Algerian wines. Tension was such that a law was introduced requiring French wine labels to state their country of origin. Over the following years, regional boundaries were drawn up. Referred to as appellations, they were codified into the modern AOC system in 1935.[13]

Upon its independence from France, a combination of mismanagement of the vineyards, the disavowal of the French government's promise to keep on purchasing wine from Algeria on a large scale due to political disagreements,[14] and the adoption of a law in France that banned all non-French wine from using blends led to a collapse of the wine production in Algeria.[15] Religious sentiments against the consumption of alcohol and difficulties brought about by climate change have further reduced production.[16] Still, there remain seven areas in Algeria that benefit from the *Vins d'Appellation d'origine garantie*—wines of guaranteed appellation of origin (VAOG), which was set up by decree in 1970.[17] Wines produced under VAOG are high-quality wines, which must respect a precise set of specifications. These wines are mainly for export.[18]

Algerian agricultural products or products of agricultural origin may further benefit from the following distinctive labels: *l'Appellation d'origine*—appellation of origin, *l'indication gèographique*—geographical indication, *l'Agriculture biologique*—organic farming, and *les labels agricoles de qualité*—quality agricultural labels.[19] Products benefiting from such labels must respect certain specifications, such as those related to the appearance of the products, production, transformation, and packaging. Of these four products, appellations of origin and geographical indications (GIs) are those with a direct link with the geographical origin. In 2018, the Ministry of Agriculture, Rural Development and Fisheries identified around sixty products that could benefit from such labels.[20]

---

[13] Joshua Malin, 'Tipsy History: The Great Boom & the Epic Bust of the Algerian Wine Industry' (*VinePair*, 27 August 2014) <https://vinepair.com/wine-blog/tipsy-history-boom-bust-algerian-wine>.

[14] Although Algeria was a major wine producer, it relied heavily on external markets as domestic consumption was nearly inexistent in a predominantly Muslim country.

[15] Malin (n 13).

[16] Aghiles Ourad, 'The Withering of Algerian Wine' (*New Lines Magazine*, 26 July 2022) <https://newlinesmag.com/reportage/the-withering-of-algerian-wine>.

[17] The seven areas are Les Côteaux de Tlemcen, Les Monts du Tessalah, Les Côteaux de Mascara, Dahra, Les Côteaux du Zaccar, Médéa, and Aïn-Bessem-Bouïra.

[18] Lamara Hadjou and Foued Cheriet, 'Contraintes institutionnelles et labellisation des produits algeriens de terroir: Cas du vin et des dattes' (2013) 103(29) CDC 73.

[19] Executive Decree No 13-260 of 7 July 2013 fixing the system of quality of agricultural products or products of agricultural origin, art 2.

[20] Lyas Hallas, 'Le ministère de l'agriculture recense 60 produits à labelliser' (*Le Soir d'Algerie*, 6 November 2018) <www.lesoirdalgerie.com/actualites/le-ministere-de-lagriculture-recense-60-produits-a-labelliser-13789>.

By 2021, twelve product names had been registered as GIs, including the *Date Deglet Nour of Tolg* and the *Dry fig of Beni Maouche* in 2016. Six of these products are registered through the Lisbon Agreement for the Protection of Appellations of Origin and their International Registration (Lisbon Agreement) of 1958.[21] Since 2021, the World Intellectual Property Organization (WIPO) has been supporting the adoption of a collective mark by producers of Chechar honey *Miel de Chechar* and manufacturers of carpets of Babar *Tapis de Babar* in the province of Khenchela, Algeria. WIPO's support includes carrying out a diagnostic of these two sectors, assessing the appropriateness of protecting them through distinctive signs, and defining the steps towards registration.[22]

1. Legal Framework

In Algeria, the legal system is based on French law (civil Napoleonian law) and the *Shariah* law with regard to family law. The judiciary is three-tiered, composed of the Supreme Court, Courts of Appeal, and tribunal courts. At the first level are the tribunals, composed of a single judge, assisted sometimes by assessors. Civil and commercial litigation and some criminal matters are submitted to the tribunal courts. Since the executive decree 23-53, twelve specialized commercial tribunals have been established around the country. At the second level are the Courts of Appeal.[23] Courts of Appeals are organized regionally and hear appeals in all matters from the tribunal courts. There are forty-eight Courts of Appeal in Algeria whose judgments may be reviewed before the Supreme Court. The Supreme Court has the highest jurisdiction and hears cassation claims. In the matter of administrative justice, there are administrative tribunals and appeal courts, in addition to the *Conseil d'État*, which is the highest jurisdiction of the administrative law.

Legal practitioners in Algeria are either an *avocat* (lawyer) or a *notaire* (notary). A lawyer renders legal advice, drafts agreements, handles commercial disputes, and may appear before the Algerian courts to which they are admitted. A notary focuses on the preparation and recording of specific acts and the administration and settlement of estates. They do not litigate in court.[24]

---

[21] Monique Bagal and others, *Manual for Geographical Indications in Africa* (2nd edn, European Union Intellectual Property Office 2023) 39.

[22] Bulletin d'information du Bureau d'Algérie, 'Protection et commercialisation du "Miel de Chechar" et du "Tapis de Babar" (Wilaya de Khenchela)' (*Bulletin d'information du Bureau d'Algérie*, 12 May 2022) <https://mailchi.mp/wipo/quatrime-dition-du-bulletin-dinformation-du-bureau-extrieur-en-algrie-avril-2022>.

[23] Administratively, Algeria is divided into forty-eight *wilayas*. The *wilaya* is an administrative district or *prefecture*.

[24] Privacy Shield Framework, 'Algeria—Local Professional Services' (*Privacy Shield Framework*, nd) <www.privacyshield.gov/article?id = Algeria-Local-Professional-Services>.

2. Domestic Legislation on GIs

Algeria has been a member of the Paris Convention for the Protection of Industrial Property since March 1966. Algeria joined the Lisbon Agreement for the Protection of Appellations of Origin and their International Registration in July 1972. However, it has not ratified the 2015 Act of Geneva. Algeria has been a signatory to the Madrid Protocol Concerning the International Registration of Marks of 2007 Madrid System) since July 2015. Algeria signed the Madrid Agreement for the Repression of False or Deceptive Indications of Source on Goods on 5 July 1972. Algeria is not a member of the World Trade Organization (WTO) but is a WTO Observer. Algeria is thus not bound to enforce the WTO Agreement on Trade-Related Aspects of Intellectual Property Rights (TRIPS) minimum standards of 1994. However, many of its provisions regarding appellations of origin are compatible with TRIPS.

The Ordinance regarding procedures for the registration and publication of appellations of origin No 76-65, 16 July 1976 (Law on AO) is the main law providing for the protection of appellations of origin. It is applied through the Decree regarding procedures for registration and publication of appellations of origin and establishing fees No 76-121, 16 July 1976 (Decree on AO). Appellations of origin and GIs for agricultural products or products of agricultural origin may further be registered under Executive Decree No 13-260, 7 July 2013 fixing the system of quality of agricultural products or products of agricultural origin (Decree 13-260). Decree 13-260 itself builds on Law 8-16, 3 August 2008 on agricultural orientation, which aims to highlight agriculture as important to national food security, sustainable development of rural areas, and economic development. It is further possible to register a collective mark in Algeria under the Ordinance regarding the protection of marks No 03-06, 19 July 2003 (the Law on Marks).

3. Registration of GIs Domestically

3.1 Appellations of origin

The Law on AO provides for registration of domestic and foreign appellation of origin, although the conditions differ. Domestic appellations of origin may only be registered by domestic entities. A foreign appellation of origin may be registered only in the context of international treaties to which Algeria is a party and subject to reciprocity provisions.[25] A foreign entity cannot register an appellation of origin in Algeria that is not registered abroad.

---

[25] Law on AO, art 6.

The Law on AO defines an appellation of origin as the geographical name of a country, region, or part thereof, as well as a location within a region, which designates goods herein produced, whose qualities or characteristics are essentially or exclusively linked to the geographic environment, including human and natural factors. This definition aligns with article 22(1) of the TRIPS Agreement and article 2 of the Lisbon Agreement. In addition, a name that is not one of a country, region, part of region, or locality will be considered as a geographical name where it refers to a specific area for specific goods.[26] Under an appellation of origin, any goods may be protected, including agricultural, industrial products, and handicrafts. Services are excluded.

A GI is defined under Decree 13-260 as a denomination used to identify a product as originating from a territory, region, or locality where a quality, reputation, or any other characteristic of the product is essentially attributable to the geographic origin and/or the production, and/or processing and/or preparation takes place in the delimited geographical area with a specification chart.[27]

3.2 Collective marks

It is also possible to register a collective mark, defined under the Law on Marks as a mark intended to guarantee the origin, composition, manufacture, or any other common characteristic of goods or services from various undertakings using the mark under its owner's control.[28] Both goods and services are registrable under a collective mark.

No specific rules and/or additional protection apply to wines and spirits under either appellation of origin or collective mark.

4. Registrability of Names

4.1 Appellations of origin

Under the Law on AO, an indication cannot be protected as an appellation of origin where it

a) does not abide to the definition of an appellation of origin;
b) is not regulated;

---

[26] ibid art 1.
[27] Decree 13-260 (n 19) art 2.
[28] Law on Marks, art 2.

c) is a generic name of a product i.e., when it is established by usage and considered by persons skilled in the field and by the public as generic;
d) is contrary to good morals, morality, or public policy.[29]

4.2 Collective marks

A mark will not be registered where the sign consists exclusively or partly of an indication that is liable to cause confusion as to the geographical origin of the goods or services concerned or which, if registered, would unduly restrict the use of the geographical indication by other persons entitled to make use of that indication.[30] A mark will not be registered for similar or identical goods and services where the proposed mark is identical, or confusingly similar to, a collective mark that has expired less than three years prior to the filing date of the proposed mark.[31]

5. Procedure and Requirements for Registration

5.1 Appellations of origin

To be protected, appellations of origin must be registered.[32] An appellation of origin may be registered in Algeria either as a national application through the Algerian National Institute of Industrial Property (INAPI) or as an international application via the Lisbon Agreement.

For a national application, the applicant must file four copies of the standard application forms with the INAPI. An applicant may be an institution legally constituted and empowered for this purpose, any natural or legal person who carries out an activity as a producer in the geographical area concerned, or any competent authority. The application indicates the name, capacity, and address of the applicant(s) or, in the case of a legal person, its business name, registered office, and activity. Where the applicant is a foreign entity, the application must be submitted through a duly authorized Algerian representative domiciled in Algeria. In this case, a signed power of attorney is necessary. The application must mention the claimed appellation of origin; the geographical area where the goods are produced; the relevant product; and the description of the particular properties and conditions behind the use of the appellation of origin, namely how the product should be

---

[29] ibid art 4.
[30] ibid art 7.
[31] ibid art 7(9).
[32] Law on AO, art 3.

labelled. Where relevant, a list of authorized users should be provided. The application should be filed in French, and a fee must be paid.

If the application is deemed in order, a report noting the filing will be issued. In case of any deficiencies, the INAPI may allow the applicant two months for corrections. Such deficiencies include the submission of incomplete particulars or supporting documents, the non-submission of particulars or supporting documents, the fact that the applied appellation does not cover the entire geographical area, insufficient characteristics indicated in the application, or the appellation not covering the product designated on the application. The two-month period may be extended for an equal period if valid reasons are given.[33]

The application is examined first formally and then substantially.

An application shall be rejected where the applicant was not entitled to file the application; the regularization of a defect was not carried out within the time limit; the applied sign does not abide by the Law on AO's definition of an appellation of origin; the applied sign is unregulated; the sign is the generic name of the product; or the applied sign is contrary to good morals, morality, or public policy. The applicant may present its observations within two months from the date of notification of the rejection of the application, prior to asserting its rights by any other legal means, if necessary.

Where an application is accepted, it is registered and published in the *Official Bulletin of Industrial Property*. There is no opposition procedure. A copy of the application, including the registration references, shall be issued to the applicant or its representative as a certificate of registration.

A foreign applicant may also register an appellation of origin through an international application in accordance with the requirements of the Lisbon Agreement.

Algerian applicants may further apply for the registration of an appellation of origin or GI under Decree 13-260 for agricultural products or products of agricultural origin. The producers and/or transformers, individually or in a group, must apply to the permanent secretary of the National Labelling Committee.[34] The National Labelling Committee regroups representatives from the public service, farmers, producers, transformers, distributors, artisans, and consumers. It is attached to the Ministry of Agriculture.[35] Upon receiving the application, the National Labelling Committee transmits the demand to a specialized subcommittee that examines the application and elaborates a specification chart together with the applicant.[36] Once the report of the specialized subcommittee is ready, it is submitted for approval to the applicant. If approved, it is transmitted to the National Labelling Committee, which publishes the application in at least two daily

---

[33] Decree on AO, art 7.
[34] Order of 5 May 2016 laying down the rules relating to the procedure for recognition of appellations of origin, geographical indications, and quality agricultural labels (Order 05-2016) art 2 and Decree 13-260 (n 19) art 28.
[35] Decree 13-260 (n 19) art 5.
[36] Order 05-2016 (n 34), art 4

newspapers for opposition. Among the possible grounds of opposition are that the denomination applied for infringes a mark registered by the Algerian Intellectual Property (IP) Office. The Ministry of Agriculture has the final word and the power to grant a distinctive sign through a decree.[37] The INAPI publishes the decree in three daily newspapers at the cost of the applicant.

5.2 Collective marks

The registration of a collective mark is open to any public or private person who belongs to and represents a business association or social organization. A foreign applicant not domiciled in Algeria need not appoint a proxy if a local address for service is provided. In practice, many foreign applicants find appointing a local agent easier. An application for a collective trade mark is filed with the INAPI by submitting a written statement specifying the designated classes and the list of goods or services, along with the regulations governing the use of a collective mark. These regulations shall define the specific conditions of use of the collective mark and provide for effective control over the use of the mark.[38] Similar to trade marks, collective marks are examined on both formal and substantive grounds by the Office. Once accepted, the application is registered and published in the *Official Gazette*. There is, however, no opposition procedure for collective marks as is the case for trade marks). It is possible for third parties feeling aggrieved by a collective trade mark application to file third-party observations, which the INAPI may consider.

6. Term of Protection

6.1 Appellations of origin

An appellation of origin is valid for ten years from the filing date. It may be renewed indefinitely for consecutive periods of ten years upon payment of the renewal fee. Information submitted for the application must be submitted again for renewal together with a reference to the previous filing and the date and number of the prior registration. The renewal of an appellation of origin must not include any changes to the previous registration as it stood on the renewal date. Members of the public may consult the register of registered appellations of origin free of charge.

Any change in the regulations governing the use of the appellation must be made in writing and is registered (free of charge) in the register of appellations of origin.

---

[37] ibid art 19.
[38] Law on Marks, art 23.

Any person showing a legitimate interest or any competent authority may request the court to order the cancellation of the registration of an appellation of origin where the appellation is excluded from protection pursuant to the provisions of article 4 of the Law (ie the appellation does not abide by the Law on AO's definition of an appellation of origin; is unregulated; generic; or contrary to good morals, morality, or public policy) or the circumstances and conditions that were decisive for the registration of the appellation have ceased to exist. Any person with a legitimate interest or a competent authority may further request the court to modify the registration of an appellation of origin where the appellation of origin does not cover the entire geographical area, the characteristics of the products indicated in the application are no longer sufficient, or not all the products described in the application are covered by the designation.[39]

Any application for cancellation or modification shall indicate the name, address, and capacity of the applicant; the object of the request; the registration whose cancellation or modification is requested; and the grounds on which the application is made.

6.2 Collective marks

A collective mark is valid for ten years as of the filing date. It is renewable for the same period. Any person may request a copy of the regulations governing the use of the collective mark. The owner of a collective mark must ensure the proper use of the mark.

The court shall revoke the registration of a collective mark at the request of the competent department or at the request of an interested third party where the legal entity that owns the mark ceases to exist; the owner uses, authorizes, or tolerates the use of the mark under conditions other than those laid down in the regulations governing the use of the mark; or the proprietor uses, authorizes, or tolerates the use of the mark in such a way as to deceive the public as to any common feature of the goods or services for which the mark is used.[40] It is not possible to have recourse to the INAPI for either the cancellation or invalidation of a mark.

7. Rights of the Owner and Enforcement Mechanisms against Infringers

Civil and criminal actions are available in case of an infringement of both appellations of origin and collective marks. In a civil action, the court may order the

---

[39] Law on AO, art 23.
[40] Law on Marks, art 25.

cessation of the counterfeiting acts or allow it subject to the indemnification of the owner of the mark. Where the right owner can prove an imminent threat to its rights, the court may order detention measures, confiscation, and even destruction.

It is illegal to use, directly or indirectly, an appellation of origin that is false, fallacious, or imitates another appellation of origin.[41] No registered appellation of origin may be used without the approval of its owner, even where the true origin of the product is indicated or where the appellation is used in translation or in combination with expressions such as 'sort of', 'kind of', 'imitation', and 'the like'.[42] The owner of an appellation of origin can address the civil court to request precautionary measures to prevent an imminent infringement or halt an ongoing infringement. Criminal penalties are also provided for. Those who counterfeit or contribute to counterfeiting of a registered appellation of origin are punished by a fine of 2.000–20.000 DZD and/or imprisonment for three months up to three years. Those who have purposefully offered for sale or sold counterfeit products bearing an appellation of origin are punished by a fine of 1.000–15.000 DZD and/or imprisonment of one month up to one year. The court may also order the posting of the judgment in such places as it shall determine and its publication, in whole or in part, in such newspapers as it shall designate, all at the expense of the convicted person.[43] There are, however, no administrative penalties against the illicit use of appellations of origin.

The Law on AO also provides for quality control of appellation of origins. Any competent authority or interested person may request the legally competent service to carry out quality control, in accordance with the laws and regulations in force, of products put into circulation under a registered appellation of origin. Using an appellation of origin for products of lesser quality than that defined by the regulatory texts in force is prohibited, taking into account any tolerances provided for.

The offence of counterfeiting is constituted by any act that infringes the owner's exclusive rights on a mark, including a collective mark.[44] The owner of the mark may act against counterfeiters and those having done acts that render likely the offence of counterfeiting. Counterfeiting is punishable by imprisonment and/or a fine; the temporary or permanent closure of the facility; the confiscation of objects, instruments, or tools used; and the destruction of the counterfeited goods.[45] Civil reparations are also possible, subject to expertise and proof of damages. Before entering a case on the basis of counterfeiting, it is highly recommended to undertake a descriptive seizure with the assistance of a bailiff to collect proof of the counterfeiting goods.

---

[41] Law on AO, art 28.
[42] ibid art 21.
[43] ibid art 30.
[44] Law on Marks, art 26.
[45] ibid art 32.

In the case of counterfeit goods, right holders may further have recourse to the Ministry of Commerce and the directorate for the control of quality and repression of fraud (*Direction générale du contrôle économique et de la répression des fraudes*) or to the police unit specialized in the fight against counterfeiting. These two entities have the power to seize suspected counterfeit goods. If the goods are, indeed, counterfeits, they will be destroyed at the expense of the counterfeiter.

8. Customs Enforcement

The Algerian Customs Administration (*Direction générale des douanes*) may seize, examine, and collect samples of suspected counterfeit imported goods upon request of the right holder or *ex officio*. Counterfeit goods are defined as those infringing IP rights. [46] This should therefore include appellations of origin, GIs, and collective marks. No legal provision allows customs to take action against infringing goods in transit not intended for the Algerian market.

A request for customs enforcement must be presented in writing to the Algerian Customs sub-directorate in charge of the fight against counterfeiting by the right holder or its representative. The applicant must provide customs with the following documents: power of attorney, letter of commitment to cover costs, copies of registration certificates, and information allowing Customs to recognize counterfeit goods. Customs may reject or accept the application. When granting an application for action, Customs shall specify the period during which Customs authorities are to take action. That period may be extended at the request of the right holder. A custom watch in Algeria usually lasts for five years.

Once accepted, an alert service bulletin is issued to all customs offices. The IP right is placed on watch, and suspected goods are monitored and inspected. Where suspected goods are found, Customs informs the right holder of the suspension of the goods, allowing the right holder to seize the competent jurisdiction.

Customs may further intervene *ex officio* (ie without an application having been filed) where it is apparent that the goods are counterfeit. Customs authorities may then intervene and inform the right holder if the identity is known. Customs suspends the release of the goods for three working days to allow the right holder to file an application. The suspension is lifted if the right holder does not file an application or the right holder's identity is unknown.

Once goods have been detained, a legal action must be filed before the court in Algeria for a judgment on the merits or provisional measures within ten working days. Otherwise, the suspected goods will be released and cleared. In appropriate cases, the delay may be prolongated by a maximum of ten working days. It is for the

---

[46] Ordinance of 4 Joumada El Oula 1423 corresponding to 15 July 2002 on the application of article 22 of the Customs Code on the importation of counterfeit goods, art 2.

right holder to seize the competent jurisdiction and to inform Customs accordingly. Goods held for presumption of infringement and for which the right holder or its representative has lodged a complaint cannot be subject to any release until a court decision deciding on their fate has been handed down.

Without prejudice to the other legal remedies open to the right holder to whom an infringement has been recognized, customs may take the necessary measures to

a) destroy goods found to infringe an intellectual property right or dispose of them outside commercial channels in such a way as to preclude injury to the right holder and this without compensation of any kind and at no cost to the Public Treasury;
b) take, in respect of such goods, any other measures effectively depriving the persons concerned of any economic gains from the transaction, on the condition that Customs administrations do not authorise:
   i. the re-exportation in its natural state of the counterfeit goods;
   ii. the removal, except in exceptional cases, of the marks unduly affixed on the counterfeit goods;
   iii. the placing of goods under a different customs procedure.[47]

The goods may further be abandoned to the profit of the National Treasury.[48]

9. Bilateral Agreements

There are no bilateral agreements between the European Union (EU) and Algeria specific to GIs. The 2005 Euro-Mediterranean Agreement between the EU and Algeria does not mention GIs or appellations of origin among protected IP rights.[49] The French and Italian Ministries of Agriculture did, however, provide technical support to the Algerian Ministry of Agriculture for the registration of the following products in Algeria: *Tolga Deglet Nour Dates*, *Beni Maouche Dry Figs*, and *Sig Olives*.[50] There are, further, no bilateral agreements between the United States and Algeria specific to GIs.

---

[47] Ordinance of 4 Joumada El Oula 1423 corresponding to 15 July 2002 on the application of article 22 of the Customs Code on the importation of counterfeit goods, art 14
[48] More information may be found on customs enforcement in Algeria in Marius Schneider and Vanessa Ferguson, *Enforcement of Intellectual Property Rights in Africa* (OUP 2020) 66–70.
[49] One reason behind this omission could be that Council Regulation (EC) No 510/2006 of 20 March 2006 on the protection of geographical indications and designations of origin for agricultural products and foodstuffs was adopted after this agreement.
[50] African Union Commission Department of Rural Economy and Agriculture, 'Continental Strategy for Geographical Indications in Africa 2018–2023' (African Union Commission Department of Rural Economy and Agriculture nd) 42.

7
Angola

Angola is found in southwest Africa between Namibia and the Republic of Congo. It is also bordered by the Democratic Republic of the Congo and Zambia, with a coastline on the Atlantic Ocean. At 1.247 million km², Angola is the seventh largest African country. In 2021, the country had a population of 34.5 million inhabitants. Portuguese is the official language. The working week is from Monday to Friday, and the national currency is the Kwanza (Kz).

Angola has an oil-driven economy, with oil exports amounting to about 90 per cent of the country's exports and one-third of its gross domestic product (GDP).[1] It is the second largest oil producer in Africa. Other significant resources for Angola include gas and various mineral resources, that is diamond, copper, and gold. High international oil prices and rising oil production allowed for strong economic growth in the country, with GDP per capita reaching an all-time high of USD 4,164 in 2014.[2] However, the country's high reliance on oil means that any decline in oil prices significantly impacts the country's economy. Angola was in a recession in 2016, with oil prices low and production dropping. Income inequality is high, with Angola having one of the highest Gini coefficients in Africa.[3] Still, Angola remains the third largest economy in sub-Saharan Africa, behind Nigeria and South Africa.

While Angola is endowed with fertile soils, abundant water, and a favourable climate, Angola imports half of its food.[4] Angolan produce is increasingly becoming available in supermarkets, but a large amount of the fruit, vegetables, and meat sold is imported from Portugal and elsewhere. Spending on food and beverages will likely increase over the years as Angola has one of the fastest-growing populations in Africa. Angola's GDP was at USD 67.4 billion in 2021.

Foreign producers entering the Angolan market will find that while the informal retail sector remains the most important retail player, the situation is evolving. Angolan customers are focused on quality and look for international brands and recognizable names. International franchises have entered the country, and there has been heavy investment in building supermarkets and shopping malls. This has

---

[1] World Bank, 'The World Bank in Angola' (*World Bank*, 4 April 2023) <www.worldbank.org/en/country/angola/overview>.
[2] World Bank Group, 'Angola: Systematic Country Diagnostic. Creating Assets for the Poor' (World Bank Group 2018) ii.
[3] World Bank, 'Angola Poverty Assessment' (World Bank 2020) iii.
[4] Exportgov, 'Angola—Agricultural Products' (*Exportgov*, 22 August 2019) <www.export.gov/apex/article2?id=Angola-Agricultural-Products>.

led to a jump in food sales in the formal market from less than 5 per cent in 2000 to 20–30 per cent in 2019.[5] E-commerce is, however, limited by the low level of internet access (only 14.3 per cent of the population had access to the internet in 2017)[6] as well as the dominance of cash. Angola has a cash-based economy: only 50 per cent of adults participate in the formal banking system. Among these, many use debit cards (aka 'multicaixa'). International credit cards, which allow for online shopping worldwide, are extremely scarce and reserved for members of the upper class.[7] Finally, e-commerce is hampered by the unreliable mail delivery system.

As of July 2023, no domestic geographical indication (GI) was registered in Angola. However, some agricultural products have been highlighted over the years as having the potential to be protected under the GI framework. These are Ambriz Coffee, Encoge Coffee, and Cazengo Coffee.

1. Legal Framework

Angola follows the Portuguese civil law tradition. The primary source of law is legislation. Precedent is accepted but not binding. The judicial system in Angola is based on a three-tiered pyramidal system, with the Supreme Court (*Tribunal Supremo*), based in Luanda, the highest court of common jurisdiction.[8] The Supreme Court hears appeals from the Courts of Appeal (*Tribunais da Relação*), which themselves hear appeals from the district courts (*Tribunais de Comarca*). The Courts of Appeal are thus second-instance courts, which hear civil and criminal matters. District courts are first-instance courts, where judicial proceedings are initiated. They are progressively being implemented in every district in the country. The Constitutional Court hears matters related to the Constitution. In most court cases, the parties have to be represented by attorneys.

Of particular relevance to the legal regime for the enforcement of intellectual property (IP) rights is the Luanda District Court (first instance), which has been appointed as a Commercial, Intellectual and Industrial Property Section (Commercial and IP Court). The Court started functioning in 2021 after the entry

---

[5] Business Wire, 'Angola Wholesale & Retail of Food, 2020—Grocery Market Is Still Far from Mature & Represents a Significant Growth Opportunity—ResearchAndMarketscom' (*Business Wire*, 7 February 2020) <www.businesswire.com/news/home/20200207005306/en/Angola-Wholesale-Retail-of-Food-2020---Grocery-Market-is-Still-Far-from-Mature-Represents-a-Significant-Growth-Opportunity---ResearchAndMarkets.com>.

[6] World Bank, 'Individuals Using the Internet (% of population)—Angola' (*World Bank*, nd) <https://data.worldbank.org/indicator/IT.NET.USER.ZS?locations=AO>.

[7] Privacy Shield Framework, 'Angola—eCommerce' (*Privacy Shield Framework*, nd) <www.privacyshield.gov/article?id=Angola-eCommerce>.

[8] Law No 29/22 of 29 August 2022, the 'Organic Law on the Organization and Functioning of the Courts of Common Jurisdiction' (hereinafter 'Law on the Judicial Courts'), which establishes the principal and general rules for the organization and functioning of the Courts of Common Jurisdiction (Judicial Courts).

into force of Resolution No 2/21 of the Judiciary Superior Council, published on 4 March 2021.[9] With regard to IP, the Commercial and IP Court is competent for all actions where the cause of action concerns IP, including copyright; actions and appeals involving company names; and appeals against decisions of the Angolan Institute of Industrial Property (IAPI), which grants, refuses, or declares the revocation of IP rights.[10] Court cases are, however, lengthy and expensive in Angola.

2. Domestic Legislation on GIs

Angola acceded to the Paris Convention for the Protection of Industrial Property of 1883 in September 2007. Angola is a party neither to the Madrid Agreement for the Repression of False or Deceptive Indications of Source on Goods of 1891 nor to the Lisbon Agreement for the Protection of Appellations of Origin and their International Registration of 1958. Angola is not a party to the Madrid Protocol Concerning the International Registration of Marks of 2007.

Angola has been a member of the World Trade Organization since 23 November 1996.

There is no *sui generis* legislation regarding GIs currently in force in Angola. The legal provisions on IP are contained in Law No 3/92 of 28 February 1992 on Industrial Property Law (IP Law), which came into force on 29 March 1992.[11] The IP Law mirrors the main principles and many of the provisions of the Industrial Property Code of 1940, which was in force in Portugal at that time. The IP Law is not compliant with the standards set by the World Trade Organization (WTO) Agreement on Trade-Related Aspects of Intellectual Property Rights (TRIPS).

The IP Law provides for the trade mark system in Angola. Theoretically, it is possible to protect GIs in Angola through collective marks. In practice, many governing bodies of GIs have opted to register a trade mark rather than a collective mark in Angola. This is the case with *Alentejo*, a European Union (EU) GI for wines produced in a specific region in Portugal,[12] and *Irish Whiskey*, an EU GI for whisky produced in Ireland.[13]

---

[9] Marques da Cruz Duarte, 'Angola: New Intellectual Property and Commercial Section Starts Working at Luanda District Court' (*Further Africa*, 25 March 2021) <https://furtherafrica.com/2021/03/25/angola-new-intellectual-property-and-commercial-section-starts-working-at-luanda-district-court>.

[10] Law on the Judicial Courts (n 8) art 67. On the issue of appeals from decisions on the IAPI, please also refer to section 5 of this chapter.

[11] For the sake of completeness, the carrying out of administrative acts for the prosecution of IP rights is governed by the Code of Administrative Procedure approved by Law No 31/22 of 30 August 2022 and which came into force on 26 February 2023 and the Code of Contentious Administrative Procedure approved by Law No 33/22 of 1 September 2022, which came into force on 28 February 2023.

[12] 'ALENTEJO' was applied for in Angola on 14 November 2014 in the name of the Comissão Vitivinicola Regional Alentejana for 'wine' under class 33.

[13] 'IRISH WHISKEY' was applied for in Angola on 27 January 2020 in the name of the Irish Whiskey Association for 'whiskey; whiskey liquor and whiskey-based drinks' under class 33.

The IP Law also mentions indication of source, defining the latter as the expression or sign used to indicate that a product comes from a given country, region, or geographical place commonly known as a centre for extracting, producing, or manufacturing the goods or products in question.[14] As there is no requirement for a link between the characteristics, quality, and reputation of the product with the location, this is not appropriate for GIs. Further, in practice, it is not possible to register and enforce an indication of source in Angola. This is most likely due to a provision in the IP Law that grants the right to use an indication of source not only to the manufacturers and producers but also to purchasers of products.[15] GIs owners may, however, have recourse to the law against unfair competition. No specific provision exists for additional protection for wines and spirits.[16]

Since 2018, Angola has started a revision process of its IP legislation to bring it in line with international standards. According to disclosed drafts, the bill provides for, and regulates, designations of origin and GIs. The bill is already at an advanced legislative stage, but it is not known when it will come into force.

3. Registration of GIs Domestically

In theory, collective marks are the most adequate means for protecting GIs in Angola within the existing legal framework. A collective mark is defined as a mark used by an economic group to distinguish the goods manufactured or sold or the services provided by each one of the members of the group.[17] It is intended for use by those on whom the relevant statutes or founding documents confer the right.[18] In practice, the authors are unaware of any GIs registered as a collective mark in Angola.

4. Registrability of Names

Under article 35 of the IP Law, trade marks that in some or all of its elements contain false indications concerning the geographical origin, manufacture, ownership, office, or establishment of the mark shall be refused. In an *a contrario* interpretation, the registration of a collective mark that contains a truthful indication of the geographical origin should be allowed.

---

[14] IP Law, art 61(1).
[15] ibid art 62.
[16] African Union Commission Department of Rural Economy and Agriculture, 'Continental Strategy for Geographical Indications in Africa 2018–2023' (African Union Commission Department of Rural Economy and Agriculture nd) 32.
[17] IP Law, art 30(3).
[18] ibid art 30(1).

Article 31(2) of the IP Law specifically mentions geographical names as a sign acceptable as a trade or service mark.[19]

5. Procedure and Requirements for Registration

An application for the registration of a trade mark or collective mark shall be filed with the IAPI. As article 30 of the IP Law sets out who shall have the right to use a mark, it is presumed that these groups shall also have the right to apply for a trade mark or collective mark. These are the:

a) manufacturers to indicate their products;
b) traders to indicate the articles or merchandise they trade in;
c) farmers and producers, to indicate agricultural or fisheries products or those products arising from any agricultural, animal husbandry, forestry or extractive enterprise;
d) craftsmen to indicate the products of their art or craft;
e) entrepreneurial groups representing an economic activity; and
f) self-employed professionals, entities, or businesses to distinguish their services or activities.[20]

Only single-class applications are possible.
An application shall contain

a) The full particulars of the applicant: name or business name of the holder of the trade mark, nationality, profession, and residence;
b) Prints of both word and device marks. The graphical representation of the mark may not exceed 8/8 cm;
c) Specification of goods or services in accordance with the Nice Classification. An application may cover any number of goods or services in the same class, but additional fees are charged for each good or service after the first five;
d) The legal or statutory provisions governing the regime and use of the collective mark; and
e) In the case of foreign applicants:
   i. Appropriate evidence that the mark is related to their activity (commercial, industrial, or professional) which is effectively and lawfully exercised in the country of origin;

---

[19] One may imagine the problems caused by the registration of a GI as a trade mark by a product not respecting the conditions attached to a GI but which truly originates from that region.
[20] IP Law, art 30(1).

ii. A power of attorney signed, notarised, and legalised up to an Angolan Embassy or Consulate appointing a local agent; and
iii. A certified copy of an official document stating the activity of the applicant company duly translated in Portuguese, notarised and legalised.[21]

The application must be accompanied by a single fee representing the filing fees, the first and second publication fees, and the granting and registration certificate fees.

After the filing of the application, it is published in the *Angolan Industrial Property Bulletin*. Although not expressly provided, any person may oppose the application within sixty days from the date mentioned in the circular letter with which the *Bulletin* is distributed. A thirty-day extension may be requested.

The IAPI examines the opposition regarding its formal admissibility and merits. If the opposition is upheld, the registration is refused. If the opposition is rejected, the application proceeds to substantial examination, in which the examiner considers both absolute and relative grounds (potential conflicting third-party rights not invoked in the opposition). An application may be refused where it

a) consists of a sign that does not allow the distinction of a company's goods or services from identical or similar ones;
b) contains false indications or indications liable to mislead the public as to the nature, characteristics, or usefulness of the products or services using the mark;
c) contains false indications concerning the geographical origin, manufacture, ownership, office, or establishment;
d) contains symbols such as insignia, flags, arms, or official signs adopted by the State, commissariats, international organizations, or any other public entities, whether Angolan or foreign, without due authorization from these bodies;
e) contains signatures, names, or establishment names that do not belong to the person applying for the mark or which said applicant is authorized to use;
f) contains reproduction or imitation, in whole or in part, of a mark previously registered by another person for the same or similar products or services, which could be misleading or could cause confusion in the marketplace;
g) contains expressions or drawings contrary to common decency or that contravene the law or public policy;
h) contains individual names or likenesses without due authorization from the persons to whom they relate.[22]

---

[21] IP Law, art 33.
[22] IP Law, art 35.

If the application is granted, the IAPI publishes the decision and issues the registration certificate.

The applicant, or the party whose opposition was rejected, can file an internal appeal with the IAPI within fifteen working days after the publication of the notice of decision in the *Bulletin*. Should the internal appeal be rejected, filing an appeal at the Ministry of Industry within thirty working days is possible. An applicant or the party whose opposition was rejected may also directly file an appeal at the Ministry of Industry, bypassing the internal appeal at the IAPI. These appeal decisions may be challenged before the administrative courts. In theory, the Commercial and IP Court is the competent court for deciding appeals against the decisions of the IAPI. In practice, the Commercial and IP Court has refused to do so, invoking a lack of jurisdiction. While the territorial jurisdiction of the Commercial and IP Court is limited to the Province of Luanda, the decisions of the IAPI are nationwide in scope.

6. Term of Protection

The registration of a mark is effective for an initial period of ten years and is renewable for like periods.

7. Rights of the Owner and Enforcement Mechanisms against Infringers

Registration grants exclusive rights to a mark. A mark owner or the recorded licensee may institute criminal and civil proceedings against infringers. The institution of criminal proceedings is also open to public prosecution.

Any person who

a) imitates or reproduces in whole or in part, a protected mark without authorization from its owner;
b) uses a counterfeit or imitation mark;
c) fraudulently uses a collective mark in conditions other than those provided for in the relevant rules;
d) uses a mark with a false indication as to the source of the products and sells or places on sale products designated with such a mark;
e) uses a mark in the conditions described for marks that are excluded from protection,[23] shall commit an offence punishable with a fine up to Kz 50,000.00 and/or a prison sentence of up to three months.

---

[23] ibid art 70.

Other remedies available for criminal and civil proceedings include final injunctions, damages, and the seizure and destruction of infringing goods.

Registered and unregistered marks and unregistered foreign GIs may further be protected under unfair competition. Any competitive act contrary to honest practices in any branch of economic activity is deemed illegal. This includes false indications as to the source, nature, or quality of products or services; the production, manufacture, importation, storage, or sale of merchandise with a false indication of source; and false statements or any other acts liable to discredit the establishment, products, services or reputation of competitors, or those made with the intention of benefiting from the reputation of a name, mark, or establishment of another, regardless of the means employed. The penalty applicable shall be a fine between Kz 20,000.00 and Kz 100,000.00, save where the offender is liable for a heavier penalty in application of the criminal article and Law No 9/89 (Law on Crimes against the Economy).[24]

Interestingly, although there is no legislation specific to GIs in Angola, the IAPI has allowed oppositions against trade mark applications by unregistered GIs for wines and spirits.[25] The IAPI relies either on the law against unfair competition (namely that false indications as to the source, nature, or quality of products are illegal) or on articles 22(2)(b) and 23(1) of the TRIPS Agreement through article 77 of the IP Law. Under article 77 of the IP Law: '(t)he provisions of international conventions relating to intellectual property and industrial property, in particular those which the country is a contracting party, shall apply in the event of divergence'.

Article 448 of the Penal Code provides that whoever, with the intent to harm a third party or enrich himself, manufactures, transforms, imports, exports, stores, transports, holds, exhibits for sale, sells, puts into circulation, or distributes counterfeit or imitation goods, passing them off as genuine or unaltered or of a different nature, or goods of a quality inferior to that attributed to it by the perpetrator, may be punished with a prison sentence of up to two years or with a fine of up to 240 days if a more severe penalty is not applicable by any other criminal provision. In case of negligence, the penalty shall be a fine of up to sixty days.[26]

8. Customs Enforcement

There is no formal procedure for registering IP rights with Angolan customs, nor does the IP Law provide for border measures. The Customs Code, however,

---

[24] ibid art 73.

[25] See, eg trade mark 59242 SUPER SCOTCH WHISKY in class 33, refused on the basis of the SCOTCH WHISKY; device mark 59243 New Port Wine in class 33, refused on the basis of the PORTO; and trade marks 41921 and 41922 in class 43 and class 41, respectively, CLUB CHAMPAGNE refused on the basis of the CHAMPAGNE.

[26] In Angola, the Penal Code at art 46 sets out the fine penalty in days, with each day corresponding to a variable reference unit, which the court fixes in accordance with the economic and financial situation of the convicted person and its personal expenses.

provides that one of the responsibilities of Customs is to protect IP rights.[27] Merchandise that infringes IP rights is prohibited and must be seized. Merchandise manufactured or produced in contravention of the rights of a GI is explicitly mentioned as a prohibited importation.[28] Based on the Customs Code, and although no formal guidelines exist, customs have been active in seizing counterfeit goods both *ex officio* and following informal applications for actions by right holders.[29] Right holders are therefore well advised to actively seek out customs collaboration to protect their GIs and collective marks.

9. Bilateral Agreements

There is no bilateral agreement between either the European Community or the United States and Angola specific to GIs.

---

[27] Customs Code (approved by Executive Decree No. 5/06 of 4 October 2006 (2007), art 19(1)(p).
[28] ibid art 71(1)–(3).
[29] More information may be found on customs enforcement in Angola in Marius Schneider and Vanessa Ferguson, *Enforcement of Intellectual Property Rights in Africa* (OUP 2020) 85–86.

8
Botswana

Botswana is located in Southern Africa, bordered by South Africa, Namibia, Zimbabwe, and Zambia. The landlocked country of 581,730 km² had a population of 2.63 million inhabitants in 2022. The official languages of Botswana are English and Tswana. English is the language of business, and most written communication is in English. The working week is from Monday to Friday, and the national currency is the Botswana Pula (BWP).

From one of the world's poorest countries at its independence in 1966, since 2005, Botswana has been classified by the World Bank as an upper-middle-income country.[1] This growth was enabled by significant mineral wealth, in particular diamonds, good governance, and a solid democratic system. Botswana now aims to become a high-income country by 2036. Living conditions have thus considerably improved, and poverty has fallen steadily in the country. Still, income inequality in Botswana remains high.[2]

Dominated by the vast Kalahari Desert, Botswana has less than 5 per cent of cultivable land area and limited available water. Crop production is low, with cattle raising making up 80 per cent of the country's agricultural output.[3] Food imports such as poultry and agricultural produce are high and are expected to grow. In 2019, 12.7 per cent of all merchandise imports in Botswana were food and beverages.[4] The leading food suppliers in order of importance are South Africa, Zimbabwe, Namibia, Eswatini, and Zambia.[5]

Due to its proximity to South Africa, Botswana's retail market is dominated by both local and South African actors. With nearly half of the population classified as middle class, retailers will find a well-developed formal retail sector with numerous shopping malls. E-commerce is, however, still in its infancy, although 47 per cent of

---

[1] The only country having enjoyed a similar high growth rate over a long period is China: Brian Mccaig, 'Stuck in the Middle? Structural Change and Productivity Growth in Botswana' in Margaret McMillan and others (eds), *Structural Change, Fundamentals, and Growth: A Framework and Case Studies* (International Food Policy Research Institute 2017) 125.
[2] ibid 129.
[3] It has often been reported that there are more cattle than people in Botswana: Kate Wilkinson, 'Do Cattle Outnumber People in Botswana?' (*AfricaCheck*, 14 December 2015) <https://africacheck.org/fact-checks/reports/do-cattle-outnumber-people-botswana>.
[4] Knoema, 'Botswana—Food Imports as a Share of Merchandise Imports' (*Knoema*, nd) <https://knoema.com/atlas/Botswana/topics/Foreign-Trade/Import/Food-imports>.
[5] World Integrated Trade Solution, 'Botswana Food Products Imports by Country in US$ Thousand 2020' (*World Integrated Trade Solution*, nd) <https://wits.worldbank.org/CountryProfile/en/Country/BWA/Year/LTST/TradeFlow/Import/Partner/by-country/Product/16-24_FoodProd>.

the population has access to the internet[6] and 51 per cent of the population has an account with a financial institution.[7] A 2014 survey found that only 4.6 per cent of Batswana purchase goods or services through e-commerce.[8] Although this figure has certainly increased over the years, fear of scams and concerns over the safety of online payment solutions are still restricting e-commerce in the country.

There are currently no local products registered as a geographical indication (GI) in Botswana, although the 2022 national policy on intellectual property (IP) highlights the desire of the government to use GIs to promote agro-tourism in rural areas.[9] Goods that have the potential to be registered as GIs are Ghanzi Beef and the Ngami/Nhabe Basket. As of May 2023, *Scotch Whisky* is the first and only GI registered in Botswana. Registration in Botswana also marked the first recognition for *Scotch Whisky* as a GI in an African country.[10] It is, however, possible to register a collective mark in Botswana. The Chobe basket collective mark was registered in 2021 by the cooperative 'Chobe Basket Weavers Cooperative Union Ltd'. With support from the World Intellectual Property Organization and the Funds-in-Trust Japan Industrial Property Global, the branding project of traditional Chobe baskets woven from palm leaves took two years to reach completion.[11]

1. Legal Framework

Botswana has a mixed legal system influenced by the Roman-Dutch model, customary law, and English common law. The court system consists of the Magistrate's Court and customary courts as the most important inferior courts. Inferior courts are subordinate to the High Court, a superior court with unlimited original jurisdiction to hear and determine any criminal and civil cases under any category of law. An appeal from a decision of the High Court is heard before the Court of Appeal.

In Botswana, attorneys and advocates are the two legal practitioners qualified to appear before the courts. Attorneys provide various services to their clients, while

---

[6] Statista, 'Internet Penetration Rate in Botswana from 2017 to 2022' (*Statista*, nd) <www.statista.com/statistics/1155039/internet-penetration-rate-botswana>.

[7] These figures relate to the year 2021: Statista, 'Share of Population with an Account at a Financial Institution in Botswana from 2018 to 2022' (*Statista*, nd) <https://www.statista.com/statistics/1155784/bank-account-owners-botswana>.

[8] Statistics Botswana, 'Botswana Household Access and Individual Use of Information & Communication Technologies Survey—2014' (Statistics Botswana 2016) 12.

[9] Republic of Botswana, 'Botswana Intellectual Property Policy BIPP 2022' (Republic of Botswana nd) 26.

[10] Afro Leo, 'An IP First for Scotch Whisky in Botswana' (*Afro-IP*, 7 August 2015) <http://afro-ip.blogspot.com/2015/08/an-ip-first-for-scotch-whisky-in.html>.

[11] World Intellectual Property Organization, 'Conclusion of the IP and Branding Strategy for Chobe Baskets Project' (*World Intellectual Property Organization*, 1 March 2023) <www.wipo.int/cooperation/en/funds_in_trust/japan_fitip_global/news/2023/news_0003.html>.

advocates or counsels are specialists in advocacy whose primary function is to conduct cases in court.

2. Domestic Legislation on GIs

Botswana has been a member of the Paris Convention for the Protection of Industrial Property of 1883 since April 1998. Botswana is a party to neither the Madrid Agreement for the Repression of False or Deceptive Indications of Source on Goods of 1891 nor the Lisbon Agreement for the Protection of Appellations of Origin and their International Registration of 1958. Botswana has been a party to the Madrid Protocol Concerning the International Registration of Marks since December 2006. Botswana has been an African Regional Intellectual Property Organization (ARIPO) member state since February 1985 and a party to the Banjul Protocol on marks in the framework of ARIPO since October 2003. Botswana is a member of the World Trade Organization (WTO), and the transition period available to put in effect national legislation implementing the WTO Agreement on Trade-Related Aspects of Intellectual Property Rights (TRIPS) expired on 31 December 1999.

GIs are protected in Botswana via a *sui generis* system under the Industrial Property Act No 8 of 2010 (IPA), which came into force on 31 August 2012. It is further possible under the IPA to register a collective mark. However, the IPA provides that a mark shall not be registered if it is a mark that consists exclusively of a sign or indication that may serve in trade to designate the geographical origin of the goods or service.[12] In practice, this might exclude a number of GIs from being registered as collective marks. The Companies and Intellectual Property Authority (CIPA) is in charge of implementing and administering the IPA.

There is no specific additional protection for wine and spirits in the IPA. There is no provision regarding homonymous GIs.

3. Registration of GIs Domestically

3.1 GIs

It is possible to register both local and foreign indications or signs in Botswana as GIs. The IPA defines a GI as an indication or sign that identifies goods as originating in the territory of a country or a region or locality in a country where a quality, reputation, or other characteristic of the goods is essentially attributable to that geographical origin.[13] This is in line with the definition provided in article

---

[12] IPA, s 74(1)(d). Section 90(1) of the IPA makes applicable s 74 of the IPA to collective marks.
[13] ibid s 2.

22 of the TRIPS Agreement. As per the definition in the IPA, registration as a GI is restricted to goods, and services are excluded. There is no explicit restriction as to the type of goods. Registration is not limited to food and drink and could thus be granted for other products such as handicrafts. The exclusive right to a GI under the IPA shall be acquired by registration.

3.2 Collective marks

A collective mark is defined as 'any visible sign belonging to a collective owner and capable of distinguishing the origin or other common characteristic, including the quality, of goods or services of different enterprises which use the sign subject to the control of that owner'.[14]

If a GI was registered as a mark before the IPA's coming into force, the mark remains in force.

4. Registrability of Names

4.1 GIs

A GI shall not be registered if it is

a) incapable of distinguishing goods originating from a particular territory, region, or locality, or it does not possess characteristics attributed to that territory, region or locality in which those goods come from;
b) contrary to public order or morality;
c) likely to mislead the public or those in the trade as regard the geographical origin of the goods concerned or their nature or characteristics;
d) in respect to goods, identical with the term usually used in common language as the common name for such goods in Botswana; or
e) not protected, has ceased to be protected, or has fallen into disuse in its country of origin.[15]

4.2 Collective marks

A collective mark cannot be registered where it is likely to mislead the public or trade circles, in particular as regards the geographical origin of the goods or

---

[14] ibid s 2.
[15] ibid s 106(2).

services concerned or where it consists exclusively of a sign or indication that may serve in trade to designate the geographic origin of the goods or service.[16]

5. Procedure and Requirements for Registration

5.1 GIs

An application for the registration of a GI shall be made to the Registrar of Marks, Patents and Designs on a prescribed form (Form 17). The IPA does not set out the quality of the applicant, although in line with international practice, this will likely be a producer association rather than an individual trader. On the form, the applicant must provide the following information:

a) Name and contact details of applicant and the agent (if applicable);
b) Name and contact details of the authority or body responsible for certifying compliance with the specification;
c) Reproductions of the GI;
d) Evidence of protection in the country of origin;
e) The list of products for which the GI is to be used;
f) a specification containing—
  i. the name of the products to which the GI applies,
  ii. a description of the product, including its raw materials, if appropriate, and principal physical, chemical, microbiological, or organoleptic characteristics,
  iii. the definition of the geographical area from which the designated product originates,
  iv. evidence that the product originates in the defined geographical area,
  v. a description of the method of obtaining or producing the product, including as appropriate, the traditional local methods, and information concerning packaging if it is claimed that the packaging is relevant to the claimed characteristics or required to safeguard the quality or ensure the genuine origin of the product,
  vi. details bearing out the link between the quality or characteristics of the product and its geographical origin.[17]

The application form shall be accompanied by a written request that the GI be registered. This can take the form of a cover letter/application letter, which should also include the applicant's personal details.

---

[16] ibid s 74(2).
[17] This may include natural factors, such as climate, and human factors, such as the traditional skills required and developed in the production area: Afro Leo (n 10).

The application should be signed by the applicant or its authorised agent and contain a durable graphic reproduction of the GI. A fee must be paid.[18]

Where the ordinary residence or principal place of business of the applicant is outside Botswana, the applicant shall be represented by a legal practitioner who has been enrolled to practice in the courts of Botswana (attorney) or persons prescribed by the minister of trade and industry. A power of attorney appointing the agent may be filed within one month of filing Form 17.

The applicant may withdraw its application at any time before the GI is registered.

The Registrar shall examine the application to determine whether it complies with the requirements of the IPA. Where so satisfied, the Registrar shall accept the application and publish that application in the *Journal of trade marks, patents and industrial designs (Journal)* for three months upon payment of a fee.[19] Within those three months, any interested person may file with the Registrar a notice of opposition on the ground that the requirements of section 106(2) of the IPA have not been satisfied or that the GI does not comply with the definition of a GI as specified in the IPA.

Where, having considered the merits of any opposition and any counterstatement, the Registrar is satisfied that the application for the registration of a GI satisfies the requirements of this Act, the Registrar invites the applicant to pay for the registration. After payment, the Registrar registers the GI in the appropriate register, issues to the applicant a certificate of registration, and publishes in the *Journal* a reference to the registration of the GI.[20]

5.2 Collective marks

The registration of a collective mark is open to both domestic and foreign applicants. The requirements and process for the application for a collective mark are similar to an application for a trade mark. The application must, however, clearly designate the mark as a collective mark and be accompanied by a copy of the rules governing the use of the collective mark drawn by the person under whose control the collective mark may be used.[21] The application is made on prescribed Form 11 to the Registrar. Similar rules of representation apply to the foreign applicant of a collective mark as a GI. The Registrar examines the mark on both relative and absolute grounds. As such, the Registrar may refuse an application that does not respect the rules regarding the registrability of certain marks. Upon acceptance of

---

[18] Industrial Property Regulations 2012 Statutory Instrument No 70 of 2012 published on 31 August 2012, s 53.
[19] IPA, s 108(2).
[20] ibid s 110(1).
[21] ibid s 90.

the application, the application is published in the *Journal*. Any person may oppose the trade mark within three months from publication. A copy of the notice of opposition filed by the opponent is shared with the applicant, who may thereafter submit its counterstatement with the grounds relied upon. The counterstatement is then shared with the opponent, and the Registrar may hear the parties if any of the two parties wishes to be heard. Should there be no opposition, or should the opposition be rejected, the Registrar will issue a certificate.

6. Term of Protection

6.1 GIs

The registration of the GI shall expire ten years after the filing date of the application, but may, upon the written request and payment of a renewal fee, be renewed for consecutive periods of ten years.[22]

The rights conferred by the registration of a mark may not be invoked to prevent a third party from using a GI registered under the IPA in the course of trade.[23] At the same time, where a mark has been registered in good faith, or where rights in the mark have been acquired through use in good faith either before 1 January 2000 or before a GI is protected in Botswana, the registration of such mark, or the use of such mark on the basis that the mark is identical to or similar to a GI, shall not be prevented or interfered with.[24]

The rights conferred by the registration of a GI may further not be invoked to prevent a national or domiciliary of Botswana who has previously used the GI to identify wines or spirits to continue such use in the same manner, provided such use was undertaken continuously

a) for at least ten years preceding 15 April 1994; or
b) in good faith preceding 15 April 1994.[25]

This section reflects article 24(4) of the TRIPS Agreement.

Any interested person may apply to the Registrar for the invalidation of the registration of a GI on the ground that the requirements of section 106(2) and the definition of a GI as specified under this Act have not been satisfied.[26] This is in

---

[22] The IPA does not explicitly specify how long a GI's registration shall remain valid. However, IPA, s 105 provides that the provisions of the Act related to marks and collective marks, and trade names apply with the necessary modifications to GI and their registration.
[23] IPA, s 82(1)(d).
[24] ibid s 75.
[25] ibid s 112.
[26] ibid s 113(1).

line with article 22(3) of the TRIPS Agreement. The applicant shall serve a copy of an application for the invalidation of a GI on the owner of the GI and on any other person having the right to use the GI. The applicant shall also file a copy with the Registrar. Where the application for invalidation is based on the ground that the geographical area specified in the register does not correspond to the GI, or that the indication of the products for which the GI is used or the indication of the quality, reputation, or other characteristic of such product is missing or unsatisfactory, the Registrar may order for the rectification of the registration. The invalidation of a registered GI shall be published in the *Journal*.

6.2 Collective marks

A collective mark is protected for ten years from the application's filing date. The mark will be renewed indefinitely for consecutive periods of ten years upon payment of the renewal fee. Any changes to the rules of the collective mark must be notified to the Registrar in writing.

Any interested person may apply to the Registrar to invalidate the registration of a mark on both absolute and relative grounds as provided for trade marks. Additional grounds of invalidation for a collective mark are that only the owner uses the mark, uses or permits its use in contravention of the rules, or uses or permits its use in a manner that is liable to deceive those in the trade or the public as to the origin or any other common characteristics of the goods or services concerned.[27] Having regard to the grounds available for opposition, one may argue that a collective mark owner can use the mark as long as it is not the only one to do so.

7. Rights of the Owner and Enforcement Mechanisms against Infringers

7.1 GIs

The right to a registered GI shall belong to the registered owner.[28]

Registration of a GI shall confer on the registered owner the right to prohibit third parties from using the GI and to institute court proceedings against any person infringing its rights. The registered GI owner, or a licensee if it has requested the owner to institute court proceedings for a specific relief and the owner has refused or failed to do so, may apply to the High Court for an interdict to prevent an

---

[27] ibid s 91(1).
[28] ibid s 111(1).

infringement or the use by a person without the authorization of the owner of the registered GI of

a) the registered GI to identify products of the same description but not originating from the place indicated by the GI, even where the true origin is indicated or the GI used is accompanied by disclaimers or expressions such as 'kind', 'type', 'style', 'imitation' or the like;
b) the registered GI to indicate that products originate in a geographical region other than their true place of origin; or
c) the registered GI for goods produced in the geographical area specified in the register in respect of the GI that do not possess the quality, reputation, or other characteristics specified in the register.[29]

Any person other than the owner of the title of protection performing these acts without the agreement of the owner commits an infringement.[30] Any person who intentionally or wilfully performs any such infringement commits an offence and shall be sentenced, on conviction, to a fine of not less than BWP 2,000 but not more than BWP 5,000 and/or to imprisonment for a term of not less than six months but not more than two years.

7.2 Collective marks

The right to a collective mark shall belong to the registered owner. Registration of a collective mark shall confer on the registered owner the right to prohibit third parties from using the collective mark and to institute court proceedings against any person infringing its rights or performing acts that make it likely that infringement will occur.[31]

Any person who, without authorization from the owner of a collective mark,

a) affixes the mark or a similar distinctive sign on goods for which the mark has been registered, on goods associated with the services for which the mark has been registered, or on containers, wrapping, or packaging of such goods;
b) suppresses or distorts the mark after it has been affixed on the goods for which the mark has been registered for commercial purposes;
c) produces, sells, offers for sale, distributes or stocks labels, containers, wrapping, packaging, or any other material on which the mark is reproduced;
d) refills or re-uses for commercial purposes, labels, containers, wrapping, packaging, or any other material bearing the mark;

---

[29] ibid s 111(3).
[30] ibid s 134(4).
[31] ibid s 81(1).

e) uses in the course of trade, a sign that is identical or similar to the mark in respect of any goods or services, where such use may cause a risk of confusion or association with the registered mark;
f) uses in the course of trade, a sign identical or similar to the mark in respect of any goods or services where such use may cause unfair economic prejudice to the registered owner through dilution of the distinctive character or advertising value of the mark, or an unfair advantage being taken from the reputation of the registered mark or of its holder; or
g) for non-commercial purposes, uses a sign identical or similar to the mark, where this may cause dilution of the distinctive character or advertising value of the mark, or an unfair advantage being taken of the reputation of the mark or its holder,

infringes the rights of the owner of the collective mark.[32]

In addition to more traditional definitions of use in the course of trade (importation, exportation, selling, use of the mark in advertising), the IPA also defines use as the use of the mark on the internet or other electronic communication media or networks open to the public, where the use is intended for Botswana or has a commercial market in Botswana. This definition widens the scope of the Act and brings in numerous infringing actions under the purview of the Batswana courts. The adoption or use of the mark as part of a domain name or other similar identification or designation on the internet or other electronic communication media or networks open to the public is also included in the definition of use.[33]

The rights over a registered mark cannot prevent a third party from using a registered GI in the course of trade.[34]

Among the remedies available in a suit for infringement, the right owner may be entitled to an interdict, delivery up, or destruction of any infringing product, article, or product of which the infringing product forms an inseparable part, damages, or an account of the profits derived from the infringement. Where the court awards damages, the court may not, for the same infringement, order that the right owner be given an account of the profits derived by it from the infringement.[35]

7.3 Unfair competition

The owner of a registered GI or a collective mark, any competent authority, any person, association, or syndicate may request an interdict from the High Court of Botswana to prevent an act of unfair competition, award damages, or grant any

[32] ibid s 81(2).
[33] ibid s 81(3).
[34] ibid s 82(1)(d).
[35] ibid s 83(5).

other remedy as the court may deem appropriate.[36] This right to apply for an interdict to prevent an act of unfair competition also belongs to a licensee if it has requested the owner of the GI or collective mark to institute court proceedings for a specific relief and the owner has refused or failed to do so.[37] Any act of competition contrary to honest practices in industrial or commercial matters shall constitute an act of unfair competition and shall be unlawful. This includes

a) any act of such a nature as to create confusion by any means whatever with the establishment, the goods, or the industrial or commercial activities of a competitor;
b) the making of a false allegation in the course of trade of such a nature as to discredit the establishment, the goods, or the industrial or commercial activities of a competitor;
c) the making of allegations which, in the course of trade, is likely to mislead the public as to the nature, the manufacturing process, the characteristics, the suitability for their purpose, or the quantity of the goods of a competitor;
d) the use of a GI that identifies specific products of a particular origin to designate products of the same description but not originating from the place indicated by the GI, even where the true origin is indicated, or the GI used is accompanied by disclaimers or expressions such as 'kind', 'type', 'style', 'imitation' or the like;
e) the use of GIs to indicate that products originate in a geographical region other than their true place of origin; or
f) any act or practice done in the course of industrial or commercial activities that results in obtaining, using, or disclosing to third parties undisclosed information without the consent of the rightful holder of that information.[38]

An offender found guilty of an act of unfair competition shall be sentenced, on conviction, to a fine of not less than BWP 2,000 but not more than BWP 5,000 and/or to imprisonment for a term of not less than six months but not more than two years.

8. Customs Enforcement

There are currently no formal recordal mechanisms available with customs in Botswana, although there have been talks of such. In practice, Botswana customs

---

[36] ibid s 114(1).
[37] ibid s 134(5).
[38] ibid s 114(3).

does seize counterfeit goods at the borders.[39] Another mechanism that is widely adopted is for the right holder to lodge a complaint with the police or an administrative authority with regard to suspected counterfeit goods. The police or administrative authority will then request customs to detain the goods for identification or verification by the right owner.[40] Detained goods are destroyed following court orders.

9. Bilateral Agreements

There is no agreement between either the European Union (EU) or the United States and Botswana regarding GIs. Botswana is part of the South African Development Community, with which the EU has entered into an Economic Partnership Agreement (EPA); however, the provisions on GIs in the EPA only apply to South Africa. These provisions do not apply to Botswana and other community members (eSwatini, Lesotho, Mozambique, Namibia).

---

[39] International Trademark Association, 'Conductor Paul Masena—Advancing Companies' IP in Botswana' (*International Trademark Association*, 27 January 2021) <www.inta.org/perspectives/interviews/conductor-paul-masena-enabling-companies-ip-in-botswana>.

[40] More information may be found on customs enforcement in Botswana in Marius Schneider and Vanessa Ferguson, *Enforcement of Intellectual Property Rights in Africa* (OUP 2020) 121–23.

9
Democratic Republic of the Congo

The Democratic Republic of the Congo, also known as the DRC or Congo-Kinshasa, is in Central Africa. It borders nine African countries: the Republic of Congo (Brazzaville), the Central African Republic, Sudan, Uganda, Rwanda, Burundi, Tanzania, Zambia, and Angola. It has a small coastline on the Atlantic. It is the largest Francophone country in Africa, the second largest country in Africa, and the eleventh largest country in the world. Sparsely populated, the DRC had 99 million inhabitants in 2022. The working week is from Monday to Friday, and the national currency is the Congolese Franc (CDF).

The gross domestic product (GDP) of the DRC in 2021 amounted to USD 53.96 billion. Most of the country's GDP is based on the extractive industry. The DRC is home to 1,110 different minerals and precious metals. The country produces 70 per cent of the world's cobalt, holds 60 per cent of the planet's coltan reserves, and is the world's fourth biggest producer of copper.[1] The DRC also has around 80 million hectares of arable land. Still, although endowed with exceptional natural resources, the DRC has been unable to reach its full economic potential due to ongoing conflicts. Erupting in the 1990s, the war has created a protracted economic and social slump. The DRC is among the five poorest nations in the world. In 2018, about 73 per cent of Congolese lived on less than USD 1.90 a day.[2]

Although two-thirds of the Congo's labour force works in the agricultural sector, only 10 per cent of the available arable land in the DRC is under cultivation. Agriculture consists mainly of subsistence farming. Therefore, it is no wonder that the DRC relies heavily on food imports. The DRC, Nigeria, Angola, and Somalia account for most of the agricultural trade deficit in sub-Saharan Africa.[3] The top four partners for food imports reflect historical ties (Belgium), language ties (France), and geographical proximity (Senegal and South Africa).[4]

---

[1] Jason Mitchell, 'Kinshasa Is Already Africa's Biggest City—Could Cobalt Make It the Richest?' (*Investment Monitor*, 15 February 2022) < www.investmentmonitor.ai/features/kinshasa-africa-democratic-republic-congo-cobalt/>.
[2] World Bank, 'The World Bank in DRC' (*World Bank*, 29 March 2023) <www.worldbank.org/en/country/drc/overview>.
[3] Louise Fox and Thomas S Jayne, 'Unpacking the Misconceptions about Africa's Food Imports' (*Brookings*, 14 December 2020) <www.brookings.edu/blog/africa-in-focus/2020/12/14/unpacking-the-misconceptions-about-africas-food-imports>.
[4] World Integrated Trade Solution, 'Congo, Rep Food Products Imports by Country in US$ Thousand 2020' (*World Integrated Trade Solution*, nd) <https://wits.worldbank.org/CountryProfile/en/Country/COG/Year/LTST/TradeFlow/Import/Partner/by-country/Product/16-24_FoodProd>.

Customers in the DRC still favour the informal sector for their purchases. Eighty-five per cent of foodstuff in the DRC is still purchased through the traditional system (open markets, proximity stores, street stalls, and kiosks). Modern retail stores, including shopping malls, are moving into the country, though it is estimated that by 2040, traditional shops will still make up 50–70 per cent of the market.[5] The formal sector caters mainly to the Congolese elite and the expatriate community. E-commerce is practically non-existent. This is due to an internet penetration rate of only 17.6 per cent in 2022, limited access to the formal banking system and the difficulties of delivering goods cheaply due to poor physical infrastructure and the size of the country.

In 2020, the provincial Minister of Agriculture announced the establishment of two certificates-of-origin labels for products from the Ituri province, namely Kawa Ituri DRC and Cacao Ituri DRC. It is unsure whether this has been put into place.[6] The Coffee of Kivu is often highlighted as having the potential to be protected under the geographical indication (GI) framework.

1. Legal Framework

The DRC's legal system is based on a mix of Belgian civil law and customary law. The highest court in the DRC is the Court of Cassation. It is the court of last resort, which hears cassation claims from decisions and judgments made by civil and military courts and tribunals on points of law only. The subordinate courts are the *Tribunal de Paix*, *Tribunal de Grande Instance*, and Courts of Appeal. The *Tribunal de Paix* hears civil cases up to 2.5 million CDF and criminal cases with a maximum penalty of five years and/or a fine. The judge at the *Tribunal de Grande Instance* or, by default, the president of the *Tribunal de Grande Instance* may authorize descriptive seizures. The *Tribunal de Grande Instance* hears all civil cases whose value exceeds 2.5 million CDF and criminal offences with imprisonment exceeding five years or penal servitude. The *Tribunal de Grande Instance* further hears appeals from the *Tribunal de Paix*. Situated within a *Tribunal de Grande Instance*, the Commercial Court decides upon cases involving bankruptcy, partnerships, unfair competition, and other commercial matters. Nine commercial tribunals have been created, including two in the capital city of Kinshasa. The Courts of Appeal hear appeals from the *Tribunal de Grande Instance* and Commercial Courts. With the exception of Kinshasa, which has the status of a province and which has two

---

[5] Llyods Bank, 'Democratic Republic of Congo: Buying and Selling' (Llyods Bank December 2023) <https://www.lloydsbanktrade.com/en/market-potential/democratic-republic-of-congo/distribution>

[6] Kji, 'Ituri: Vers la mise en place d'une brigade agricole pour l'encadrement de la jeunesse' (*Agence Congolaise de Presse*, 13 August 2020) <https://acpcongo.com/index.php/2020/08/13/ituri-vers-la-mise-en-place-dune-brigade-agricole-pour-lencadrement-de-la-jeunesse>.

Courts of Appeal (Gombe and Matete), a Court of Appeal is installed in each provincial capital and a *Tribunal de Grande Instance* in each district or city, and there is a *Tribunal de Paix* for each group of municipalities or territory. There are no courts in the DRC specializing in intellectual property (IP) rights.[7]

Lawyers in the DRC are advocates or *défenseur judiciaire*. An advocate can appear in all courts, while a *défenseur judiciaire* may only appear at *Tribunal de Grande Instance* and *Tribunal de Paix* in a specific area. Advocates will appear before the courts and advise, conciliate, and draw up private deeds. A *défenseur judiciaire* will assist and represent parties before the Tribunal.

2. Domestic Legislation on GIs

The DRC acceded to the Paris Convention for the Protection of Industrial Property (Paris Convention) of 1883 in October 1974. The DRC is a party to neither the Madrid Agreement for the Repression of False or Deceptive Indications of Source on Goods of 1891 nor the Lisbon Agreement for the Protection of Appellations of Origin and their International Registration of 1958. The DRC is a member of the World Trade Organization (WTO). As a least-developed country member, the DRC is not required to apply the provisions of the World Trade Organization (WTO) Agreement on Trade-Related Aspects of Intellectual Property Rights (TRIPS), other than articles 3, 4, and 5, until 1 July 2034 or until the date when it ceases to be a least developed country, whichever date is earlier.[8] Currently, the DRC's IP legislation is not in line with the TRIPS Agreement.

Law No 82-001 of January 1982 on Industrial Property (IP Law) provides for the protection of IP rights in the country. The IP Law clearly mentions GIs—which designates *Appellations d'origine* (appellations of origin) and *Indications de provenance* (indications of source)—as the subject of an IP title, and articles 101–105 are dedicated to GIs. The practice, as seen in this chapter, is more complicated.

3. Registration of GIs Domestically

3.1 Appellations of origin and indications of source

The IP Law provides for the *sui generis* protection of GIs. Registration as a GI is open to DRC nationals as well as foreigners under certain conditions. Nationals of

---

[7] World Trade Organization, 'Trade Policy Review Report by the Secretariat Democratic Republic of the Congo WT/TPR/S/339' (World Trade Organization 2016) para 3.161.
[8] WTO, 'WTO Members Agree to Extend TRIPS Transition Period for LDCs until 1 July 2034' (*WTO*, 29 June 2021) <www.wto.org/english/news_e/news21_e/trip_30jun21_e.htm>.

non-member countries of the International Union for the Protection of Industrial Property whose domicile or establishment is located outside the DRC may only benefit from the provisions of the IP Law if Congolese nationals benefit from reciprocity of protection in the application of the provisions of the Paris Convention for the Protection of Industrial Property. A *contrario*, nationals of member countries of the International Union for the Protection of Industrial Property benefit from the provisions of the IP Law.[9]

Under the IP Law, a GI refers to either an appellation of origin or an indication of source. An appellation of origin refers to a specific place—a locality, region, or country—used to distinguish one or more products which come from that place and whose characteristics are essentially due to the geographical environment. An indication of source refers to an expression or any sign used to indicate that one or more products come from a specific geographical place, locality, region, or country. Appellations of origin or indications of source only apply to a product: natural products, crafts, or agricultural or industrial goods.[10] While the definition of an appellation of origin closely follows article 22(1) of the TRIPS Agreement, an indication of source would likely not be considered as a GI as there are no requirements for any characteristics linked to the region.

The same rules apply to all products bearing an appellation of origin and indication of source: no specific rules and/or additional protection are applicable to wines and spirits.

3.2 Collective marks

It is also possible under the IP Law to register a GI as a collective mark. A collective mark is defined as any sign used to distinguish one or more common characteristics of products or services from different firms that affix said signs as a mark under the control of the grouping, body, or community that owns the collective mark.[11]

A collective trade or service mark may be registered in the name of any group, body, or community under public or private law that has been legally constituted and has legal capacity for the purposes of general, industrial, commercial, or agricultural interest or in order to promote the development of commerce or industry among their members.

Certification marks are not available in the DRC.

---

[9] IP Law, art 3. The Paris Convention created the International Union for the Protection of Industrial Property. As of 10 February 2023, 179 states were party to the Paris Convention. Nationals of the vast majority of countries can thus benefit of the protection of IP Law and theoretically register their GI in the DRC.
[10] IP Law, art 159.
[11] ibid art 141.

4. Registrability of Names

Under the IP Law, appellations of origin or indications of source that are false or contrary to public order or morality may not be protected.[12] In addition, appellations of origin, indications of source, and collective marks cannot be registered where they contain indications likely to mislead the public.[13]

No legal provisions or jurisprudence exist on the interrelation of appellations of origin, indications of source, and collective marks.

5. Procedure and Requirements for Registration

5.1 Appellations of origin and indications of source

The requirements and procedure for registering an appellation of origin and indication of source are similar to the requirements for registering a mark, including a collective mark. An application must be filed at the Directorate of Industrial Property at the Ministry of Industry and Small and Medium-Sized Enterprises (SMEs).[14] There is no IP Office in the DRC. There is, further, no prescribed form for the registration of an appellation of origin and indication of source, and no official fees are provided. Based on the requirements for a trade mark registration, it seems that an application for an appellation of origin and indication of source must contain details as to the applicant, designation of the appellation of origin or indication of source, the relevant product, and proof of payment of taxes. There is likely no opposition procedure similar to trade marks.

5.2 Collective marks

The IP Law is more explicit regarding collective marks. Any grouping, body, or community under public or private law, which has been legally constituted and enjoys legal status, may, for general, industrial, commercial, or agricultural interest or to promote the development of the trade or industry of its members, apply for a collective mark.[15] A copy of the rules for use and control of the mark must

---

[12] ibid art 161.
[13] ibid art 133.2.
[14] ibid art 24(2) provides that 'the ad hoc services' of the regional administration may receive and transmit application to the Ministry in charge of industrial property. Since it has never been clarified who these ad hoc services are and what the deadline for transmission is, applicants or their agents file directly with the Directorate of Industrial Property at the Ministry of Industry and SMEs.
[15] IP Law, art 140.

accompany an application for the registration of a collective mark. The rules must, under pain of invalidity, state the conditions on which the use of the mark depends, the common characteristics of the products and services the mark intends to guarantee, and the procedures for controlling these characteristics. The rules must also provide for appropriate sanctions and be subject to the rights of anyone who can claim a prior right in a non-collective mark. Those rules may not contain provisions contrary to public order or morality.[16]

Once an application is received and payment effected, the Ministry should provide the applicant with a note (*proces-verbal*) attesting to the filing. In practice, obtaining such a document is laborious and time-consuming. Once obtained, the mark is examined on absolute grounds. There is no examination on relative grounds and no opposition procedure. Following the examination, the mark is registered. It must, however, be published in the *Official Journal* to be enforceable against third parties. This is generally done at the initiative of the right holder.

6. Term of Protection

6.1 Appellations of origin and indications of source

The validity period of an appellation of origin and indication of source is not provided for in the IP Law and is therefore unclear.

6.2 Collective marks

A collective mark is valid for ten years from the filing date and may be renewed for further periods of ten years. Any amendment to the rules of a collective mark must be notified to the Ministry responsible for industrial property by the collective mark's owner. The amendments shall only take effect after the notification.[17]

Any interested party, including the Public Prosecutor's Office, may institute invalidity proceedings against a collective mark whose regulations for use and control do not comply with the law's requirements.[18] Collective marks rendered invalid or which have lapsed may not be appropriated by a new filing or be used for any purpose for the same products, objects, or services before three years.[19]

---

[16] ibid art 142.
[17] ibid art 147.
[18] ibid art 149.
[19] ibid art 151.

7. Rights of the Owner and Enforcement Mechanisms against Infringers

7.1 Appellations of origin and indications of source

The unlawful use, directly or indirectly, of an appellation of origin and indication of source belonging to a third party constitutes an act of unfair competition without prejudice to the penalties contained in other specific legislations.[20] These penalties are those provided under the Penal Code, the Code of Commerce, and Ordinance Law No 41/63 of 24 February, 1950 regulating unfair competition (Ordinance Law). Under the Ordinance Law, the judge may apply the following sanctions: the award of damages, the cessation of the act of unfair competition, penalty payments where the injunctions or prohibitions pronounced in a final court decision are not respected, the posting of the judgment for a certain period determined by the judge, the publication of the judgment in newspapers at the offender's expense, and penal servitude of between seven days and two months in the event of a repeat offence.

7.2 Collective marks

The collective mark holder may oppose any manufacturing, import, sale, placing on sale, rental, offer to rent, exhibition, delivery, use, or possession for one of these purposes, for an industrial or commercial aim, of a product bearing the collective mark. The right to bring legal proceedings to claim the protection of a collective mark is reserved for its holder. Nevertheless, the regulations for use and control may grant persons authorized to use the mark the right to act jointly with the holder or to be a party to the proceedings brought by or against it. The same regulations may also provide that the holder, acting on its own, may mention the special interest of users of the mark and take into account, in its request for compensation, the specific damage suffered by one or more of them.[21]

8. Customs Enforcement

The Customs Code in the DRC provides for customs enforcement either at the right holder's request or *ex officio*. The request is open for the importation or exportation of counterfeit trade mark goods and pirated goods. The Customs Code further provides that all foreign goods, natural or crafted, that do not respect

---

[20] ibid art 161.
[21] ibid art 148.

Congolese law related to GIs are excluded from importation and prohibited from warehousing, transit, and circulation.[22] It is unclear whether customs recordal will apply in those circumstances. The applicant must file a request with customs, who shall respond within thirty days. Once the application is in place, customs may detain suspected goods. Customs will inform all interested parties within ten days of a detention of suspected goods. Legal proceedings must be instituted within those ten days, renewable once. If not, the goods shall be released. Customs may further, of its own initiative, suspend the clearance of goods for which it suspects a *prima facie* case of infringement of an IP right. In the case of an *ex officio* detention, customs may request from the right holder any information relevant to the processing of the file. The importer or exporter and the right holder are immediately informed of the suspension measures.[23] Detained goods can be destroyed once a court order is obtained.

The procedure provided under the Customs Code is in line with the procedure provided under the TRIPS agreement. In practice, customs recordal is not possible. There have been no implementing regulations, and customs officials are wary of detaining counterfeit goods, being unsure as to the procedures to be applied. Even the content of the application form for customs enforcement, which is to be determined by the Director General of Customs,[24] is yet to be made available.[25]

9. Bilateral Agreements

There are no bilateral agreements between either the European Union or the United States and the DRC specific to GIs.

---

[22] Customs Code, art 77.
[23] ibid art 82.
[24] ibid art 78(2).
[25] More information may be found on customs enforcement in the DRC in Marius Schneider and Vanessa Ferguson, *Enforcement of Intellectual Property Rights in Africa* (OUP 2020) 230–33.

10
Egypt

Egypt is found in northeast Africa. It shares borders with the Gaza Strip, Israel, Libya, and Sudan. Its population was estimated at more than 105 million in 2022, making it the third most populated country on the continent. Its population is expected to grow annually at nearly 2 per cent and will double to 210 million by 2083.[1] Most of the population lives along the banks of the Nile River, and two-fifths of the population lives in urban areas. The capital city is Cairo, a megalopolis of nearly 20 million inhabitants. In 2015, the Egyptian government started building a new administrative capital (NAC) between the Nile River and the Suez Canal, east of Cairo. The NAC is one of the biggest planned cities ever and aims to be Egypt's new capital. The official language of Egypt is Arabic. While Modern Standard Arabic is used in most written documents, Egyptian Arabic is the most widely spoken. It is also the *de facto* national language in the country and is widely used in the media. The working week is from Sunday to Thursday. The currency used is the Egyptian Pound (LE).

Egypt's gross domestic product (GDP) stood at USD 396.33 billion in 2021. Its top exports are crude petroleum, gold, and insulated wire. Its top imports are refined petroleum, petroleum gas, and food products such as wheat and corn. Eight key sectors constitute about two-thirds of the country's GDP: telecommunications, construction, wholesale and retail trade, non-oil manufacturing, natural gas, real estate, agriculture, and government spending.

Egypt is both an importer and exporter of food products. While the country is largely self-sufficient in producing most agricultural products, it imports wheat, oil, and sugar. In fact, with a growing population and a territory where less than 3 per cent of the land is arable and where water is a precious resource, it is no surprise that 40 per cent of Egypt's imports are of food and agricultural products.[2] In 2019, the main import partners for Egypt for food products were Brazil, Thailand, the United States, France, and Ukraine.

Egypt holds the second highest number of ultra-rich individuals in Africa, just below South Africa. Knight Frank's 2020 Wealth Report predicted that Egypt will

---

[1] World Population Review, 'Egypt Population 2023 (Live)' (*World Population Review*, nd) <https://worldpopulationreview.com/countries/egypt-population>.

[2] Privacy Shield Framework, 'Egypt—Agricultural Sectors' (*Privacy Shield Framework*, nd) <https://www.privacyshield.gov/article?id = Egypt-Agricultural-Sectors>.

be the second-fastest-growing ultra-high-net-worth country in the coming years.[3] Close to 30 per cent of the population can be considered middle class.[4]

Only 8 per cent of Egyptians make regular purchases online.[5] Although this might seem small, this figure obscures the compounded 14.7 per cent annual growth and the USD 7,909 million expected value of e-commerce in Egypt by 2023.[6] With an internet penetration rate of 71.9 per cent at the start of 2022 and the COVID-19 pandemic reinforcing social distancing, e-commerce is here to stay in Egypt. E-commerce will further grow as challenges such as the availability of debit/credit cards and lacklustre protection for online transactions are resolved.

Geographical indications (GIs) are not unknown to Egypt, with brickmakers in ancient Egypt already using GIs to indicate the strength of the bricks according to their origin.[7] As of April 2023, there were three Egyptian GIs registered domestically: *Black Grapes from Baranni*, *Matrouh Olives*, and *Figs from Matrouh*. In a study published in 2020, 426 terroir products were identified in Egypt. Of these, 300 products had existed for over 500 years, 46 between 200 and 500 years, and 80 for 60–200 years. This is reflective of the long history of Egypt. Fruits, particularly date varieties, comprised 50 per cent of the identified products.[8] The most famous Egyptian indication of origin is protected as a trade mark. Since 2000, the Egyptian Cotton mark guarantees that the product is made of 100 per cent Egyptian Barbadense cotton. The mark is jointly registered as a trade mark by the Egyptian Ministry of Economy and Foreign Trade and Alexandria Cotton Exporters Association. It is now protected as either a certification or trade mark in fifty-eight countries worldwide. The Egyptian government also maintains a licensing scheme for the commercialization and promotion of Egyptian cotton.

1. Legal Framework

The Egyptian legal system combines an Islamic (*Shariah*) law and a civil law system with French legal concepts and methods. Laws are embodied in codes and statutes. At the top of the court system is the Court of Cassation in Cairo, where appeals

---

[3] Knight Frank Research, *The Wealth Report: The Global Perspective on Prime Property & Investment* (14th edn, Knight Frank Research 2020) 20.
[4] World Bank Group Poverty & Equity, *Understanding Poverty and Inequality in Egypt* (World Bank Group Poverty & Equity 2019) 1.
[5] International Trade Administration, 'Egypt—Country Commercial Guide eCommerce' (*International Trade Administration*, 8 August 2022) <www.trade.gov/country-commercial-guides/egypt-ecommerce>.
[6] Ecommerce DB, 'ECommerce Market in Egypt' (*Ecommerce DB*, nd) <https://ecommercedb.com/markets/eg/all>.
[7] Claire Durand, 'L'émergence des indications géographiques dans les processus de qualification territoriale des produits agroalimentaires' (Doctoral thesis, Institut National D'études Supérieures Agronomiques de Montpellier—Montpellier Supagro 2016) 130.
[8] Enroot, 'Final Report: Inventorying of Egyptian Typical/Terroir Food Products' (United Nations Industrial Development Organization 2020) 24.

on issues of law are heard. In rare cases, the Court of Cassation can reverse judgments unsupported by sufficient evidence as erroneous as a matter of law. Courts of Appeal are second-degree courts that review the awards of the courts of first instance, covering questions of fact and law. There are seven Courts of Appeal in Egypt, all in major cities. Primary courts and district courts are first-degree courts. Cases are primarily divided between both courts based on their value, with cases of less than 40,000 LE decided by the district courts. Appeals from judgments rendered by the district courts are brought in front of a primary court with an appellate body, which has the same standing as the Court of Appeal.

The specialized Economic Courts hear economic and commercial matters in both criminal and civil proceedings. Created by Law No 82 of 2002 pertaining to the Protection of Intellectual Property Rights (Law on Intellectual Property), the courts have so far promptly adjudicated matters (on average between six and fourteen months) and proven generous in awarding damages for counterfeiting. Litigants in Egypt will encounter well-trained judges and an independent judiciary. In Egypt, a licensed lawyer may appear before courts, provide legal advice, draft agreements, and take the necessary measures to declare and notarize them.

2. Domestic Legislation on GIs

Egypt has been a member of the Paris Convention for the Protection of Industrial Property of 1883 since July 1951 and acceded to the Madrid Agreement for the Repression of False or Deceptive Indications of Source on Goods in March 1951. Egypt is not a party to the Lisbon Agreement for the Protection of Appellations of Origin and their International Registration of 1958. Egypt is party to the Madrid Protocol Concerning the International Registration of Marks of 2007, in force since 3 September 2009. Egypt is a World Trade Organization (WTO) member, and the WTO Agreement on Trade-Related Aspects of Intellectual Property Rights (TRIPS) came into force on 1 January 2005.

The Law on Intellectual Property covers the protection of GIs, certification marks, and collective marks. The Ministry of Supply and Internal Trade of Egypt started the registration of GIs in Egypt for Egyptian products in March 2020. The registration began with *Black Grapes from Baranni*, *Matrouh Olives*, and *Figs from Matrouh* and should move on to onions.[9] Ultimately, the registration will be extended to a broader range of products. As for foreign GIs, they may, subject to reciprocity provisions and their protection in their country of origin, be protected in Egypt.[10] No specific protection is granted to wine and spirits, although contrary to

---

[9] Abeer Hamdi, 'The Geographical Indication Protects Egyptian Products' (*Tridge*, 23 November 2020) <www.tridge.com/news/after-japanese-mallow-the-geographical-indication->.
[10] The Law on Intellectual Property, art 104.

many Arab countries, Egypt does allow for the registration and protection of wine and spirits. GIs can also be protected as a certification or collective trade mark. A foreign certification or collective mark must be protected in its country of origin.

3. Registration of GIs Domestically

3.1 GIs

Registration as a GI is open indistinctly to domestic and foreign indications. The Law on Intellectual Property does not define what constitutes a GI. The element of an answer may, however, be found in article 104, which provides for a geographical origin that has 'become descriptive of the quality, reputation or other characteristics of a certain product so as to be largely instrumental in its marketing'. One clear requirement for GI registration is that the applicant must have produced, in a continuous manner, the products in the reputed geographical area. The reputation attached to the GI is not explicitly stated as a requirement for registration.

As the Law on Intellectual Property refers to 'product' with regard to GI, one can assume that only goods may be protected, to the exclusion of services. There is no explicit provision as to the nature of the product, and both agricultural products and handicrafts should be registrable.

3.2 Collective and certification marks

The Law on Intellectual Property does define a collective mark as one 'used to distinguish a product of a group of persons who belong to a specific entity, even where such entity has no industrial or commercial enterprise of its own'.[11]

A certification mark is a mark that certifies the control or examination of a product in respect of its origin, components, method of manufacture, quality, authenticity, or any other distinctive characteristic.[12]

4. Registrability of Names

Under the Law on Intellectual Property, marks and GIs that are likely to mislead or confuse the public or contain false descriptions of the origin of products, whether goods or services, or their other qualities may not be registered as trade marks.[13] A trade mark including a GI may not be registered where such an indication is

---

[11] ibid art 69.
[12] ibid art 70.
[13] ibid art 67(8).

likely to mislead the public as to the real origin of the goods.[14] Where, however, a geographical name has become descriptive to indicate, in a commercial sense, the nature of any products and not their geographical place of origin, the geographical name may be used in connection with such products.[15]

Where a person resides in a place especially reputed for producing a given product, it may not affix on the products of its trade GIs in such a manner as to lead the public to believe that the products were produced in that place of special reputation.[16]

A trade mark including a GI may be registered if the right conferred by the mark was acquired in good faith before the entry into force of the Law on Intellectual Property in 2002 or before the GI was granted in the country of origin.[17] This provision is in line with article 24(5) of the TRIPS Agreement.

In practice, the Egyptian Trade Mark Office (ETO) often rejects any trade mark that includes a GI, city name, or national or international identifier. Where the GI is not the main element of the trade mark, the Registrar may issue a conditional acceptance asking for the disclaimer or deletion of the same from the trade mark since it is considered misleading to the public about the origin, quality, and characteristics of the product.

5. Procedure and Requirements for Registration

5.1 GIs

The registration of a GI is addressed to the Internal Trade Development Authority (IDTA) of the Ministry of Supply and Internal Trade. The applicant shall be any natural person or legal entity in Egypt for a domestic GI. For foreign GIs, the applicant shall be any natural person or legal entity belonging to or having the centre of its effective activity in a country or entity member of the WTO or who applies reciprocity to Egypt.

For both domestic and foreign GIs, there is no requirement that the application be made on an official form; suffice that all the necessary information is provided. These include the GI to be protected; the relevant good; the geographic region; a statement that the region is in Egypt, a member of the WTO, or applies reciprocity to Egypt; the name, address, and legal status of the entity seeking registration; the nationality of the applicant; the agent's details (where applicable); and a statement describing the basis on which the protection is claimed. If the protection is based

---

[14] ibid art 110.
[15] ibid art 108.
[16] ibid art 105.
[17] ibid art 111.

on the reputation of the goods, proof of the reputation must be provided. Foreign GI applicants must further provide proof that the GI is protected in the country of origin.[18] This may be established by any means consistent with the general rules of evidence. All documents must be in Arabic or accompanied by a translation into the Arabic language.

The Department examines the application formally and substantially. GIs that are likely to mislead or confuse the public or that contain false descriptions as to the origin of the products or their qualities are rejected.[19] Refusals may be appealed. Once accepted, the GI is published for opposition for a sixty-day period. Opposition is open on both formal (ie does not respect conditions laid down in the law to be considered a GI) and relative (ie former rights) grounds.[20] Should there be no opposition or the opposition is rejected, the GI is registered. Upon registration, the GI will be placed on the official Register of Geographical Indications in the Trade Mark Office in the Commercial Registration Authority.[21]

Egyptian producers who would like to use a GI previously registered by an official government body can request permission from the relevant body to use the GI. There is no need to file an application.

5.2 Collective and certification marks

The procedure for registering a certification or collective trade mark is quite similar to registering any trade mark in Egypt. The representative of the applicant entity must apply at the IDTA by providing the completed prescribed application form with the name, address, and nationality of the applicant. The full particulars of goods are required. Although the law provides that one application may cover several classes, in practice, the IDTA requires a separate application for each class. A certified extract of the entry of the applicant company in the commercial register or a certified copy of the certificate of incorporation, including the name, address, nationality, legal status, and nature of the applicant's business, must be included. For foreign applicants, these documents must be certified by an Egyptian Consulate. A local agent must further represent foreign applicants. The application and the accompanying documents must be in Arabic or accompanied by a translation into the Arabic language. The law does not clearly state which additional documents must be provided for certification or collective marks. However, one

---

[18] Judy Goans, *Guidelines for the Protection of Geographical Indications* (United States Agency for International Development & Technical Assistance for Policy Reform II 2008) 7–8.

[19] The Law on Intellectual Property, art 110.

[20] International Association for the Protection of Intellectual Property (AIPPI), 'Rapport de synthèse Question Q191 Les relations entre les marques et les indications géographiques' (*AIPPI*, nd) 4, <www.aippi.fr/upload/Gothenburg%202006%20Q189%20Q190%20191%20192/sr191french.pdf>.

[21] Goans (n 18) 3.

may imagine that a copy of the relevant rules will be required. The application is examined on both absolute and relative grounds. The IDTA may accept, accept conditionally, or reject the application. If accepted, the applicant must pay the publication fees within six months. The application is then published in the Trade Mark and Industrial Design Gazette for opposition for sixty days from filing. Any interested party may oppose a published trade mark by indicating the grounds for the opposition. The applicant must file a counter-statement in response within thirty days of being notified of the opposition. If there is no opposition, or the opposition is rejected, the certificate shall be issued after payment of the certification fee.

6. Term of Protection

GIs, as well as certification or collective marks, are protected for ten years, renewable for an identical period.[22]

A court may cancel the registration of a registered mark.

Interestingly, in Egypt, a GI may be transferred within producers of the same geographical area.[23]

7. Rights of the Owner and Enforcement Mechanisms against Infringers

7.1 GIs

It is an offence for any person to

a) affix on products it trades, a GI in a manner that misleads the public to believe that those products were produced in that reputed place;
b) use any means for the designation or exhibition of products in a manner that may mislead the public as to the production of those goods in a geographical place especially reputed rather than the real place of origin of such products; or
c) manufacture a product in a place especially reputed for its production and affix a GI on similar products it produces in other places in such a way as to suggest that such goods were produced in the said place.[24]

Interestingly, the offences mentioned concern the use of the GI in a misleading manner rather than preventing others from using the GI. No explicit provision

---

[22] The Law on Intellectual Property, art 90.
[23] AIPPI (n 20) 3.
[24] The Law on Intellectual Property, art 114

grants the owner of a GI exclusive rights over the GI. It seems that others may use a GI where the correct product is produced in the right region in a non-misleading manner, consistent with honest business practices.[25]

The infringing use of false or misleading information regarding the product's origin, nature, or essential qualities is punished by at least one month of imprisonment and/or a fine between 2,000 and 10,000 LE. In case of repetition, the punishment is increased to imprisonment of not less than one month and a fine between 4,000 and 20,000 LE. Protection from the misuse of certain misleading expressions (eg 'like', 'style', 'way', etc) is not clearly provided for. The law further provides that any interested party may institute court proceedings to request the prohibition of the use of any misleading GI not included in a registered trade mark, where such use is likely to mislead the public as to the real origin of the products. These proceedings shall take place in the court having jurisdiction where the GI is used.[26]

Interestingly, the owner of a GI does not own the GI and cannot prevent others from using the GI as long as they are doing so truthfully. However, where the owner uses a distinctive logo or font for its GI, the owner may act against unauthorized use of the logo.

7.2 Collective and certification marks

As for a collective or certification mark, it is an offence for any person to counterfeit a mark; imitate a mark in a manner that is likely to mislead the public; fraudulently use counterfeit or imitated marks; fraudulently affix to its product a mark belonging to a third party; or knowingly sell, offer for sale, distribute, acquire for the purpose of sale a product bearing counterfeit or imitated mark or on which a mark has been unlawfully affixed.[27] These offences are punishable by imprisonment of at least two months and/or a fine between 5,000 and 20,000 LE. In case of repetition, the punishment is increased to imprisonment of not less than two months and a fine between 10,000 and 50,000 LE. The court shall order the confiscation of the infringing products, the revenue and returns of such products, and the implements used. The court may order the closure of the business used to commit the infringement for up to six months. In the event of repetition, the enterprise must be closed.

For collective and certification marks and GIs, civil actions are possible. In case of an infringement, the mark or GI owner may serve a cease-and-desist letter to the infringer. If the response is unsatisfactory, the owner may file a civil action against the alleged infringer. Often, right owners will request a court order for a descriptive

---

[25] Goans (n 18) 5.
[26] The Law on Intellectual Property, art 112.
[27] ibid art 113.

or physical seizure of the infringing goods prior to, or at the time of filing, the civil suit. The seizure allows for establishing the infringement of the right, drawing up an inventory of items used in the commission of the offence, and (more rarely) seizing the infringing product and the equipment used in their production. Such a request must be accompanied by financial security. Once the court order has been granted, the right owner must file a case within fifteen days before the courts, failing which the order shall lapse. In civil cases, the court may appoint an expert to gather evidence. Such evidence may be in favour or challenge the plaintiff's case, as the expert is independent. Upon conviction, the court may order confiscation; the destruction of the products, advertising materials and relevant machinery; publication of the decision in the local newspaper; and damages for actual loss suffered. The quantum of damage must be proven by evidence. The recovery of litigation costs, including legal fees, must be initiated through a separate civil action.

The owner may also file a complaint before the Infringement Department of The Ministry of Supply and Internal Trade or the Consumer Protection Agency for investigation. The owner must provide evidence of the infringement committed and proof of its right. The authorities will likely raid the infringer's premises, seizing infringing products. The matter is then referred to the public prosecutor, who decides whether to file a criminal case. The prosecutor may conduct further investigation including interviewing suspects. In a criminal prosecution, the file shall be transferred to the Misdemeanour Court of the Egyptian Economic Court, the competent court for registered GIs and collective marks. In a criminal case, the involvement of the owner is limited. However, the owner may join the proceedings by filing a civil case for damages. Once the matter of the criminal infringement has been resolved in favour of the right owner, the court will decide upon the issue of compensation. The prosecutors also review the verdicts on IP crimes and initiate appeals in case of erroneous application or interpretation of the law. Criminal prosecution is also possible for the claimant of a civil right through direct prosecution.

It is further possible to file a criminal case followed by a civil one. If the criminal case is successful, the civil case will be prosecuted based on the criminal conviction. However, an unsuccessful criminal case will likely negatively affect the civil case.

In both civil and criminal cases, the GI must be used (ie continuously produced by the applicant in the reputed geographical area) to be protected.

Egyptian law also provides for acts of unfair competition. Article 66 of the Unfair Competition Law provides that all acts contravening the customs and norms observed in commercial dealings shall be considered unfair competition. This includes encroachment on a third party's trade mark; acts; or claims that cause confusion about the products or weaken confidence in its owner, those in charge of its management, or on products. The offender must compensate for the harm suffered due to the act of unfair competition. The court may further order the removal of the harm and the publication of a summary of the sentence at the expense of the unsuccessful party in a daily newspaper.

8. Customs Enforcement

Customs may seize products that infringe GIs, certification, and collective marks. These apply only to imports of goods intended to be used in the country. Exported goods, goods in transit, and goods bearing unregistered IP rights are excluded.

There are two means through which customs will act. Where the right holder has detailed knowledge of incoming products which customs have not released, it may request Customs enforcement against those goods. The right holder must file a complaint in Arabic, providing details as to the owner of the right, the representative (where applicable), the ownership of the IP rights, and details as to the suspicious consignment.[28] Customs may reject or accept the application. Customs will notify both the applicant and the importer of the suspension. The suspension lasts ten working days, which may be extended, based on cogent reasons, by another ten working days. During the Customs seizure, the right holder must file a request for an order from the Urgent Matters Court to seize the goods, that is an attachment order or injunctive relief. Once the Customs Authority receives notice of the order granted by the court, it will hold the shipment until the court issues a final decision. The court action on the merits will determine whether the shipment is infringing. The right holder may pursue a civil or criminal case against the importer.

The right holder must therefore have detailed knowledge of the incoming products to ask for customs enforcement. There is no general preventative application whereby Customs is allowed to suspend goods infringing the rights of registered right holders. It is, however, possible to submit some kind of 'informal preventive application' against any future importation of items similar to or resembling the products of the right holder. Such an application can be made to the Department of Agreements at Customs. This procedure is not provided by any law but is based upon the tacit acceptance by the head of this department in person. No decree or provision obliges the head of the Department of Agreements at Customs to accept such applications since acceptance engages its responsibility. The head of the department may therefore accept or reject the application at its discretion.

The GI or collective mark owner or its legal representative may also file a complaint, along with proof of infringement, to prevent the release of goods that have not been released or are on course to reach the Egyptian ports once the right holder or its representative submits an intellectual property right. Right holders who had previously obtained a judicial decision confirming that the subject items entering Egypt are counterfeit products and are not allowed to enter the Egyptian territory may use this decision to support a later application for the same products.[29]

---

[28] Decree No 770/2005, art. 28.
[29] More information may be found on customs enforcement in Egypt in Marius Schneider and Vanessa Ferguson, *Enforcement of Intellectual Property Rights in Africa* (OUP 2020) 264–70.

9. Bilateral Agreements

The European Union (EU)-Egypt Association Agreement governs the relationship between Egypt and the EU, the leading trading partner of Egypt. The Association Agreement, which entered into force on 1 June 2004, promotes the protection of intellectual property rights, including GIs. Article 23(1) of the Agreement provides that Egypt shall 'grant and ensure adequate and non-discriminatory protection of intellectual property rights and provide for measures for the enforcement of such rights'. In case of problems in the area of intellectual property affecting trading conditions, urgent consultations shall be undertaken to reach mutually satisfactory solutions. The practical impact of the Association Agreement for individual GIs is, however, limited by the fact that the Association Agreement does not include a list of European GIs to be protected in Egypt. Further, there are no European GIs registered in Egypt. Still, the EU promotes attention to GIs through technical assistance through promotion in the Joint Rural Development policy (2016–19) and by including GIs as one of the future areas of EU–Egyptian cooperation.[30]

There are no bilateral agreements between the United States and Egypt specific to GIs.

---

[30] European Commission, Consumers, Health, Agriculture and Food Executive Agency, *The Food and Beverage Market Entry Handbook Egypt: A Practical Guide to the Market in Egypt for European Agri-Food Products and Products with Geographical Indications* (Publications Office 2019) 43.

11
Ethiopia

Located in East Africa in the Horn of Africa, Ethiopia is a landlocked country bordered by Sudan, Somalia, Djibouti, Eritrea, and Kenya. The tenth largest country in Africa in size, Ethiopia is 1,104 million km^2. It had a population of 123,3 million in 2022, making it the second most populous country on the continent after Nigeria and the most populous landlocked country in the world. It is a largely rural country with only 20.3 per cent of the population living in urban areas, mainly in the capital city of Addis Ababa. There are approximately 100 languages spoken in Ethiopia, but until recently, only Amharic was used as the official federal government language. Since February 2020, Afaan Oromo, Tigrinya, Somali, Afar, and English are also recognized as working federal government languages. English is the most taught foreign language in school and the medium of instruction in universities. All laws and proclamations are available in both Amharic and English. The working week is from Monday to Friday, and the national currency is the Ethiopian Birr (ETB).

In 2000, Ethiopia was the third poorest country in the world. Today, Ethiopia is one of the fastest growing economies in the world, and there has been a 33 per cent reduction in the share of its population living in poverty between 2000 and 2011.[1] From 2010 to 2020, Ethiopia's economy grew at 10 per cent on average. Over eight years, gross domestic product (GDP) per capita tripled.[2] Ethiopia is currently the eighth richest country in Africa based on GDP. The agricultural sector contributes to about one-third of Ethiopia's GDP and employs more than two-thirds of the workforce. Ethiopia is the fifth largest coffee producer in the world, the third largest producer worldwide of oilseeds, and the twelfth largest producer of dry beans.[3] Ethiopia is also home to one of the largest livestock populations in Africa. Construction, services (such as hospitality and transportation), and manufacturing have also been drivers of the Ethiopian economy.

Although landlocked, Ethiopia benefits from its strategic position between Europe and Asia and is close to the Middle East. The country has taken advantage of its position and has developed export-orientated industries, especially ready-made garments, semi-processed hides, and agro-processing. The country's

---

[1] World Bank Group, 'Ethiopia Poverty Assessment 2014' (World Bank Group 2015) 4.
[2] African Development Bank Group, 'Development Effectiveness Review 2015—Ethiopia Country Review' (African Development Bank Group 2015) 11.
[3] Santander Trade Markets, 'Ethiopia: Economic Outline' (*Santander Trade Markets*, nd) <https://santandertrade.com/en/portal/analyse-markets/ethiopia/economic-outline>.

Protecting Geographical Indications in Africa. Marius Schneider and Nora Ho Tu Nam, Oxford University Press.
© Marius Schneider and Nora Ho Tu Nam 2024. DOI: 10.1093/9780191955082.003.0011

large-scale investment in infrastructure development, the low labour cost, and the stability of large parts of the country will, no doubt, continue to lure investors and feed into economic growth.

Still, Ethiopia is confronted with many issues. Although poverty rates are declining, Ethiopia remains one of the poorest countries in the world based on per capita annual income. The country's reliance on antique and rainfall-dependent methods for agricultural production means that it is particularly vulnerable to droughts, pests, and natural disasters. The civil war with the Tigray region has had not only huge human costs, with millions killed, displaced, or in need of humanitarian assistance, but is also damaging the economy, with factories and mining sites closed. In addition, the war has impacted the reputation of Ethiopia as a stable, conflict-free country. This will, no doubt, deter future investors.

Still, the consistent economic growth over the past years has led to a reduction in the unemployment rate and growth in the middle class in Ethiopia. Ethiopia's middle class is expected to be one of the most important in Africa by 2030. There is also a growing upper class. The number of millionaires in USD in Ethiopia grew by 23 per cent from 2019 to 2022.[4] For the moment, for those part of the low and middle class, price remains the main determining factor in purchasing decisions in Ethiopia. This will likely change as income increases. Modern retail space in Ethiopia is less widely available than in other East African countries such as Kenya. Many people still shop at medium-sized stores and local supermarkets. Nonetheless, several small and medium shopping malls are present in the capital, and new international retailers are entering the market.

E-commerce is still in its infancy in Ethiopia. This is likely due to a low internet penetration rate of 20.6 per cent and slow, expensive, and unreliable internet provision.[5] In addition, 66 per cent of Ethiopia's adult population does not have access to the formal financial system.[6] Although debit cards and automated teller machines (ATMs) are available, local banks do not issue credit cards.[7] In the coming years, one can expect a democratization of online shopping. Mobile money, which is quite popular in neighbouring East African countries and allows for financial transactions through a mobile phone,[8] was launched in May 2021. Interest is high: over

---

[4] H&P Henley & Partners, 'Africa Weath Report 2023' (H&P Henley & Partners 2023) 21.
[5] Figure as of January 2021. Simon Kemp, 'Digital 2021: Ethiopia' (*Datareportal*, 11 February 2021) <https://datareportal.com/reports/digital-2021-ethiopia#:~:text = There%20were%2023.96%20 million%20internet,at%2020.6%25%20in%20January%202021.>.
[6] Tawanda Karombo, 'One Million Ethiopians Signed Up for the Country's First Mobile Wallet in One Week' (*Quartz*, 26 May 2021) <https://qz.com/africa/2012992/one-million-sign-up-to-ethio-telec oms-telebirr-mobile-money-wallet>.
[7] International Trade Administration, 'Ethiopia—Country Commercial Guide' (*International Trade Administration*, 22 January 2024) < www.trade.gov/country-commercial-guides/ethiopia-ecomme rce-0>.
[8] Mobile money allows customers to send, receive, and store money and pay utility bills using their mobile phones. Other possible applications include access to loans, remittances, and insurance.

1 million cell phone subscribers registered for mobile money in Ethiopia in the week of its launch.[9]

When thinking of potential geographical indications (GIs) from Ethiopia, the first product which comes to mind is coffee. The country is the birthplace of coffee, and Ethiopian coffee is already highly reputed worldwide as quality coffee. Interestingly, instead of setting up a protection mechanism based on GIs, the Ethiopian government has chosen to protect three of Ethiopia's heritage coffees, *Harar*, *Sidamo*, and *Yirgacheffe*, via the trade mark regime in thirty-six countries[10] since 2004 through the Ethiopian Coffee Trademarking and Licensing Initiative. Trade marking as an individual trade mark was seen as the most effective and practical solution. About 50 per cent of the coffee in Ethiopia is grown on very small plots, often by subsistence farmers. This would make a collective or certification mark particularly impractical and expensive.[11] A collective or certification mark would also have imposed a specification chart on small producers. A GI was also considered inappropriate as, although these coffees are named based on locations in Ethiopia, they are not grown just in the namesake regions. This would have led to the exclusion of many small farmers. The trade mark applications have all been initiated by the government of Ethiopia and are therefore owned by the government and not coffee producers.[12]

However, the Ethiopian Coffee Trademarking and Licensing Initiative has not proven to be without challenges. In the United States, Starbucks had previously filed for the *Shirkina Sun-Dried Sidamo* trade mark with the United States Patent and Trademark Office (USPTO), which then prevented the processing of the *Sidamo* application filed by the government of Ethiopia. It is only following extensive pressure from international organizations, the media, political figures, and negative public opinion that Starbuck's prior application was withdrawn. This was not the end of the tunnel for the government of Ethiopia, as two weeks before the withdrawal of the application by Starbucks, the United States National Coffee Association (NCA) filed a letter of protest against the application of the government of Ethiopia at the USPTO against trade mark applications *Harrar* and *Sidamo*. The NCA argued that these names were generic and could not be registered. It was widely reported that the NCA, a lobbying association for US coffee, was supported by Starbucks.[13] No doubt, Starbucks wanted to avoid further

---

[9] Karombo (n 6).
[10] The thirty-six countries are either major coffee import destinations or potential future markets: Australia, Brazil, Canada, China, India, Japan, the countries of the European Union, Saudi Arabia, South Africa, and the United States: Getachew Mengistie, 'Ethiopia: Fine Coffee' in Michael Blakeney and others (eds), *Extending the Protection of Geographical Indications: Case Studies of Agricultural Products in Africa* (Routledge 2012) 157.
[11] World Intellectual Property Organization (WIPO), 'The Coffee War: Ethiopia and the Starbucks Story' (*WIPO*, nd) <www.wipo.int/ipadvantage/en/details.jsp?id = 2621>.
[12] There is no trade mark registration for those coffees in Ethiopia.
[13] WIPO (n 11).

negative press. The USPTO initially sided with the NCA and first considered the trade marks as generic. Its decision was only reversed after a letter of rebuttal by the government of Ethiopia. *Sidamo* was registered in April 2008 and *Harar* in June 2008.[14] Meanwhile, Starbucks and the Ethiopian government managed to find a solution to the distribution, marketing, and licensing of Ethiopia's coffee. Starbucks agreed to a voluntary licensing agreement recognizing Ethiopia's ownership of the *Harrar*, *Sidamo*, and *Yirgacheffe* trade marks. In Europe, a German company opposed the trade mark application for *Sidamo*. The opposition was finally withdrawn after an agreement was reached between Ethiopia and the German company. In Japan, the Patent Office first invalidated the trade marks *Sidamo* and *Yirgacheffe*, which were later reinstated by the Intellectual Property (IP) High Court in 2010. In Australia, all three trade mark applications were rejected on the grounds that they were names of geographical areas and lacked distinctiveness.[15] The refusal to register has become final, and there is no trade mark registration in Australia. Nevertheless, this must not minimize the achievements of the Ethiopian government, which holds trade marks for *Harar*, *Sidamo*, and *Yirgacheffe* in more than thirty-six countries, including Brazil, the European Union, Great Britain, and South Africa. Today, Ethiopia operates a royalty-free licensing scheme: the government owns the trade marks that licensees must use on Ethiopian coffee products, free of charge. In addition to *Harar*, *Sidamo*, and *Yirgacheffe*, a fourth 'umbrella mark', *Ethiopian Fine Coffee*, has been created. The Ethiopian Intellectual Property Authority (EIPA) manages the licensing scheme through licensing management units in various countries supported by the Ethiopian diplomatic missions.

Other products highlighted as potential GIs in Ethiopia are honey, which has distinctive regional characteristics in Ethiopia, and Ambo herbs from the Western Highlands.

1. Legal Framework

The Ethiopian legal system is a civil law system. Ethiopia has federal and regional courts, reflecting the federal state structure. Disputes involving IP are heard before the Federal High Court. Decisions of the High Court may be appealed before the Federal Supreme Court. The Cassation Bench, which is part of the Supreme Court, hears appeals from decisions of the Supreme Court. There is still a two-tier regulation system for the legal profession. Advocates who appear before the federal courts and courts in Addis Ababa and Dire Dawa, a city in Eastern Ethiopia, are regulated by the federal government, while lawyers appearing before the regional courts are regulated by the state. The frequent postponement of cases, excessive

---

[14] Mengistie (n 10) 157.
[15] ibid 157.

backlog, and the lack of competent judges are some of the problems litigants face in commercial matters. The average time to resolve a commercial dispute in the Federal High Court is twenty months, with the longest period being six years and three months.[16]

2. Domestic Legislation on GIs

Ethiopia is a member of the World Intellectual Property Organization (WIPO). Ethiopia is not a party to the Paris Convention for the Protection of Industrial Property of 1883, the Madrid Agreement for the Repression of False or Deceptive Indications of Source on Goods of 1891, and the Lisbon Agreement for the Protection of Appellations of Origin and their International Registration of 1958[17] Ethiopia is not yet a member of the World Trade Organization (WTO) and is thus not bound to enforce the WTO Agreement on Trade-Related Aspects of Intellectual Property Rights (TRIPS) minimum standards. Ethiopia formally applied for membership at the WTO in January 2003 and has since been going through accession negotiations. After a pause in the nearly eight-year negotiations, the WTO membership negotiations resumed on 30 January 2020. One area of focus in the negotiations is Ethiopia's IP regime.

The 1994 Constitution of Ethiopia recognizes the right of every citizen to ownership of private property, which includes IP.[18] There is, however, no specific law on GIs. The EIPA drafted a Proclamation for the Registration and Protection of Designations of Origin and a GI Proclamation in 2012, but no laws have up to now been enacted. The draft intellectual property policy of the country made a few mentions of GIs, highlighting that new laws should be enacted to protect GIs but providing no practical solution in that regard.[19] A three-year project aimed at elaborating a national legal framework for GIs suited to the Ethiopian local context and implementing a pilot GI in the Ethiopian coffee value chain was launched on 23 May 2023. The project 'Geographical indications for origin-linked products in Ethiopia' (GOPE) is carried out by various actors, including the EIPA, with the technical and financial assistance of the French government.[20] GIs may, however,

---

[16] Zemedkun Mekasha, 'The Scope and Structure of Specialized Commercial Court for Ethiopia: Lessons from Abroad' (LLM thesis, University of Hawassa 2017) 82.

[17] Ethiopia is not a party to any multilateral conventions or treaties on IP except the 1981 Nairobi Treaty on the Protection of the Olympic Symbol and the Convention Establishing WIPO.

[18] Constitution of the Federal Democratic Republic of Ethiopia 1994, art 40(2).

[19] International Trademark Association (INTA), 'Comments on Draft Intellectual Property Policy of the Federal Democratic Republic of Ethiopia' (*INTA*, nd) <www.inta.org/wp-content/uploads/public-files/advocacy/committee-reports/INTA-Comments-Ethiopia-IP-Policy.pdf> 4–5.

[20] Facilité IG, 'Supporting the Development of a Geographical Indication System in Ethiopia: Launch of the Project' (*Facilité IG*, 12 July 2023) <www.facilite-ig.fr/actualites/launch-of-the-project-for-the-development-of-a-gi-system-in-ethiopia>.

be protected indirectly as collective marks by the Trademark Registration and Protection Proclamation 501/2006 (TMP), which entered into force in early 2013. There is no additional level of protection for wines and spirits under the TMP.

3. Registration of GIs Domestically

The EIPA is the domestic body mandated to implement laws and regulations on IP rights in Ethiopia. Ethiopia does not have a GI-specific legislation. This applies to both domestic and foreign GIs. GIs can, however, be registered via the trade mark regime as a collective trade mark. A collective trade mark is defined under article 2(1) of the TMP as 'a trade mark distinguishing the goods or services of members of an association, which is the owner of the trade mark, from those of other undertakings'.

Certification marks are not available in Ethiopia.

4. Registrability of Names

Any visible sign capable of distinguishing the goods or services of one person from those of other persons, including words, designs, letters, numerals, colours, or the shape of goods or their packaging or the combinations thereof, may be registered as a collective mark.[21] Non-traditional trade marks like smell and sound, not being visible signs, are excluded.

As the provisions on the registration of trade marks apply to the registration of collective marks,[22] the requirements for the distinctiveness of ordinary trade marks also apply to collective marks. A trade mark will not be considered distinctive and will not be admissible for registration where the trade mark consists 'exclusively of signs or indications which designate [...] geographical origin of goods or services'.[23] These trade marks will be rejected *ex-officio* by the EIPA upon examination or, if registered mistakenly, can be subsequently invalidated either at the initiative of the Office or any interested party.

The exclusion of signs with a geographic origin from protection as collective marks poses a serious problem for most GIs as many consist exclusively of the geographical indication of the goods.[24] The TMP does, however, provide for an

---

[21] TMP, art 2(12).
[22] ibid art 18(2).
[23] ibid art 6(1)(e).
[24] Some authors have argued that since GIs identify the geographic origin of goods and the relevant quality, reputation, or other quality, this provision does not exclude GIs, as GIs are not mere indications but link the attributes to the product. It remains to be seen whether the EIPA will be convinced by such an argument: Sileshi Hirko, 'The Legal Framework for the Protection of Geographical Indications in Ethiopia: A Critical Review' (2014) 58(2) J Afr Law 219.

exception: the restriction as to the designation of the geographical origin will not apply where it is proven that, by the date of receipt of the collective mark application, the trade mark has, as a result of its use, become well known in Ethiopia.[25] An applicant wishing to avail itself of this exception should provide the EIPA with evidence of acquired distinctiveness of the applied sign.

5. Procedure and Requirements for Registration

An application for the registration of a collective trade mark shall be filed at the EIPA. The application shall designate the trade mark as a collective trade mark and be accompanied by

(1) full name address and nationality of the applicant(s). Only trade unions, trade union federations, or associations may apply for the registration of collective trade marks. As a legal person, the applicant must also provide a copy of the certificate of its registration and evidence authorizing the person who has signed the application to represent the legal person;

(2) two copies of the statutes governing the use of the collective mark.[26] The statutes shall specify the name, headquarters, objectives, and representatives of the association. It shall also indicate the group of persons entitled to use the trade mark, the conditions for use, and the rights and obligations of the parties concerned in the event of an infringement of the mark;[27]

(3) registration certificate certified up to Ethiopian consular level for any foreign applicant;

(4) when the application for registration is filled through an agent, a duly authenticated power of attorney certified up to Ethiopian consular level;

(5) three copies of the reproduction of the mark and a brief written description of pictures, if the mark is pictorial or includes pictorial elements;

(6) where the mark contains characters other than Amharic or Latin, or numerical expressions other than Amharic, Arabic, or Latin numerals, their transliteration into Amharic or Latin characters and Arabic numerals;

(7) a list of goods and services classified in accordance with the international classification of goods and services for which registration of the mark is requested and the class numbers of the classification;

(8) a document certifying payments of the filing fee.

---

[25] TMP, art 6(2).
[26] ibid art 18(1).
[27] ibid art 18(3).

All documents filed with the EIPA shall be either in Amharic or English. Any document in a language other than Amharic or English shall be accompanied by a translation into Amharic or English.

The EIPA will conduct its examination on both absolute and relative grounds. Where the requirements for the application of the registration of a collective mark have not been complied with, the EIPA shall notify the applicant in writing to file the necessary correction within ninety days from the date of the notification. Should the applicant fail to do so within the time limit, the EIPA shall reject the application and the applicant shall forfeit the fees paid, if any. On the contrary, where an application passes the examination on absolute grounds, the EIPA shall issue a notice of acceptance to the applicant.

The EIPA shall also conduct a substantive examination, looking *inter alia* at the distinctiveness of the mark, at whether the trade mark is admissible for registration,[28] and third-party prior rights. Where the EIPA finds that the trade mark has not passed the substantive examination, the EIPA shall notify the applicant, in writing, together with the reasons thereof. The applicant may respond to the Office within ninety days from the date of receipt of the notice (renewable twice). The applicant may, in its response, either take the proper measures to satisfy the specified additional requirements or to overcome the grounds impeding the registration or request an amendment to the application. The Office shall re-examine the application upon receipt of the applicant's response. If the Office finds, upon re-examination, that the applicant has failed to fully satisfy the specified additional requirements or to overcome the grounds impeding the registration, the application shall be rejected and the decision communicated to the applicant in writing, together with the reasons. The applicant may appeal the decision before the EIPA Tribunal. If rejected, the applicant may then appeal to the court. Prior to the expiry of the period of appeal on the rejection, the applicant may take measures to satisfy the outstanding requirements, overcome the grounds impeding the registration, or amend the application to take such measures.

Where an application passes both the formal and substantive examination, the EIPA publishes the application for opposition. While the law mentions that such publication should occur in the intellectual property gazette, in practice, publication occurs in one of two newspapers with a national reach. The publication period is of sixty days. During this period, the applicant enjoys a seniority right from the day of application if the trade mark later gets registered. From the time an application is made known to the public until the grant of the trade mark, the applicant enjoys the legal protection that it would get if it had been granted a trade mark. The only exception to this rule is legal infringement. A trader may not initiate proceedings for legal infringement until the trade mark has been registered and certified.

---

[28] A trade mark that is likely to mislead the public, or the business community in particular, as regards the geographical origin of the goods or services concerned is not registrable (ibid art 6(1)(g)).

If an application faces no opposition or is successfully refuted, the EIPA issues the registration certificate.

6. Term of Protection

A collective mark is valid seven years from the date of submission of the application, renewable for consecutive periods of seven years.

The statute governing the use of a registered collective mark is open to public inspection. Any changes made to the statutes shall be notified to the EIPA by the owner of the registered collective mark.[29] Amendments shall not be effective unless the amended statute is filed with the EIPA and registered. The EIPA, before registering any amended statute, may publish the amendment where it finds it necessary, with a view to inviting opposition and observations.

The registration of a collective mark shall be cancelled

a) upon dissolution of the registered owner;
b) when the registered owner no longer satisfies the requirements of the TMP:
c) when the registered owner has used the mark or knowingly allowed it to be used in conditions other than those prescribed in the statutes;
d) when the statutes contain provisions contrary to public order or morality.[30]

Where a collective mark has been cancelled, it may neither be appropriated in respect of the same goods or services by a new registration nor be used in any other way until a period of seven years has lapsed.[31]

7. Rights of the Owner and Enforcement Mechanisms against Infringers

The owner of a collective mark may use or authorize any other person to use the trade mark in relation to any goods or services for which it has been registered. While the TMP clearly states, at article 30(3), that a collective mark owner or applicant may not license the collective mark, nothing is said about an assignment.

The owner may preclude others from

a) using a trade mark or a sign resembling it such as to be likely to mislead the public for goods or services in respect of which the collective mark is

---

[29] ibid art 18(4).
[30] ibid art 20(1).
[31] ibid art 20(2).

registered, or for other goods or services in connection with which the use of the mark or sign is likely to mislead the public;
b) any use of a collective mark or a sign resembling it, without just cause and in conditions likely to be prejudicial to his interests; and
c) other similar acts.[32]

The collective mark owner may institute civil trade mark right infringement proceedings before the Federal High Court. Prior to instituting a civil suit, the trade mark owner may apply for prompt and effective provisional measures to prevent any infringement from occurring, in particular to prevent the entry into the channels of commerce, or the import and export of goods after completing customs formalities, or to preserve relevant evidence in regard to an alleged infringement of a right.[33] Where any delay is likely to entail irreparable harm or the destruction of evidence to the prejudice of the applicant, provisional measures may be granted *ex parte* without summoning the defendant.[34] The defendant may request the modification or revocation of the provisional measures after having received due notice after the execution of the measures. Interestingly, although Ethiopia is not a party to the TRIPS Agreement, this provision at article 39 on provisional measures is a verbatim copy of article 50 of the TRIPS Agreement. Where provisional measures are revoked due to any act or omission by the applicant or upon subsequently ascertaining that there has been no infringement or threat of infringement to a trade mark, the court may, on the request of the defendant, order the applicant to compensate the defendant for any injury caused by such measures.

Where the case succeeds on the merits of the case, the court may order an injunction prohibiting the defendant from continuing the act of infringement, damages, and/or the reimbursement of expenses incurred for the case. The quantum of damages is calculated either on the basis of the infringer's net profit from the use of the trade mark or the estimated royalty rate the defendant would have been charged had it used the trade mark under a licence, whichever is the highest.

A collective mark owner may also act under the Trade Competition and Consumers Protection Proclamation (Competition Law).[35] The Competition Law enumerates acts of unfair competition at its article 8. Under article 8(1) of the Competition Law, no businessperson may, in the course of trade, carry out an act that is dishonest, misleading, or deceptive and harms, or is likely to harm, the business interest of a competitor. Particularly interesting is sub-article 2(e), which defines the dissemination to consumers or users of false or equivocal information in connection with the manufacturing place of goods and services as unfair competition. Such false information concerning the place of manufacturing

[32] ibid art 26.
[33] ibid art 39(1).
[34] ibid art 39(2).
[35] Trade Competition and Consumers Protection Proclamation (Proclamation No 813/2013).

could therefore relate to the geographic origin. Any business person who violates the provisions of article 8 is punishable with a fine of 5–10 per cent of the annual turnover. Where a person other than a business person has participated directly or indirectly in the offence under article 8, the person is punishable with a fine from 10,000 to 100,000 ETB. Article 22(1) and 22(15), respectively, lay down the prohibition for any business person to furnish false information on the source of goods and services and the falsification of the country of origin of goods. The violation of these provisions under article 22 is punishable with a fine ranging from 5 to 10 per cent of the person's annual turnover and imprisonment from one to five years. In addition, article 14(1) provides that consumers have the right to receive sufficient and accurate information about the quality and type of goods or services. Once again, this can be linked back to the right of consumers (and the corresponding duty of traders) to provide accurate information as to the origin of a product.

The Civil Code also provides for unfair competition as an extra-contractual liability. Article 2057 of the Civil Code provides that the offence of civil unfair competition is constituted by the offender acting in a manner that is contrary to good faith. Again, GIs are not mentioned explicitly, but infringing acts may fall within the purview of this article.

On the other hand, it is also possible to prosecute trade mark rights infringers criminally. Unless a heavier penalty is provided for under the Criminal Code, whoever intentionally violates a right protected under the TMP shall be sentenced to imprisonment for not less than five years and not more than ten years.[36] Where the violation occurs through gross negligence, the sentence ranges from one year to a maximum of five years.[37] Other penalties include seizure, forfeiture, and destruction of the infringing goods and of any materials and implements used in the commission of the offense.

The relevant offence for collective mark owners under the Criminal Code is article 720, which concerns intentional acts of infringement; imitation, or passing off committed in such a manner as to deceive the public about another mark or distinctive sign; and the declaration of origin on any produce or goods or their packing, whether industrial or agricultural. Such infringements are punished with imprisonment not exceeding ten years. Where the infringement is committed through negligence, the sentence shall be imprisonment not exceeding five years.

8. Customs Enforcement

The collective mark owner may request the seizure and detention of infringing goods by the Ethiopian customs authority at ports and other customs stations. The

---

[36] TMP, art 41(1).
[37] ibid art 41(2).

request shall be made in writing and must be accompanied by the collective mark certificate, any other relevant evidence, and the provision of sufficient guarantee.[38] Customs is thereafter required to inform the applicant and the owner of the goods of the measures taken to detain the said goods.[39] Unless the applicant brings a court injunction within ten days of seizure, the goods are released. Although provided by law, in practice, customs enforcement upon application by the right holder is rare in Ethiopia.[40]

9. Bilateral Agreements

There is no bilateral agreement between Ethiopia and either the European Union or the United States specific to GIs.

---

[38] ibid art 42(1).
[39] ibid art 42(2).
[40] More information may be found on customs enforcement in Ethiopia in Marius Schneider and Vanessa Ferguson, *Enforcement of Intellectual Property Rights in Africa* (OUP 2020) 320–21.

12
Kenya

Kenya is found across the equator in East Africa, with a coastline on the Indian Ocean. It is bordered by Somalia, Tanzania, and the landlocked countries of South Sudan, Ethiopia, and Uganda. Kenya is 580,367 km² and had a population of 54 million inhabitants in 2022. Its capital city, Nairobi, is the largest city between Cairo and Johannesburg and its port, the port of Mombasa, is the most important deep-water port in the region. The main languages in Kenya are English and Swahili. The working week is from Monday to Friday, and the national currency is the Kenyan Shilling (KES).

Kenya is East Africa's economic powerhouse. It is the largest economy in Central and East Africa and one of the fastest-growing economies in Africa, averaging a sustained 5.9 per cent economic growth between 2010 and 2018.[1] With a gross domestic product (GDP) of USD 95.5 billion in 2019 and an increased per capita income, Kenya is now classified as a lower-middle-income economy. The Kenyan economy relies heavily on agriculture, the latter contributing to one-third of the country's GDP. Around 75 per cent of Kenya's population works at least part-time in the agricultural sector.[2] Other important sectors are tourism, manufacturing of small-scale consumer goods, horticulture, and oil refining.

Kenya is not only a diverse and dynamic economy, with tremendous potential for producers, but also the entry point to the larger East African Community (EAC) market with over 146 million people and the Common Market for Eastern and Southern Africa (COMESA) market with over 460 million people.[3] Many entrepreneurs interested in East Africa have set up their economic, commercial, financial, and logistics hubs in Kenya.

Although over one-third of the population lived under the poverty line in 2016, there is a large and growing middle class in Kenya. Around 44.9 per cent of the population earn 3,900 USD or more annually and are classified as middle-class.[4]

---

[1] United States Agency for International Development (USAID), 'Economic Growth and Trade: Overview' (*USAID*, nd) <www.usaid.gov/kenya/economic-growth-and-trade>.
[2] CIAgov, 'The World Factbook: Kenya' (*CIAgov*, 26 April 2023) <www.cia.gov/the-world-factbook/countries/kenya/#economy>.
[3] East African Community, 'Market Size, Access, Trade Policies' (*East African Community*, nd) <www.eac.int/agriculture/investment-opportunities/75-sector/investment-promotion-private-sector-development/162-184-706-market-size-access-trade-policies#:~:text=The%20internal%20EAC%20market%20has,are%20all%20members%20of%20COMESA>.
[4] Oxford Business Group, 'Consumer Goods Producers Benefit from Kenya's Growing Middle Class' (*Oxford Business Group*, nd) <https://oxfordbusinessgroup.com/analysis/top-shelf-growing-middle-class-encouraging-consumer-goods-producers>.

In addition, Kenya is home to Africa's fifth-highest number of wealthy individuals.[5] The super-rich and middle class are driving high consumer spending. Private spending in Kenya has nearly tripled over the past ten years, reaching USD 78.78 billion in 2019.[6] The increased disposable income has led to a growth in the demand for consumer-orientated agricultural products. Kenya imports more than 72 per cent of consumer-orientated agricultural products, mainly from Uganda, Europe (Italy, France, Belgium, and the Netherlands), South Africa, and Egypt.[7]

Investors looking to enter the Kenyan market will find a formal retail market— the second highest in sub-Saharan Africa—with large shopping malls.[8] Many international retailers are already present in the country in response to the demand by Kenyans for high-end shopping experiences and international trends.[9]

With a digitally connected population and a high acceptance rate of mobile money, Kenya is, and will continue to be, a promising area for online retailing. In 2021, 40 per cent of the Kenyan population were internet users. Mobile phone penetration was at almost 109 per cent (many people have more than one sim card) and almost 73 per cent of Kenyans aged fifteen and above had a mobile money account, which allows them to deposit, withdraw, transfer money, and pay for services with their mobile phone.[10] It is estimated that the Kenyan e-commerce *market will be worth USD 3.98 billion by 2028*.[11]

Kenyan tea and coffee, two highly reputed products from Kenya, are registered as certification marks. The Coffee Board of Kenya, a state corporation, has registered 'Coffee Kenya so rich so Kenyan' as a certification mark in Kenya and abroad. The Tea Board of Kenya has registered 'Mark of Origin' as a certification mark for tea. The first collective mark registered in Kenya was 'Maasai/masai' for jewellery, precious stones, leather products, home textile, clothing and footwear, entertainment, and cultural activities.[12] Taita baskets, sisal baskets handwoven by women in Taita Taveta County, and Echuchuka, cosmetics made of Aloe Vera by a community living on Lake Turkana, are also registered as collective marks.

---

[5] Afrasia, 'Africa Wealth Report 2021' (NWWealth 2021) 6.
[6] CEIC, 'Kenya Private Consumption Expenditure' (*CEIC*, nd) <www.ceicdata.com/en/indicator/kenya/private-consumption-expenditure>.
[7] Export.gov, 'Kenya—Agriculture' (*Exportgov*, 13 August 2019) <www.export.gov/apex/article2?id=Kenya-Agriculture>.
[8] Oxford Business Group, 'Kenya's Retail Sector Ranks as Second-Most Formalised in Africa' (*Oxford Business Group*, 12 February 2016) <https://oxfordbusinessgroup.com/articles-interviews/kenyas-retail-sector-ranks-as-second-most-formalised-in-africa>.
[9] Cytonn, 'Kenya Retail Sector Report 2020' (*Cytonn*, 22 November 2020) <https://cytonn.com/topicals/kenya-retail-sector-report-2020>.
[10] Gilbert Paula, 'Kenya Internet Usage Lags Mobile Penetration' (*Connecting Africa*, 14 April 2021) <www.connectingafrica.com/author.asp?section_id=761&doc_id=768744&>.
[11] Statista, 'Digital Commerce-kenya' (*Statista*, n.d) < https://www.statista.com/outlook/dmo/fintech/digital-payments/digital-commerce/kenya>.
[12] Michael Blakeney and Getachew Mengistie, 'Kenya: Tea' in Michael Blakeney and others (eds), *Extending the Protection of Geographical Indications: Case Studies of Agricultural Products in Africa* (Routledge 2012) 218.

Other products that have been identified as agricultural products with the potential of being registered as collective or certification marks are Gathuthi Tea, Kisii Tea, Kericho Tea, Mt Kenya Coffee, Kangeta Miraa, Kikuyu Grass, Meru Potato, Mombasa and Assembo Mangoes, Muranga and Kisii Bananas and Molo Lamb. Protectable handicrafts could include Lamu Doors and Chests, Kisii Soapstone, and Akamba Carvings.[13]

1. Legal Framework

Kenya's legal system is based on English common law. There are two levels of courts in Kenya: the Superior Courts, which include the Supreme Court, the Court of Appeal, and the High Court, and the subordinate courts, which include the Magistrates' Courts, the Kadhis' Courts, the Court Martial, and any other court or local tribunal, such as the small claims courts.

The Supreme Court is the highest court in Kenya, with exclusive jurisdiction to determine presidential elections and appeals from the Court of Appeal on matters related to the interpretation of the Constitution or on matters of general public importance. The Supreme Court's decisions bind all other courts.

The High Court may hear all criminal and civil cases as well as appeals from the lower courts and tribunals. The High Court further supervises subordinate courts and bodies exercising judicial and quasi-judicial functions. The jurisdiction of the High Court includes disputes involving unfair competition, trade secrets, and trade dress. The High Court may hear appeals from the Trade Mark Registrar and the Intellectual Property Tribunal. It has exclusive jurisdiction to deal with matters regarding passing off and infringement of trade marks in Kenya. Appeals from the High Court are heard before the Court of Appeal. Due to the limitations imposed for appeals before the Supreme Court, it is unlikely, in practice, that an appeal regarding intellectual property (IP) rights will end up before the Supreme Court. The High Court has forty-one stations across the country. Plaintiffs or appellants are required to file their suit at the High Court station closest to the location where the cause of action arose. Where plaintiffs or appellants do not respect this practice, the court may, at its discretion, either hear the matter or direct that it is heard at the High Court station that is closest to the location of the cause of action arose.

IP tribunals have been established by law to deal with disputes arising from regulating and administering specific IP matters. Kenya has three main specialized IP tribunals: the Industrial Property Tribunal for patents, industrial designs, utility models and technovations; the Seeds and Plant Varieties Tribunal, and the

---

[13] ibid 230.

Kenya Copyright Board Authority. The Office of the Registrar of Trade Marks is also competent to deal with disputes arising in the regulation of trade marks.

In Kenya, attorneys are known as advocates. They may represent their clients before the courts, both superior and subordinate, and also advise on non-contentious matters.

2. Domestic Legislation on Geographical Indications (GIs)

Kenya acceded to the Paris Convention for the Protection of Industrial Property of 1883 in June 1965. Kenya is a party to neither the Madrid Agreement for the Repression of False or Deceptive Indications of Source on Goods of 1891 nor the Lisbon Agreement for the Protection of Appellations of Origin and their International Registration of 1958. Kenya has been a party to the Madrid Agreement Concerning International Registration of Marks, and the Protocol relating to that Agreement since 1998. Kenya is a member of the World Trade Organization (WTO) and the transition period available to put in effect national legislation implementing the WTO Agreement on Trade-Related Aspects of Intellectual Property Rights (TRIPS) expired on 31 December 1999.

Although Kenya is a member of the informal Group of Friends of Geographical Indications that advocates for the extension of GI protection beyond wines and spirits through the TRIPS Agreement, there is no specific legislation regarding GIs currently in force in Kenya. Kenya has been in the process of drafting a Bill on GIs since 2007, when the process was initiated by the Kenya Industrial Property Institute (KIPI), the Kenyan IP Office. [14] The draft Bill has been commented upon by various stakeholders and approved by the Attorney General but has yet to be presented to Parliament. [15] The Bill's definition of a GI is in line with article 22(1) of TRIPS. The Bill meets the minimum requirements prescribed by articles 22 and 23 of TRIPS. Natural, agricultural, food, and handicrafts can all be protected as GIs. Interestingly, although the Bill provides for the ability to register GIs, section 4(a) provides that protection is available regardless of registration.[16] It is, however, unlikely that this Bill on GIs will be going forward, as the IP Bill of 2020 also makes provisions for the *sui generis* protection of GIs. The IP Bill was drafted jointly by the KIPI, the Kenya Copyright Board (KECOBO), and the Anti-Counterfeit Authority

---

[14] ibid 216.
[15] The use of the term 'bill' here is incorrect. A bill is only a bill once legally published by the Government of Kenya. Here, the document should be referred to as 'drafting instructions for a geographical bill 2012'. The term 'bill' is used by the authors here only for convenience purposes: Geoffrey M Ramba, 'Policy Framework for Promoting GIs in Kenya. What the Law and the Policy Prescribe' (First Training Workshop for a Branding Project Using Intellectual Property (IP) for the Taita Basket, February 2016) slide 12.
[16] Blakeney and Mengistie (n 12) 216.

(ACA) under the guidance of the Kenya Law Reform Commission. The IP Bill is rather classic in its protection of GIs, with the addition that GIs are protected whether registered or not.[17] Interestingly, the IP Bill provides for a tribunal on GIs that would adjudicate on proceedings related to the use of a GI for identical or similar products not originating in the place indicated by the designation; identical or similar products in non-compliance with the requirements of a registered GI; or for other products not originating in the place indicated by the designation, in a manner which is deceitful or confusing as to the geographical origin or exploits the reputation of a GI.[18] The IP Bill further provides for certification and collective marks. In June 2020, members of the public were invited to present their comments on the IP Bill. As Parliament has not yet passed the IP Bill, this chapter focuses on the current law in place in Kenya for the protection of GIs: the Trade Marks Act of 2002 (TMA).[19]

3. Registration of GIs Domestically

There is currently no specific provision regarding the registration of GIs in Kenya. This applies to both domestic and foreign GIs. GIs can, however, be registered via the trade mark regime as a certification mark for goods or a collective mark for goods and services by foreign and local applicants. Registration through the trade mark regime is open to domestic and foreign applicants.

Under section 40 of the TMA, a mark may be registered as a certification mark where it is

> adapted in relation to any goods to distinguish in the course of trade goods certified by any person in respect of origin, material, mode of manufacture, quality, accuracy or other characteristic from goods not so certified [. . .] in respect of those goods in the name, as proprietor thereof, of that person: Provided that a mark shall not be so registrable in the name of a person who carries on a trade in goods of the kind certified.

Under section 40A of the TMA, a mark may be registered as a collective trade mark or service mark where it is 'capable of distinguishing, in the course of trade, the goods or services of persons who are members of an association, from goods or services of persons who are not members of such association [. . .] in respect of the goods or services in the name of such an association'.

---

[17] Intellectual Property Bill, s 192(1).
[18] ibid s 208(1).
[19] Trade Marks Act, Cap 506.

4. Registrability of Names

Geographical names may be registered as either collective or certification marks. The TMA does not explicitly set out the particulars of a mark that would be acceptable as a certification mark. However, the Act excludes certification marks from restrictions applicable to trade marks whereby a trade mark cannot be a word or words that, according to its ordinary signification, is a geographical name.[20] A certification mark may therefore reference a geographical location. Section 40A(5) of the TMA explicitly provides that geographical names or other indications of geographical origin may be registered as collective trade marks or service marks.

5. Procedure and Requirements for Registration

Trade mark registration in Kenya is processed at the KIPI, with the managing director acting as the Registrar of trade marks. An applicant for a collective or certification mark in Kenya may apply for domestic registration through the KIPI or through the Madrid Protocol for the International Registration of Trade Marks of 2007 (Madrid System).

The application process at the KIPI for the registration of a certification trade mark and a collective trade or service mark is similar. In fact, the same application form is used. The certification or collective mark applicant must identify the trade mark and provide its name, trade, or business address, and trading style (if any) on the form. The applicant must also indicate the class(es) in which the collective mark is to be registered and a list of goods and/or services. Kenya is a multi-class jurisdiction. Where the applicant is not a resident or has its principal place of business outside Kenya, the applicant is required to use a local trade mark agent. An application must therefore be accompanied by an acceptable form of authorization or a power of attorney duly completed and signed, with a duty stamp affixed to it. The form for entry of the address of service in Kenya should also accompany the application. The fee payable for an application will depend on the residence or location of the applicant's business. A foreign fee is payable if the person paying the fee, or on whose behalf the fee is being paid, does not reside in Kenya and does not have a principal place of business in Kenya.

There are, however, some specificities to the registration of a certification and collective mark. For a certification mark, the person proposed to be registered as proprietor shall send to the Registrar, either with the application or when required by the Registrar, a case setting out the grounds on which it relies in support of its application, together with draft regulations for governing the use of the mark, all in

---

[20] TMA, s 12(d).

PROCEDURE AND REQUIREMENTS FOR REGISTRATION   147

duplicate. The regulations shall include provisions as to the cases in which the proprietor is to certify goods and authorize the use of the trade mark. The regulations may contain any other provisions that the Registrar may require or permit to be inserted therein (including provisions conferring a right of appeal to the Registrar against any refusal of the proprietor to certify goods or to authorize the use of the trade mark in accordance with the regulations).[21] The Registrar may communicate to the applicant any observations it may have to make on the sufficiency of the case or the suitability of the draft regulations, and the applicant may modify either of those documents.[22]

In an application for a certification mark, the Registrar will examine whether the mark is adapted to distinguish. The Registrar shall consider the extent to which the mark is inherently adapted to distinguish in relation to the goods in question and the extent to which, by reason of the use of the mark or any other circumstances, the mark is, in fact, adapted to distinguish in relation to the goods in question.[23] The Registrar is required to consider the application with regard to the following matters:

a) whether the applicant is competent to certify the goods in respect of which the mark is to be registered;
b) whether the draft regulations are satisfactory; and
c) whether in all the circumstances the registration applied for would be to the public advantage.[24]

The Registrar may either reject or accept the application and approve the regulations, either without modification and unconditionally or subject to any conditions or limitations or to any amendments or modifications of the application or other regulations that the Registrar thinks requisite having regard to any of the foregoing matter.

Except where the Registrar accepts and approves the application without modification and unconditionally, the Registrar must inform the applicant of his or her objections in writing and allow the applicant to be heard before deciding on the matter.

An application for the registration of a collective trade mark shall designate the mark as a collective trade mark and be accompanied by a copy of the rules made by the person controlling the collective mark and that will govern the use of the mark.[25]

---

[21] ibid s 40(7).
[22] The Trade Marks Rules, Rule 39.
[23] TMA, s 40(2)
[24] ibid first schedule, s 1(1).
[25] ibid s 40A(2).

An application for a certification and collective trade mark will undergo both formal and substantive examination. Once the Office has decided that there are no grounds for refusal, the trade mark is published in the *Industrial Property Journal* or the *Kenya Gazette*. In the case of a certification mark, if the Registrar decides to accept the application, the regulations governing the use of the mark approved by the Registrar and the form of application must be open to public inspection.[26] Any person may oppose the published application within sixty days.[27] Although the law uses the term 'any person', in practice, the Registrar requires that the opponent has *locus standi* to bring the opposition proceedings, such as being a GI or trade mark owner.[28] In the case of the *Agricultural and Processed Food Products Export Development Authority (APEDA) v Krish Commodities Limited*, on an appeal from a ruling of the Registrar, the High Court agreed with the latter that the appellant had no *locus standi* to oppose six applications, all including the words 'BASMATI RICE'. The fact that the appellant had lodged an application to register BASMATI as a GI in India after the opposition was deemed insufficient. Where there is no opposition or an opposition has been decided in favour of the applicant, the certification and collective trade mark is registered.

Further to the registration, the regulations governing the use of the certification mark are deposited at the office of the Registrar. These regulations are open to inspection in the same manner as the Register.[29] The registered owner of a collective trade or service mark shall notify the Registrar in writing of any changes to the rules governing the use of the collective mark.[30]

6. Term of Protection

Registered certification and collective marks are protected for ten years and renewable indefinitely for consecutive periods of ten years, provided renewal fees are paid in time.

Any aggrieved person or the Registrar may apply to the High Court for an order expunging or varying any entry in the Register relating to a certification trade mark, or for varying the deposited regulations, on the ground that

a) the proprietor is no longer competent, in the case of any of the goods in respect of which the trade mark is registered, to certify those goods;

---

[26] The Trade Marks Rules, Rule 40.
[27] TMA, s 21(2).
[28] *The Agricultural and Processed Food Products Export Development Authority (APEDA) v Krish Commodities Limited* (No 338 of 2013) High Court of Kenya.
[29] TMA, s 40(7).
[30] ibid s 40A(4).

b) the proprietor has failed to observe a provision of the deposited regulations to be observed on his part;
c) it is no longer to the public advantage that the trade mark should be registered; or
d) it is requisite for the public advantage that if the trade mark remains registered, the regulations should be varied.[31]

The Registrar shall rectify the Register and the deposited regulations in accordance with the court order.

Any aggrieved person or the Registrar (in case of fraud in the registration or assignment or transmission of a registered trade mark) may apply to the court for an order expunging a collective trade mark on the ground that the trade mark:

a) is registered without sufficient cause, or is wrongly remaining on the register; or
b) contravenes or fails to observe a condition entered on the register in relation to its registration.[32]

7. Rights of the Owner and Enforcement Mechanisms against Infringers

A valid registered trade mark, including a certification and collective mark, gives the proprietor the exclusive right to use the trade mark in relation to the goods or in connection with the provision of any services. This right is infringed where any person who, not being the proprietor of the trade mark or a registered user using by way of permitted use, uses a mark identical with or so nearly resembling it as to be likely to deceive or cause confusion in the course of trade or in connection with the provision of any services in respect of which it is registered, and in such manner as to render the use of the mark likely to

a) be taken as use of a trade mark;
b) import a reference to some person having the right either as proprietor or as licensee to use the trade mark or goods with which such a person is connected in the course of trade, where the use is upon the goods or in physical relation thereto or in an advertising circular or other advertisement issued to the public;
c) import a reference to some person having the right either as proprietor or as licensee to use the trade mark or to services with the provision of which

---

[31] ibid first schedule, s 4(1).
[32] Ibid, sect 16(1) read with sect 40A(6)

such a person as aforesaid is connected in the course of business, where the use is at or near the place where the services are available for acceptance, performed, in an advertising circular or other advertisement issued to the public or any part thereof;
d) cause injury or prejudice to the proprietor or licensee of the trade mark.[33]

There are also certain specific provisions related to the use of a certification mark. The registered proprietor of a certification trade mark has the exclusive right to use the trade mark in relation to those goods. This right is deemed to be infringed by any person who, not being the proprietor of the trade mark or a person authorized by the proprietor, uses a mark identical to it or so nearly resembling it as to be likely to deceive or cause confusion, in the course of trade, in relation to any goods in of which it is registered, and in such manner as to render the use of the mark likely to be taken either as being used as a trade mark or, in a case in which the use is used upon the goods or in physical relation thereto or in an advertising circular or other advertisement issued to the public, as importing a reference to some person having the right either as proprietor or by its authorization under the relevant regulations to use the trade marks or to goods certified by the proprietor.[34]

The right to use a certification trade mark given by registration is subject to any conditions or limitations entered on the Register. It is not deemed to be infringed by the use of any such mark in any mode, in relation to goods to be sold or otherwise traded in any place, in relation to goods to be exported to any market, or in any other circumstances, to which, having regard to any such limitations, the registration does not extend.[35]

Likewise, the right to use a certification mark shall not be deemed to be infringed where it is used by any person in relation to goods certified by the proprietor of the trade mark if, as to those goods or a bulk of which they form part, the proprietor or another in accordance with his authorization under the relevant regulations has applied the trade mark and has not subsequently removed or obliterated it, or the proprietor has at any time expressly or impliedly consented to the use of the trade mark. This limitation, however, shall not apply where the use consists of applying the certification mark to goods if such an application is contrary to relevant regulations.[36] The right to use a certification mark shall not be deemed to be infringed where any person uses it in relation to goods adapted to form part of or to be an accessory to other goods in relation to which the trade mark has been used without infringement of the right given or might, for the time being, be so used if the use of the mark is reasonably necessary in order to indicate that the

---

[33] TMA, s 7(1).
[34] ibid s 40(3).
[35] ibid s 40(4).
[36] ibid s 40(5)(a).

goods are so adapted and neither the purpose nor the effect of the use of the mark is to indicate otherwise than in accordance with the fact that the goods are certified by the proprietor.[37]

Where a certification trade mark is one of two or more registered trade marks that are identical or nearly resemble each other, the use of any of those trade marks in the exercise of the right to the use of that trade mark given by registration shall not be deemed to be an infringement of the right so given to the use of any other of those trade marks.[38]

A certification mark and a collective mark are enforced under the general provisions related to trade marks under the TMA. The proprietor of a registered trade mark is entitled to institute proceedings if its rights are infringed. Subject to any provisions in the licence agreement, the licensee may call on the proprietor to institute infringement proceedings where any of the licensee's rights are infringed.

Infringement actions are brought before the High Court. Both documentary and oral evidence may be tendered in proceedings before the High Court. In a departure from the general rule of evidence, the TMA allows the production of documents by persons other than their makers in offences related to the importation of counterfeit goods.[39]

The courts in Kenya may issue a temporary injunction where it is brought to their attention that the subject matter is in imminent danger of destruction or disposal. A temporary injunction only lasts up to twelve months, subject to a fresh application, and is only meant to apply pending the hearing and determination of the main suit. Such applications may be made and granted *ex parte* if they are found by the court to be urgent. A right holder may also make an *ex parte* application to the court to obtain a court order for searching the premises where infringing products are stored, together with sales and purchase records. The infringing products and the sales and purchase records may be seized and used as evidence.

Upon a successful civil suit, the high court may order the following remedies: permanent injunctions, accounts for profit, a claim for damages, delivery of or destruction of the offending goods, or cost of the suit to the successful plaintiff as well as damages. In Kenya, the court may choose from different types of damages, the aim being to restore the plaintiff to the position that it would have been had the offence not been committed. Nominal damages are awarded to the plaintiff as a matter of right where the plaintiff proves that infringement of its right has occurred. Punitive or exemplary damages can also be awarded where the defendant's conduct is shown to have been calculated to make a profit that far outweighs any compensation payable and where there is an injury to the plaintiff's reputation. Special damages are awarded to compensate a claimant for actual costs incurred

---

[37] ibid s 40(5)(b).
[38] ibid s 40(6).
[39] ibid s 58G.

due to the defendant's actions or behaviour. Special damages are quantified precisely, and the plaintiff must provide clear evidence of the out-of-pocket expenses and provable loss and expense incurred.

Criminal proceedings are also possible for infringements under the TMA. Any person who

a) forges a registered trade mark;[40] or
b) falsely applies a registered trade mark to goods[41] or in relation to services;[42] or
c) makes a die, block, machine, or other instruments for the purpose of forging or of being used for forging, a registered trade mark; or
d) disposes of, or has in his possession, a die, block, machine, or other instrument for the purpose of forging or of being used for forging, a registered trade mark; or
e) without the consent of the proprietor of a registered trade mark-
   i. makes, imports or has in his possession any device for applying that registered trade mark to goods or in relation to services or representations of that trade mark; or
   ii. makes any reproduction, replicas or representations of that trade mark; or
   iii. imports any reproductions, replicas or representations of that trade mark otherwise than on goods to which they have been applied; or
f) makes, imports or has in his possession–
   i. any device for applying to any goods or in relation to any services a mark so nearly resembling a registered trade mark as to be likely to deceive or cause confusion; or
   ii. any reproduction, replica or representation of a mark so nearly resembling a registered trade mark as to be likely to deceive or cause confusion for the purpose of applying it to goods or in relation to services contrary to the provisions of this Part; or

---

[40] A person forges a registered trade mark if it makes a trade mark or a mark so nearly resembling that trade mark as to be likely to deceive or cause confusion without the consent of the proprietor of the registered trade mark or the authority of the TMA or the person falsifies a registered trade mark, whether by alteration, addition, effacement, or otherwise: ibid s 58C.

[41] A trade mark is applied to goods if it is applied to the goods themselves; or it is applied to a covering on, in, or attached to which the goods are sold; or the goods are placed in or around, enclosed by or annexed to any covering to which the trade mark or other mark has been applied; or it is used in any manner likely to lead to the belief that the goods in connection with which it is used are designated by that trade mark or other mark: ibid s 58B(1).

[42] A trade mark is applied in relation to services if used in any manner likely to lead to the belief that the services in connection with which it is used are designated by that trade mark: ibid s 58B(3). A registered trade mark is falsely applied to goods or in relation to services if the registered trade mark or a mark so nearly resembling it as to be likely to deceive or cause confusion is applied to the goods or in relation to the services without the consent of the proprietor or the authority of this Act: ibid s 58B(4).

iii. any covering bearing a mark so nearly resembling a registered trade mark as to be likely to deceive or cause confusion for the purpose of using it to cover or contain, or in relation to, goods contrary to the provisions of this Part; [43]

g) sells or imports any goods or performs any services to which a forged registered trade mark is falsely applied or a registered trade mark is falsely applied[44]

shall be guilty of an offence, and liable to a fine not exceeding 200 000 KES and/or imprisonment for a term not exceeding five years. The TMA provides for defences to such charges.

On conviction of any person under the criminal offences highlighted under the TMA, the court may, in addition to any sentence passed, declare any goods in respect of or by means of which the offence was committed to being forfeited to the Government unless the owner of the goods or any person acting on its behalf or any other person interested in the goods shows cause to the contrary.[45]

While the persecution of offences under the TMA is reserved for trade marks registered in Kenya, owners of both registered and unregistered trade marks may institute passing-off actions.[46] The remedies available include injunctions (interim and permanent), claim for damages, accounts for profits, orders for the delivery of or destruction of the offending goods, and costs of the suit. It is easier to prove an infringement under the TMA since registration is, in itself, proof that the registered proprietor has the exclusive right to exploit the mark. In contrast, in a passing-off action, the offended person must prove that the misrepresentation by the other trader caused actual damage to its business or goodwill.

The holder of an IP right, including a collective and certification mark, his successor in title, licensee or agent, upon reasonable cause to suspect that an offence under section 32 of the ACA has been, is, or is likely to be committed, may lay a complaint with the Executive Director.[47] Section 32 of the ACA provides that it shall be an offence for any person to

a) have in his possession or control in the course of trade any counterfeit goods;[48]
b) manufacture, produce, or make in the course of trade, any counterfeit goods;

---

[43] ibid s 58D(1).
[44] ibid s 58E(1).
[45] ibid s S 58H(1).
[46] ibid s 5.
[47] ACA, s 33(1).
[48] Counterfeit goods are defined at s 2 of the ACA as amongst other goods that are identical to or substantially similar copies of the protected goods, goods that are colourable imitations so as to be confused with or to be taken as being the protected goods, and copies that violate an author's rights or related rights.

c) sell, hire out, barter or exchange, or offer or expose for sale, hiring out, barter or exchange any counterfeit goods;
d) expose or exhibit for the purposes of trade any counterfeit goods;
e) distribute counterfeit goods for purposes of trade or any other purpose;
f) import into, transit through, transship within, or export from Kenya, except for private and domestic use of the importer or exporter, as the case may be, any counterfeit goods;
g) in any other manner, dispose of any counterfeit goods in the course of trade;
h) have in his possession or control in the course of trade any labels, patches, stickers, wrappers, badges, emblems, medallions, charms, boxes, containers, cans, cases, hand tags, documentations, or packaging of any type or nature, with a counterfeit mark applied thereto, the use of which is likely to cause confusion, to cause mistake, or to deceive;
i) aids or abets or conspires in the commission of any offence under the ACA;
j) import into Kenya, any goods or items bearing a trade mark, trade name or copyright that has not been recorded with the Anti Counterfeiting Authority;
k) import into Kenya, in the course of trade, any goods or items except raw materials that is unbranded;
l) fail to declare the quantity or the intellectual property right subsisting in any goods being imported into Kenya;
m) falsely declare the quantity or the intellectual property rights subsisting in any goods being imported into Kenya; or
n) import into or transit through Kenya any labels, patches, stickers, wrappers, badges, emblems, medallions, charms, boxes, containers, cans, cases, hand tags, documentations, or packaging of any type or nature, with a counterfeit mark applied thereto, the use of which is likely to cause confusion, to cause mistake, or to deceive.

Upon being satisfied that the complainant is entitled to lay such a complaint, the goods referred to in the complaint are *prima facie* counterfeit goods, the IP rights alleged to be offended *prima facie* exists, and the suspicion on which the complaint is based appears to be reasonable in the circumstances, the ACA may, amongst others, inspect and seal off any premise or vehicle, seize any goods, and arrest suspects. The ACA may also act without a complaint upon suspicion that an act of dealing with counterfeits has been committed. Upon conviction of an offence under section 32 above, a person shall be liable in the case of a first conviction, to imprisonment for a term not exceeding five years, and/or to a fine not less than three times the value of the prevailing retail price of the goods, in respect of each offending article or item. In the case of a second or any subsequent conviction, a person shall be liable to imprisonment for a term not exceeding fifteen years and/or to a fine not less than five times the value of the prevailing retail price of the offending goods.[49] The determination of the penalty by the court shall take into account, *inter alia*, any risk to human or animal life, health or safety, or danger to property, whether movable or immovable, that may arise from the presence or use of the counterfeit goods in question. Mitigating factors with regard to the sentencing include cooperation by the offenders as to the source of the counterfeit goods; the identity of those involved in the importation, exportation, manufacture, production, or making of those counterfeit goods; the identity and, if reasonably demanded, the addresses or whereabouts of the persons involved in the distribution of those goods; and the channels for the distribution of those goods.[50] In addition, where a court has concluded the hearing of a matter in any criminal proceedings whether the suspect is convicted or acquitted and the goods in the opinion of the court are counterfeit and it appears that the suspect has benefited or obtained some monetary advantage from dealing in counterfeit goods the subject matter of the criminal proceedings, the court shall, on application of the prosecutor, order the suspect to forfeit that benefit or monetary advantage to the ACA within a period of three months, and in default, the ACA may trace and recover that benefit or advantage from the suspect.[51]

The Penal Code also provides for the counterfeiting of trade marks. Any person who

a) forges or counterfeits any trade mark;
b) applies any trade mark, or any forged or counterfeit trade mark, to any chattel or article, not being the merchandise of any person whose trade mark is so forged or counterfeited;
c) applies any trade mark, or any forged or counterfeited trade mark, to any chattel or article, not being the particular or peculiar description of merchandise denoted or intended to be denoted by such trade mark or by such forged or counterfeited trade mark;
d) applies any trade mark, or any forged or counterfeited trade mark, to any thing intended for any purpose of trade or manufacture, or in, on or with which any chattel or article is intended to be sold, or is sold or offered or exposed for sale;
e) encloses or places any chattel or article in, upon, under or with any thing to which any trade mark has been falsely applied, or to which any forged or counterfeit trade mark has been applied;
f) applies or attaches any chattel or article to any case, cover, reel, ticket, label or other thing to which any trade mark has been falsely applied, or to which any false or counterfeit trade mark has been applied;

---

[49] ibid s 35(1).
[50] ibid s 35(3).
[51] ibid s 35(5).

g) encloses, places or attaches any chattel or article in, upon, under, with or to any thing having thereon any trade mark of any other person, is guilty of a misdemeanour, unless he proves that he acted without intent to defraud any person.[52]

Quite surprisingly, a trade mark is defined under the Penal Code as a mark, other than a trade mark registered under the TMA, lawfully used by any person to denote any chattel to be an article or thing of the manufacture, workmanship, production, or merchandise of such person or to be an article or thing of any peculiar or particular description made or sold by such person or any mark or sign which, in pursuance of any law in force for the time being relating to registered designs, is to be put or placed upon or attached to any chattel or article during the existence or continuance of any copyright or other sole right acquired under the provision of such law.[53]

Upon conviction, a person is liable to imprisonment for a term not exceeding two years and/or a fine. The amount of the fine is not provided for under the law and is dependent upon the discretion of the court. The offender shall also forfeit all counterfeit goods and every instrument used in their manufacture.

Under the Trade Descriptions Act (TDA), it is an offence to import into Kenya or handle any goods to which there is applied a trade description containing a direct or indirect reference to any country, town, or place other than the country, town, or place in which the goods were manufactured or produced.[54] It is further an offence to apply, supply, or have in one's possession for supply goods with a false trade description. A false trade description is defined under the Act as including any mark made to so nearly resemble a registered trade mark or monogram as to be likely to deceive.[55] In both offences, the offender shall be liable to a fine not exceeding 2 million KES and/or to imprisonment for a term not exceeding five years.[56] Inspectors appointed under the Weight and Measures Act may seize and detain goods to which a false trade description is applied. They will also prosecute offences committed under the TDA.

Under the Competition Act, it is an offence for any person, in trade in connection with the supply or possible supply of goods or services, or in connection with the promotion by any means of the supply or use of goods or services, to make a false or misleading representation concerning the place of origin of goods.[57] The Competition Authority receives complaints directly from customers whether by post, email, telephone call, or walking into the Authority's office. The Authority may investigate complaints related to such offences and apply administrative remedies

[52] Penal Code, s 381(1).
[53] ibid s 380.
[54] TDA, s 7(1)(a).
[55] ibid s 9(1)(e).
[56] ibid s 15.
[57] Competition Act, s 55(b)(iii).

to resolve the complaint, including withdrawal of goods bearing misleading representations. Complaints that are not solved through administrative remedies are forwarded to the Office of the Director of Public Prosecution after completion of full investigation. Upon conviction, an offender is liable to imprisonment for a term not exceeding five years and/or to a fine not exceeding 10 million KES.

8. ACA Enforcement

In order to fight against the availability of counterfeits in Kenya, the ACA has come up with a mandatory recordal scheme for the IP rights of goods imported into the country. This obligation applies to all goods with valid IP rights imported into the country. Goods transiting or trans-shipping in Kenya are excluded from the recordation process. It is irrelevant whether the IP right is registered in Kenya or abroad as long as the IP right is still registered. Since being registered in Kenya is not a requirement, and all IP rights are to be included, one may argue that a GI registered abroad could successfully be recorded with ACA, although *sui generis* GIs do not exist under Kenyan law.

As stated by the ACA, it shall be an offence to import into Kenya any goods or items bearing an IP right that has not been recorded with the ACA. The requirements for recordation include a certified copy of the IP right registration, samples or photographs of relevant goods, a description of the goods, and details of the place of manufacture of the goods. Other requirements, where the applicant is a company, include a copy of the applicant's certificate of incorporation and its tax registration number. It is necessary to act through an authorized agent for the recordal. A fee must also be paid. The ACA reviews and process all applications within thirty days. In practice, the process suffers from undue delay and rights owners often wait months for the processing of their applications. All recorded IPs are published in the ACA's monthly newsletter. A recordal lasts for one year from the date of approval or as long as the IP right is valid, whichever is shorter.[58] The recordal should allow the ACA to scrutinize imports and prevent the entry of counterfeits at the border points.

9. Bilateral Agreements

The EU and Kenya finalised negotiations for a bilateral Economic Partnership Agreement (EPA) at the end of 2023. Under the EPA, both parties 'recognise the

---

[58] More information may be found on the ACA recordal in Marius Schneider and Nora Ho Tu Nam, 'Kenya Mandatory IPR Recordal: An Innovative Measure with an Uncertain Future' (2022) 17(12) JIPLP 6 and, on customs enforcement in Kenya, in Marius Schneider and Vanessa Ferguson, *Enforcement of Intellectual Property Rights in Africa* (OUP 2020) 424–26.

importance of geographical indications for sustainable agriculture and rural development'.[59] The parties have agreed to collaborate in identifying, recognising, registering and protecting products that could benefit from being protected as GIs.[60] GIs are explicitly highlighted as an area of cooperation. Parties will thus cooperate to develop policies and legal frameworks on GIs, establish regulations on GIs, and develop code of practice to define products in relation to their origin. In relation to capacity building, both parties must cooperate to facilate the coordination of local stakeholders on GIs and product conformity by local organisations and institutions and to build capacity on identification, registration, marketing, traceability and conformity of GIs. The EPA further provides for the parties to develop any other area of cooperation on GIs that may arise in the future.[61] The EPA will come into force once the European Parliament consents to it.[62]

There is no bilateral agreement between the United States and Kenya specific to GIs.

---

[59] EPA, art 74(1).
[60] Ibid, art 74(2).
[61] Ibid, art 83(n).
[62] Jean-Philippe Mergen, 'EU and KENYA sign ambitious Economic Partnership Agreement' (*enterprise Europe network*, 5 January 2024) <https://www.brusselsnetwork.be/eu-and-kenya-sign-ambitious-economic-partnership-agreement/>

13
Mauritius

Mauritius is found in the Indian Ocean, off the south-eastern coast of Africa. The island nation of 2,040 km² had a population of 1.2 million inhabitants in 2022. English is the accepted official language, being used by the administration and in court. On a day-to-day basis, the most commonly used languages are French and Creole. The working week is from Monday to Friday, and the national currency is the Mauritian Rupee (MUR).

The Republic of Mauritius includes its outer islands, such as Agalega, Rodrigues, and St Brandon. All goods going to the outer islands pass through Mauritius. From a monocrop and low-income economy based on sugarcane after its independence from Britain in 1968, Mauritius has grown to a well-diversified economy based on services and innovation. Hospitality, financial services, and information and communication technology are now pillaring the Mauritian economy. This translated into a gross domestic product (GDP) growth from USD 704 million in the 1970s to USD 14 billion in 2019.[1] The economic progress of Mauritius has been such that Joseph Stiglitz, a Nobel Laureate in economics, labelled it 'the Mauritius Miracle', a term that has been adopted by many over the years.[2] Since 2020, the World Bank has classified Mauritius as a high-income country, making it the second African country to achieve such status after the Seychelles.

A small but densely populated country with few economies of scale and rising labour costs, Mauritius is heavily reliant on food imports. In 2018, 20 per cent of total Mauritian imports were food imports. France is the main source of imported food products.[3] Products from France enjoy high recognition and are appreciated by the Mauritian consumer. This is likely due to a combination of factors: Mauritius was previously a French colony, the population speaks French, and French television channels (and the accompanying advertisements for French products) are popular among the Mauritian population. Other important food supplier countries, in order of importance, are South Africa, India, Australia, and New Zealand.[4]

---

[1] World Bank, 'GDP (Current US$)—Mauritius' (*World Bank*, nd) <https://data.worldbank.org/indicator/NY.GDP.MKTP.CD?locations=MU>.
[2] Joseph Stiglitz, 'The Mauritius Miracle' (*Project Syndicate*, 7 March 2011) <www.project-syndicate.org/commentary/the-mauritius-miracle?barrier=accesspaylog>.
[3] Export.gov, 'Mauritius—Agricultural Sectors' (*Exportgov*, 19 August 2019) <www.export.gov/apex/article2?id=Mauritius-Agricultural-Sectors>.
[4] ibid.

E-commerce is becoming increasingly popular among the population, with a sharp boom during and after the COVID-19 pandemic. COVID-19 and the resulting lockdown increased acceptance and familiarity among the general population of online shopping and payment solutions. Social media, particularly Facebook, remains one of the most important means for companies to reach their target audience in Mauritius.[5]

As of May 2023, the only geographical indication (GI) registered in Mauritius is *Champagne*. However, numerous agricultural products have been highlighted over the years as having the potential to be protected under the GI framework. These are Demerara Sugar, Bois Cheri Tea,[6] Onion Toupie, and Chamarel Coffee. The following products from Rodrigues, an autonomous island forming part of the Republic of Mauritius, have also been identified as suitable for GI protection: Rodrigues Limes and Chillies, Rodrigues Honey, and Baie Topaz Red Beans.[7]

1. Legal Framework

As a result of its colonial past, Mauritius has a hybrid system of law combining civil and common law. The substantive law is based on Codes of French inspiration, written in French, and complemented with statutes voted by Parliament and written in English. The substantive law is then applied in a British-inspired court architecture with British-inspired procedures. The court system consists of the Supreme Court and other subordinate courts. The Supreme Court of Mauritius is the superior court of the island and has unlimited jurisdiction to hear and determine civil or criminal proceedings other than under disciplinary law. The Supreme Court, which comprises the Court of Civil Appeal and the Court of Criminal Appeal as its divisions, acts as a court of appeal and a court of first instance for any civil claim above MUR 2 million. The subordinate courts include the Intermediate Court, the Commercial Court, and the district courts. The appropriate court is the district court for a civil claim of less than MUR 250,000. The appropriate court is the Intermediate Court for a civil claim ranging from MUR 250,001–MUR 2 million.

---

[5] International Trade Administration Mauritius, 'Country Commercial Guide: eCommerce' (*International Trade Administration Mauritius*, 10 April 2023) <www.trade.gov/country-commercial-guides/mauritius-ecommerce>.

[6] It is surprising to the authors that Bois Cheri Tea has been selected as although Bois Cheri refers to a locality in Mauritius, there are several well-known trade marks comprising BOIS CHERI registered for tea in Mauritius.

[7] Michael Blakeney, 'Mauritius: Sugar' in Michael Blakeney and others (eds), *Extending the Protection of Geographical Indications* (Routledge 2012) 246.

Mauritian lawyers are either barristers or attorneys (known as *avoués*), and litigation will require the services of both. It is common for the client to first contact the barrister for legal advice and afterwards to contact the attorney to start legal proceedings.

2. Domestic Legislation on GIs

Mauritius has been a member of the Paris Convention for the Protection of Industrial Property of 1883 since September 1976. Mauritius is a party to neither the Madrid Agreement for the Repression of False or Deceptive Indications of Source on Goods of 1891 nor the Lisbon Agreement for the Protection of Appellations of Origin and their International Registration of 1958. Mauritius is a member of the World Trade Organization (WTO), and the transition period available to put in effect national legislation implementing the WTO Agreement on Trade-Related Aspects of Intellectual Property Rights (TRIPS) expired on 31 December 1999.

The Industrial Property Act (IPA) governs the protection of GIs and collective and certification marks. It was voted by Parliament in 2019 but only came into force on 31 January 2022. The accompanying Regulations, published under Government Notice No 36 of 2022, came into force on the same day. The IPA and the accompanying Regulations provide for the domestication and application, respectively, of the Madrid Protocol. The Madrid Protocol for the International Registration of Trade Marks (Madrid System) of 2007 has been in force in Mauritius since 6 May 2023. It is possible to designate Mauritius in an international application to register a collective and certification mark.

3. Registration of GIs Domestically

3.1 GIs

The IPA provides for the *sui generis* protection of GIs. Registration as a GI is open indistinctly to domestic and foreign indications. Under the IPA, a GI is defined as an indication 'which identifies a good as originating in the territory of a country, or a region or locality in that country, where a given quality, reputation or other characteristic of the good is essentially attributable to its geographical origin'.[8] This definition closely follows article 22(1) of the TRIPS Agreement.

---

[8] IPA, s 2.

3.2 Collective and certification marks

It is also possible under the IPA to register a GI as either a certification or collective mark. A certification mark is defined as a sign certified by the owner of a mark as being capable, in respect of the origin, material, or mode of manufacture of goods, the performance of services, or their quality, standard, or other characteristics, of distinguishing goods or services from other goods or services not so certified.[9] A collective mark is defined as a sign capable of distinguishing the origin or any other common characteristic, including the quality of goods or services, of different enterprises that use the sign under the control of the registered owner of the collective mark.[10]

The rules applicable under a GI, a collective, or a certification mark apply to all goods and services. No specific rules and/or additional protection apply to wines and spirits.

4. Registrability of Names

4.1 GIs

Under the IPA, an indication may not be protected as a GI where

a) the indication is contrary to public order or morality;
b) the GI is not protected in its country of origin or ceases to be protected, or has fallen into disuse in the country of origin;
c) the indication is identical to a term customary in common language in Mauritius as the common name for relevant goods or services.[11]

4.2 Collective and certification marks

The IPA explicitly provides that a sign may not be registered as a mark, including a collective or certification mark, where it consists solely of a sign or indication that may serve in trade to designate the geographical origin of the goods or services[12] or where the sign is likely to mislead as regards the geographical origin of the goods or services concerned.[13]

---

[9] ibid s 2.
[10] ibid s 2.
[11] ibid s 105(2). This is in line with art 24(6) of the TRIPS Agreement.
[12] IPA, s 91(2)(b).
[13] ibid s 91(2)(f).

5. Procedure and Requirements for Registration

The Industrial Property Office (IPO), which is headed by the Director, receives applications for GIs and collective and certification marks. Although French is commonly spoken in Mauritius, every application must be filed in English, and any document forming part of the application or submitted to the Director shall be accompanied, where necessary, by an English translation. For GIs, certification, and collective marks, where the applicant's ordinary residence or principal place of business is outside Mauritius, the applicant must be represented by a law practitioner residing and practicing in Mauritius or an agent approved by the minister in charge of intellectual property. In such a case, the applicant must provide the agent or law practitioner with a signed power of attorney. The power of attorney must then be registered at the Registrar General in Mauritius before it is filed with the IPO, either with the application or within two months without additional cost from the filing date of the application.

5.1 GIs

An application for the registration of a GI shall be filed with the IPO and be subject to the payment of a non-refundable fee. The application may be filed by a group of producers, a legal entity which groups the producers that operate in a specified geographical area to produce specified goods, or a government department on behalf of the group of producers or legal entity. It is open to both local and foreign applicants. The application for registration should contain the

a) name, address, and domicile of the person filing the application;
b) GI for which registration is sought;
c) geographical area to which the GI applies;
d) goods designated by the GI. These goods are classified as follows: wine and spirit; manufactured goods being either handicraft or food; natural products being either mineral or agricultural, and all other goods;
e) specific characteristics of the goods for which the GI is used;
f) area and method of production of the goods;
g) link between the characteristics of the goods and the area and method of production;
h) the manner in which the specific characteristics are controlled;
i) Code of Practice which establishes the rules for the use of the GI;
j) proof that the name of the product is protected in the country of origin; and
k) the Internal Control Plan relating to the GI.[14]

---

[14] ibid s 106(3).

The Director shall examine the application. The Director shall refuse the application if all the requirements are unmet. Where the requirements are met, the Director shall publish the application for opposition.[15] Any interested person may lodge an opposition within two months from the date of publication. Where the opposition fails or there is no opposition, the Director shall register the GI, issue a certificate of registration, and give notice of the registration in the *Government Gazette*.

5.2 Collective and certification marks

Registering a certification or collective mark is open to domestic and foreign applicants. The same procedure applies to both certification and collective marks. An application for registration shall be made on the prescribed form. Official fees must be paid upon filing the application. The application form is similar to the one used for service and trade marks. The applicant should clearly identify the mark, and where the collective or certification mark takes the form of a logo or device, the correct title of the mark shall be inserted. If a mark is a foreign word, the application must be accompanied by a transliteration and/or translation of such word, stating the language to which it belongs. The applicant must indicate the class(es) in which the mark is to be registered as well as a list of goods and/or services. For a collective mark, the application should be accompanied by a copy of the agreement governing the use of the collective mark. The registered owner shall notify the Director of any change made to the agreement. Changes shall be kept on record and published where the Director finds it appropriate. For a certification mark, the application shall be accompanied by a copy of the agreement governing the use of the mark. The Director shall publish the relevant particulars of the application and agreement in the *Government Gazette* and make the agreement available for public consultation on payment of a fee. The registered owner shall notify the Director of any change made to the agreement. Changes shall be kept on record and published where the Director finds appropriate.

The Mauritian IPO examines a mark on both relative and absolute grounds. As such, the Director may refuse an application that does not respect the rules regarding the registrability of certain marks. The Director may request the applicant to furnish additional information or amend the application where information is missing from the application. Should the application be refused on relative grounds, it is possible to make written representations to the Director to reconsider the application for registering a mark within six months of receiving the refusal notice. Within one month from receipt of the written representations, the Director

---

[15] ibid s 108(1).

shall inform the applicant of his or her decision and the reasons thereof. Once an application is accepted, the IPO will issue a notice of acceptance, and the mark will be scheduled for publication in the *Government Gazette*. Any interested party may oppose the application within two months of its publication in the *Gazette*. Should there be no opposition or should the opposition be rejected, the IPO shall issue a certificate.

6. Term of Protection

6.1 GIs

GIs are protected for ten years from the filing date of the application. GIs may be renewed indefinitely for consecutive periods of ten years upon payment of the renewal fee. The Director may, however, on an application for the renewal of the registration of a GI, request the applicant to furnish such other information and documents as he or she may determine.[16]

Where there are homonymous GIs for identical products, the Director shall, in cases of permitted concurrent use of the indications, determine the practical conditions under which the homonymous indications shall be differentiated from each other, considering the need to ensure the equitable treatment of the producers concerned and that consumers are not misled.[17] The Director may require that the country of origin of every homonymous indication or that a representation of a map showing the country of origin of every homonymous indication appears prominently on the labels used for every GI.[18] This provision which in the TRIPS Agreement at article 23(3) is an additional protection for wines and spirits, applies to all goods in Mauritius.

The validity of the registration of a mark or the right to use a mark shall not be affected on the ground that the mark is identical with or similar to a GI where the mark has been applied for and registered in good faith or where the rights to the mark have been acquired through use in good faith before the commencement of the IPA Act or before a GI is protected in its country of origin.[19] This provision is in line with article 24(5) of the TRIPS Agreement.

A national or resident of Mauritius who has used a GI in connection with goods and services in Mauritius in a continuous manner with regard to the same or related goods or services for at least ten years preceding 15 April 1994 or in good faith any time before that date shall be allowed continued and similar use in Mauritius of

---

[16] ibid s 111.
[17] ibid s 105(1).
[18] IPA Regulations, Reg 109.
[19] IPA, s 110(1).

that foreign GI.[20] This provision in the TRIPS Agreement at article 23(4) applies to GIs identifying wines and spirits but applies to all goods and services in Mauritius.

Any person who has an interest in a GI may apply to the Director for rectification of the Register on the grounds that

   a) the geographical area specified in the register does not correspond to the GI;
   b) the indication of the goods for which the GI is used is missing or unsatisfactory;
   c) the indication of the quality, reputation, or other characteristic of the goods is missing or unsatisfactory.[21]

The Director shall rectify the Register where he or she is satisfied that such rectification is necessary.[22]

A GI may be cancelled at the request of the person having an interest where it does not qualify or no longer qualifies for protection as a GI in Mauritius having regard to sections 105 and 106 of the IPA. Where the Director cancels the registration of a GI, he or she shall remove the relevant entry from the Register.

A GI may be invalidated by the Industrial Property Tribunal (Tribunal) on application of an interested person where the GI does not qualify for protection; the geographical area specified in the registration does not correspond to a GI; or the indication of the products for which the GI is used or the indication of the quality, reputation, or other characteristic of such products is missing or unsatisfactory.[23]

6.2 Collective and certification marks

A collective and certification mark is protected for ten years from the filing date of the application. The mark may be renewed indefinitely for consecutive periods of ten years upon payment of the renewal fee.

A collective mark shall be invalidated by the Tribunal where an interested person proves that the

   a) mark is being used exclusively by the registered owner;
   b) registered owner is using or permitting its use in contravention of the terms of the collective agreement;

---

[20] ibid s 110(2).
[21] Ibid, s 112(1).
[22] ibid s 113.
[23] ibid s 112(1).

c) registered owner is using or permitting its use in a manner liable to deceive any person as to the origin or other common characteristics of the goods or services concerned.[24]

The Tribunal shall invalidate a certification mark upon request of any interested person where the registered holder

a) has used the mark to certify its own goods and services;
b) has allowed the use of the mark in contravention of the agreement governing the use of the certification mark or in a manner liable to deceive as to the origin or any other common characteristics of the goods or services concerned.[25]

In both cases, the invalidation of the registration of a mark shall be effective from the date of registration of the mark. The decision of the Tribunal shall be notified to the Director, who shall record it and forthwith give notice of the decision in the *Government Gazette*.

An appeal from a determination of the Tribunal may be made to the Supreme Court within twenty-one days from the date of determination.

7. Rights of the Owner and Enforcement Mechanisms against Infringers

The owner of a collective or certification mark and a GI may file a civil or criminal complaint in case of infringement. There has never been any decision rendered by the local courts regarding a GI, collective, or certification mark infringement.

No person shall, without the written agreement of the registered owner, use a registered GI or mark in relation to goods and services for which it has been registered.[26] No person other than a group of producers or a legal entity that groups the producers and carries on an activity in the relevant geographical area has the right to use a registered GI in the course of trade with respect to the goods specified in the relevant Register.[27] The owner of a GI may, where use of any sign similar to the GI or whether the use of such sign in relation to goods and services similar to those for which the GI has been registered is likely to cause confusion in the public, institute court proceedings.[28] Such use by any person other than the owner of the

---

[24] ibid s 101(5).
[25] ibid s 102(5).
[26] ibid s 98(1).
[27] ibid s 109.
[28] ibid s 110(1)(a).

title of protection or licensee and without the owner's agreement is unlawful and is punishable by a fine not exceeding MUR 250,000 and by imprisonment for a term not exceeding five years.[29] The holder of a GI may apply to the Supreme Court for a remedy against an infringer who was infringing its right or is likely to infringe that right. No proceedings shall be initiated after the expiry of five years from when the claimant became aware or had reason to know of the infringing act.[30]

The owner of the registered mark may institute court proceedings against any person who, without its written agreement, uses the mark or does any act likely to cause an infringement. A registered owner may further object, where the use of any sign similar to the registered mark or where the use of such sign in relation to goods and services similar to those for which the mark has been registered is likely to cause confusion in the public.[31]

Under criminal proceedings, the offender is liable to a fine not exceeding MUR 250,000 and imprisonment not exceeding five years. The owner of the right may also lodge a civil complaint. At the owner's request, the court may grant an injunction to prevent an unfair practice or an unlawful act, order damages, and grant any other remedy provided for in law. The damages may cover both economic and moral damages. Mauritian law and practice do not provide any general guidance on how these damages are calculated. In practice, judges have been reluctant to award high damage payments for trade mark infringement. The court may also provide for destroying the infringing goods at the cost of the offender.

The offences mentioned under the IPA also amount to an act of unfair practice and are sanctioned under the Protection against Unfair Practices (Industrial Property Rights) Act (PAUPA). The PAUPA further non-exhaustively enumerates acts that would constitute unfair practices such as acts or practices that are contrary to honest commercial practice, including causing confusion with respect to another's enterprise or activities; damaging another's goodwill or reputation; misleading the public; discrediting another's enterprise or activities; and disclosing, acquiring, or using secret information without the consent of the person lawfully in control of such information. Confusion and damage may occur with regard to a business identifier other than a trade mark or trade name. Specific reference is made to misleading the public with regard to the geographical origin of the products or services.

A complaint of *concurrence déloyale* (unfair competition) may also be brought under articles 1382 and 1383 of the Civil Code based on tortious liability. It should be noted that the offence of passing off, as it exists under English common law, does not apply to Mauritius.

The proceedings for initiating a collective or certification mark infringement case apply to the infringement of a GI. The owner may start civil proceedings either

---

[29] ibid s 139.
[30] ibid s 137.
[31] ibid s 98(3).

by lodging an injunction under section 74 of the Courts Act before the Judge in Chambers and/or by lodging a plaint pursuant to the provisions of the Courts Act, the Supreme Court Rules 2000, the District and Intermediate Courts (Civil Jurisdiction) Act (DICCJA), and any other enabling enactments. The decision should be taken in view of the urgency of the situation. If there is a risk that the infringer might dispose of and/or commercialize the infringed goods, then it would be most suitable to lodge an injunction. To collect evidence prior to a civil court case, it is recommended to have recourse to a bailiff report.

Before initiating proceedings on the merits, the right holder may ask for an interlocutory injunction restraining, prohibiting, and forbidding the other party either personally or through its agents, servants, and employees from dealing in goods that infringe the mark of the right holder; cause confusion or mislead the public; and any other act which constitutes an unfair practice. An application for an injunction is drafted by an attorney and made by means of a *Proecipe* and with a supporting affidavit establishing the facts of the case, together with relevant evidence such as the bailiff report. A prolonged delay between the discovery of an alleged infringement and the lodging of an application before the Judge in Chambers will not entitle the applicant to have recourse to the remedy of an injunctive relief.[32]

The Judge in Chambers may either grant, at the risks and perils of the applicant, an interim order in the nature of an injunction and issue a summons for a subsequent date where the respondent must show cause why the interim order should not be made interlocutory pending the main case, or the judge may decline to grant the interim order, instead issuing a summons for the respondent to appear on a subsequent date to show cause as to why the orders prayed for should not be granted. The court may refuse to issue an interim injunction where 'the correctness of the complaints is not so evident as to be beyond dispute, the defence raised by the respondents denying an infringement is not patently frivolous, any damage suffered as a result of wrongful commercial action will normally be adequately compensated by damages'.[33] Under Mauritian law and practice, an injunction will not lie in favour of the holder in the event that the prejudice caused to it can be adequately compensated in damages if such damages are prayed for in a plaint with summons before the hearing of the injunctive relief. Consequently, if the right holder wishes to initiate an injunction, then it should generally refrain from seeking any damages in the plaint with summons.

The matter is then called on the said date and will be postponed several times to allow for the exchange of affidavits. This takes, at most, eight months. Once the affidavits have been exchanged, the judge sets down the matter for hearing, where respective counsels will offer their arguments and/or submissions. Prior to the hearing, the applicant must lodge a main case in the form of a plaint with

---

[32] *Unilever plc v Manufrance (Ile Maurice) Ltee* (2003) SCJ 167.
[33] *Beau Bebe v Comanu Ltee and Pharmacie Nouvelle Ltee* (2003) SCJ 208.

summons. Otherwise the judge will not grant the interlocutory order. An interlocutory order remains in force as long as the main case is not disposed of.

The judge will take time to deliberate, either converting the interim order into an interlocutory order or discharging the interim order and setting aside the application. The judge will perform a proper balancing exercise between the claim of the parties.

Where an attorney lodges the plaint in court, a first appearance date known as 'Pro Forma New' is granted. The court summons the defendant to be present on that day to give its stand. If the defendant retains the services of legal advisers, the latter shall then apply for a Demand of particulars. The plaintiff will file the Answer to particulars. Once the Answer to particulars is filed, the defendant will file its plea (defence). Once the plea is filed, the matter will be set down for trial by the magistrate/judge. The parties need not be present during the formal matters but should be present, personally or through a legal proxy, on trial day.

Criminal proceedings are triggered by a complaint to the Anti-Piracy Unit of the Mauritian police claiming an infringement of the IPA. In practice, police will request the right holder to provide evidence of the infringing activity by submitting a product purchased from the infringer either through a bailiff or an investigator. In its complaint, the right holder must explain why the products are infringing and how the police can recognize them. If the right holder is represented by an attorney or a trade mark enforcer, the latter has to provide for a power of attorney. If the police are satisfied with the *prima facia* evidence that there has been an infringment, they will proceed to raid the infringer's premises. Contrary to what is the case in most countries, the right holder is never authorized to be present during the raid. As a result of the raid, the litigious products will be seized and carried to the police station, where the right holder has to provide a statement and explain why the products are infringing. The goods are sealed until the trial. The police will complete the investigation and the case file will be transferred to the Director of Public Prosecution (DPP). The DPP has complete power over how the criminal trial will be prosecuted.

8. Customs Enforcement

The owner, authorized user, or nominated representative of a collective mark and a GI may file a preventive border protection application. This allows the Mauritius Revenue Authority, the Mauritian Customs, to suspend the clearance of any goods imported or being exported on the grounds that a collective mark or a GI is likely to be infringed. Customs may further seize suspected infringing goods inland, that is on the domestic territory. The right holder must fill in the prescribed form, show proof of ownership, and provide a bank guarantee to customs. Foreign right holders must be represented by a local agent. Customs process the application and notify the applicant in writing of its decision within seven working days of receipt of the application. When granting an application, the period during which Customs authorities are to act is specified. It is usually two years.

When Customs suspends the release of goods and detains them, the right holder, the importer, the exporter, or his agent are informed of the suspension. The suspension lasts ten working days, renewable once. The right holder must either find an agreement with the importer or file a civil action before the courts. Otherwise, the goods shall be released.

Customs may also suspend, on its own initiative (*ex officio*), the clearance of imported or exported goods that infringe, or are likely to infringe, a GI or collective right for twenty-one working days. Notice may be given electronically or otherwise. This power also extends to the detention of any goods sold on the local market. Where an application is not lodged within twenty-one working days, the Director General shall immediately waive the suspension and clear the goods imported or exported or release the goods being detained.

Goods subject to a court procedure will be kept under customs surveillance until the court renders a judgment. In practice, customs enforcement of intellectual property rights works very efficiently in Mauritius and Customs regularly informs the right holder or its representative of the suspension of suspected infringing goods.[34]

9. Bilateral Agreements

Mauritius, together with three other countries (Madagascar, Seychelles, and Zimbabwe), signed an interim Economic Partnership Agreement (EPA) with the European Union (EU) in August 2009. The Agreement is provisionally applied since 14 May 2012. Comoros signed in July 2017.[35] The EPA provides for a 'rendezvous clause' to continue negotiations on intellectual property rights (which presumably includes GI) with a view to concluding a full and comprehensive EPA.[36] At the tenth round of negotiations between the EU and the five signatories, the signatories refused to engage in a textual discussion on GIs.[37]

---

[34] More information may be found on customs enforcement in Mauritius in Marius Schneider and Vanessa Ferguson, *Enforcement of Intellectual Property Rights in Africa* (OUP 2020) 541–46.

[35] European Commission, 'Eastern and Southern Africa (ESA)' (*European Commission*, nd) <https://policy.trade.ec.europa.eu/eu-trade-relationships-country-and-region/countries-and-regions/eastern-and-southern-africa-esa_en>.

[36] 'Interim Agreement establishing a framework for an Economic Partnership Agreement between the Eastern and Southern Africa States, on the one part, and the European Community and its Member States, on the other part' (*Official Journal of the European Union*, 24 April 2012) art 53(e)(iv).

[37] European Commission, 'Report on the 10th Round of Negotiations between the European Union and Five Eastern and Southern Africa (ESA5) Countries for the Deepening of the Currently Implemented Economic Partnership Agreement 12–16 December 2022 in Brussels' (20 December 2022) 2.

14
Morocco

Morocco is located in the Maghreb region in North West Africa. It borders the Atlantic Ocean, the Mediterranean Sea, Algeria, and Mauritania. It has an area of 710,850 km² for a population of 37.45 million in 2022. The official languages in Morocco are Arabic and Berber. Most Moroccans, however, speak an Arabic dialect called 'Darija'. French is widely used in governmental institutions and large companies and is the language of diplomacy and business. Over 10 million Moroccans are French speakers (one-third of the population). Spanish is spoken mainly in North Morocco by about five million Moroccans; English is the third most-spoken foreign language with two million speakers, most of them graduates. The working week is from Monday to Friday, and the local currency is the Moroccan Dirham (MAD).

With its rich and fertile land, it is no surprise that the agricultural sector is integral to Morocco's economy. Agriculture employed 34.14 per cent of the workforce in 2020[1] and contributed to 12 per cent of the country's gross domestic profit (GDP) in 2021.[2] The country's main crops are cereals, olives, argan, and fruits. Still, Morocco consistently imports more agricultural products than it exports.[3] The main trading partners for food imports for Morocco in 2019 were, in order of importance, Brazil, the United States, France, Argentina, and Mexico.[4] The industrial sector, comprising of textiles, food processing, and oil refineries, contributes 26.1 per cent of the GDP and employs 23 per cent of the workforce. Finally, the services sector, spearheaded by tourism, employs 43.6 per cent of the workforce and accounts for over half of the country's GDP.[5]

Morocco is the fifth largest economy in Africa based on a GDP of USD 124 billion in 2021. It is estimated that the upper and middle class in Morocco account

---

[1] Trading Economics, 'Morocco—Employment in Agriculture (% of Total Employment)' (*Trading Economics*, nd) <https://tradingeconomics.com/morocco/employment-in-agriculture-percent-of-total-employment-wb-data.html>.

[2] Statista, 'Morocco: Distribution of Gross Domestic Product (GDP) across Economic Sectors from 2011 to 2021' (*Statista*, nd) <www.statista.com/statistics/502771/morocco-gdp-distribution-across-economic-sectors>.

[3] Fatima Ezzahra Mengoub and others, 'The Russia–Ukraine War and Food Security in Morocco' (Policy Center for the New South 2022) 17.

[4] World Integrated Trade Solution, 'Morocco Food Products Imports by Country in US$ Thousand 2019' (*World Integrated Trade Solution*, nd) <https://wits.worldbank.org/CountryProfile/en/Country/MAR/Year/2019/TradeFlow/Import/Partner/by-country/Product/16-24_FoodProd>.

[5] Lloyds Bank, 'Morocco: Economic and Political Overview' (*Lloyds Bank*, April 2023) <www.lloydsbanktrade.com/en/market-potential/morocco/economical-context>.

for 66 per cent of the population.[6] The luxury goods market is well developed, amounting to USD 480.3 million in USD and expected to grow by 5.63 per cent annually.[7] No doubt, this market segment also takes advantage of the presence of tourists in Morocco. Although traditional retailing is still dominant, modern retail formats are coming up, particularly in the cities of Casablanca, Marrakech, Tangiers, and Rabat.

E-commerce is expected to rise over the coming years, boosted by the high internet penetration rate of about 75 per cent (the second highest in Africa) and rising smartphone use. Currently, e-commerce is dominated by Jumia Technologies AG and Hmizate, holding around 80 per cent of the business. Cash-on-delivery is the preferred mode of payment.[8] Credit card use is slowly becoming more common but is plagued by high instances of credit card fraud.[9]

Morocco's agricultural policy valorizes locally made produce, as can be seen in *Plan Maroc Vert* ('Green Morocco Plan'), a state-driven plan to transform agriculture into a pillar of the economy. The concept of *terroir* and the use of a distinctive sign as an indication of origin and quality are widely accepted. It is thus possible in Morocco to register geographical indications (GIs), *Appellations d'origine* (designations of origin), and *labels agricoles* (agricultural labels). By February 2022, sixty-one GIs and six designations of origin were registered in Morocco.[10] Protected GIs include *Argan Oil*, *Clementines of Berkane*, and *Majhoul Dates of Tafilalet*. Protected designations of origin include *Tyout Chiadma Olive Oil*, *Taliouine Saffron*, and *Oulmes Lavender Essential Oils*. Najda dates and lamb are protected under the agricultural label.[11] *Argan Oil* was the first African GI registered under a *sui generis* system in 2010.[12]

Moroccan wines and handicrafts are also protected under specific Moroccan intellectual property (IP) regimes. Wines benefit from the guaranteed designation of origin. Handicrafts may be recognized either under the national or regional label of the craft industry or the GI of the craft industry.[13] While 'Morocco Handmade' is the umbrella national label for handicrafts, there are a number of regional labels

---

[6] Florence Batsy-Hamimi, 'Une classe moyenne au Maroc ?' (2011) 2(102) Les Cahiers de l'Orient 35.
[7] Statista, 'Luxury Goods—Morocco' (*Statista*, nd) <www.statista.com/outlook/cmo/luxury-goods/morocco#revenue>.
[8] Kearney, 'Leapfrogging into the Future of Retail: The 2021 Global Retail Development Index' (*Kearney*, nd) <www.kearney.com/global-retail-development-index/2021>.
[9] Privacy Shield Framework, 'Morocco—eCommerce' (*Privacy Shield Framework*, nd) <www.privacyshield.gov/article?id=Morocco-eCommerce>.
[10] Moroccan Industrial and Commercial Property Office (OMPIC), 'Registre National des Indications Géographiques et Appellations d'Origine' (*OMPIC*, nd) <www.ompic.ma/sites/default/files/Registre%20National%20IG-AO.pdf>. The authors could not find the latest updated figure for products bearing an agricultural label. The latest figure available is two by the end of 2015.
[11] ibid.
[12] Monique Bagal and others, *Manual for Geographical Indications in Africa* (2nd edn, European Union Intellectual Property Office 2023) 4.
[13] Law No 133-12 relating to the Distinctive Signs of Handicraft Products promulgated by the Dahir of 27 April 2016.

such as 'Handicraft Marrakesh Safi' and 'Artisanat Souss Massa'.[14] By February 2022, there was yet to be a GI for the craft industry, although the Ministry of Tourism and Handicrafts had made progress on the topic.[15]

Morocco applied to the European Commission to register Argan oil as a protected GI in October 2011. This application was among the first applications coming from the African continent. It has yet to be accepted. Some have argued that this could be due to the existence of prior rights,[16] others to the fact that the Argan tree is also indigenous to south-west Algeria.[17] However, Argan oil is produced only in Morocco.

1. Legal Framework

The Moroccan legal system is based on both civil law (French system) and Islamic law. Even today, French case law can have authoritative value in Morocco in specific areas of the law.

The court system in Morocco is composed of neighbourhood courts (formerly community and district courts), courts of first instance, the appeal courts, and the Supreme Court. Neighbourhood courts hear all personal estate actions of less than 1,000 MAD brought against individuals who reside under their jurisdiction. Cases are heard before a single, non-professional judge. Courts of first instance hear all civil, social, and commercial matters, personal status, and real property cases. In cases where the value of the matter is less than 30,000 MAD, the court is the first and final instance. In cases where the value of the matter exceeds 30,000 MAD, the judgment is susceptible to appeal. Courts of first instance also hear criminal cases involving petty offences and misdemeanours and offences that are punishable by a sentence of more than one month in prison and a fine of more than 1,200 MAD. The presiding judge of the court of first instance has personal jurisdiction in summary and urgent matters as well as for *ex parte* orders. Appeal courts try criminal cases and hear appeals against judgments passed by courts of first instance. The highest court with the ultimate power of review is the Supreme Court. The Supreme Court is a Court of Cassation, which means it hears appeals only on issues of law. When a petition is granted and ruled on, the case is referred back to an appeal court to decide on questions of both fact and law.

---

[14] Royaume du Maroc Ministère du Tourisme, de l'Artisanat et de l'Economie Sociale et Solidaire, 'L'innovation dans le secteur de l'artisanat' (*Royaume du Maroc Ministère du Tourisme, de l'Artisanat et de l'Economie Sociale et Solidaire*, nd) <https://mtaess.gov.ma/fr/artisanat/qualite-et-innovation>.
[15] Republique francaise and National Industrial Property Institute (INPI), *La propriété intellectuelle au Maroc* (2022) 3.
[16] Annarita Antonelli and Hélène Ilbert, 'Legal Protection of Mediterranean Products' in International Centre for Advanced Mediterranean Agronomic Studies (CIHEAM) (ed.), *MediTERRA 2012: The Mediterranean Diet for Sustainable Regional Development* (Presses de Sciences Po 2012) 339.
[17] Dirk Troskie, 'Africa on the Rise' (2022) 19(1) Agriprobe 30.

Special commercial courts have exclusive jurisdiction to hear trade disputes and the sole competence to entertain cases involving industrial property rights, irrespective of the nature of the parties. From filing an action until judgment, the average case takes eighteen months. Still, the lack of training for judges on general commercial and IP matters, the resource-intensive nature of litigation, and the fact that there is no legal requirement with respect to case publishing all prove challenging to effective commercial dispute resolution in the country.

The legal profession in Morocco comprises lawyers who act as legal counsel and may draft any legal but not authenticated documents and notaries who draw authenticated legal documents.

2. Domestic Legislation on GIs

Morocco has been a member of the Paris Convention for the Protection of Industrial Property of 1883 since February 1917. Morocco is a party to the Madrid Protocol for the International Registration of Trade Marks of 2007(Madrid System) since October 1999 and to the Lisbon Agreement for the Protection of Appellations of Origin and their International Registration of 1958 since October 1958. Morocco is a member of the World Trade Organization (WTO). The transition period available to put into effect national legislation implementing the WTO Agreement on Trade-Related Aspects of Intellectual Property Rights (TRIPS) expired on 31 December 1999.

Law No 17-97 as amended and completed by Law Nos 23-13 and 31-05 as amended over the years (Umbrella Law No 17-97) governs the protection of GIs and designation of origin. This is the umbrella IP law for Morocco. A number of other product-specific legislations complement Umbrella Law No 17-97. Law No 25-06, related to distinctive signs of origin and quality of food and agricultural and fish products (Law No 25-06 on food) adopted in 2008 provides for the registration of three different labels for food, agricultural, and fish products: agricultural or fishing labels, protected designations of origin (PDO) and protected geographical indications (PGI). Article 16 of Law No 25-06 on food provides that every registered foreign GI or designation of origin may be recognized in Morocco in accordance with Law No 25-06 on food.

Designations of origin for wines are protected under Decree No 2.75.321 of 12 August 1977 regulating wine-making and the stocking, circulation, and trading of wines and Order No 869-75 of the Minister of Agriculture and Agrarian Reform regulating the designation of origin regime for wines of 15 August 1977. The law provides for fourteen geographical areas in Morocco whose wine production is entitled to the title *Appellation d'origine garantie* ('guaranteed designations of origin'). Moroccan wines may also benefit from the indication *Appellation d'origine contrôlée* ('controlled designation of origin') under Decree No 1955-98 of 8 October 1998 relating to the general conditions of production of controlled designation of origin. There are currently three controlled designations of origin in Morocco.[18] A controlled designation of origin imposes more stringent conditions than a guaranteed designation of origin. Wines produced out of Morocco are also protected under the Decree No 2.75.321. The Decree provides for what may be labelled as wine and which wines may benefit from the denominations 'selected wine', 'old wine', 'sparkling wine', 'semi-sparkling wine', and 'liqueur wine'. *Champagne* is the only GI that is mentioned by name in the Decree at article 19(3). It is forbidden to use any derivative of the term 'Champagne' to designate sparkling wine that is not entitled to be designated as *Champagne*. This prohibition applies to packaging, stoppers, labels, invoices, and advertisements. The term *méthode champenoise* ('champagne method') may, however, be used for wines made sparkling by natural fermentation in the bottle subject to certain conditions.

Another important law is Law No 133-12 on distinctive signs for handicrafts (Law No 133-12 on handicrafts). Law No 133-12 on handicrafts created two distinctive signs for handicrafts: the national or regional label for handicrafts and the GI of handicrafts. A product benefiting from the national or regional label of the craft industry is a high-quality product with a series of characteristics and qualities due to its condition of production, manufacture, or geographical origin.[19] In practice, while the regional label guarantees that the product possesses particular characteristics due to its origin, whether raw material or particular know-how, the national label is concerned with manufacturing the products in Morocco. It does not require any specific link or characteristics attached to this origin. The regional label is thus more akin to a GI than the national label. A product benefiting from the GI of the craft industry is a product whose quality, reputation, or other characteristic is due essentially to the geographical origin of the product.[20] Law No 133-12 on handicrafts is silent as to the possibility for foreign right holders to register any sign under the law. Upon seeing the signs adopted for Morocco's national and regional labels, these are clearly intended for Moroccan handicrafts. Foreigners may, however, have recourse to Umbrella Law No 17-97, which puts no restriction as to the type of goods to register handicrafts.

Collective and certification marks are also available in Morocco. The Agency for Agricultural Development thus registered the collective mark 'Terroir du Maroc' on behalf of the Ministry of Agriculture to promote Moroccan products.[21]

---

[18] Office national de Sécurité Sanitaire des produits Alimentaires, 'Obtention du label d'appellation d'origine garantie (AOG) et contrôlée (AOC) des vins' (*Office National de Sécurité Sanitaire des produits Alimentaires*, nd) <www.onssa.gov.ma/controle-des-produits-alimentaires/produits-vegetaux-et-d-origine-vegetale/agrements-et-labels-qualite/obtention-du-aog-et-controlee-aoc-des-vins>.
[19] Law No 133-12 (n 13) art 3.
[20] ibid.
[21] Agence pour le developpement agricole, *Guide de l'investisseur dans le secteur agricole au Maroc* (2018) 19.

3. Registration of GIs Domestically

3.1 GIs

Umbrella Law No 17-97 defines a GI as any indication designating a product as originating from the region or locality of a territory, where the quality, reputation, or other characteristics can be essentially attributed to the geographic origin.[22] Law No 133-12 on handicrafts retains a somewhat similar definition. The definition under Law Nos 17-97 and 133-12 closely follow article 22(1) of the TRIPS Agreement. In comparison, Law No 25-06 on food defines a GI as the name used to identify a product as originating in a territory, region, or locality where a given quality, reputation, or other characteristic of the product can be essentially attributed to that geographical origin and the production, and/or processing, and/or preparation takes place in the defined geographical area.[23] Law No 25-06 on food is thus more stringent.

Umbrella Law No 17-97 defines a designation of origin as the geographical name of a country, region, or locality used to designate a product originating from and whose quality, reputation, or other characteristics are due exclusively or essentially to the geographical environment, including human and natural factors.[24] Law No 25-06 on food retains the same definition for a designation of origin with the additional requirement that production, processing, and preparation take place in the defined geographical area.[25] The requirements for a designation of origin are thus more stringent than for a GI. There is no provision for a designation of origin for handicrafts under Law No 133-12 on handicrafts.

Law No 25-06 on food also provides for agricultural labels. A product benefiting from an agricultural label is one that is recognized as having a set of special qualities and properties and that shows a high-quality level, higher than that of similar products over which it is distinguished because of its production and manufacturing circumstances and, if any, because of its geographical origin.[26] The product's geographical origin could be one of a number of characteristics, but there is no compulsory link as for a GI or designation of origin. The agricultural label is not open to foreign right holders. Likewise, the distinctive signs for wines are open only to Moroccan wines.

3.2 Collective and certification marks

Morocco offers the possibility to register both collective and certification marks. The mark is said to be collective when it can be used by any person respecting the

---

[22] Umbrella Law No 17-97, art 180.
[23] Law No 25-06 on food, art 2.
[24] Umbrella Law No 17-97, art 181.
[25] Law No 25-06 on food, art 2.
[26] ibid.

rules of use established by the owner of the registration. A certification mark is applied to the product or service that has as regard its nature, properties, or qualities, certain characteristics specified in its regulations.[27] The use of a certification mark does not imply belonging to an association.

4. Registrability of Names

4.1 GIs

Under Umbrella Law No 17-97, a GI may be any sign or combination of signs such as words, including geographical and personal names, letters, numerals, figurative elements, and colours, including single colours, in any form.[28] A designation of origin must be the name of a county, region, or locality.[29]

Law No 25-06 on food excludes as a designation of origin or GI any name that

a) conflicts with the name of a plant variety or animal breed and is therefore liable to mislead the consumer as to the true origin of the product;
b) has become generic;
c) is homonymous with the name of the product. However, a homonymous name may be recognized if it is a traditional name.[30]

As to handicrafts, under article 9 of Law No 133-12 on handicrafts, the generic name of a product cannot be recognized as a protected name.

4.2 Collective and certification marks

Although a geographical name may constitute a sign registerable as a mark,[31] a sign or denomination that may serve to designate a characteristic of the product or service, including its geographical origin is not considered distinctive and cannot be registered as mark.[32] It is further not possible to register as a mark or as part of a mark a GI or designation of origin of a product or service that is likely to mislead the public, namely as to the nature, quality, or origin of the goods or services, the geographical origin, or the designation of origin.[33] Finally, a sign may not be

---

[27] Umbrella Law No 17-97, art 166.
[28] ibid art 180.
[29] ibid art 181.
[30] Law No 25-06 on food, art 24.
[31] Umbrella Law No 17-97, art 133(a).
[32] ibid art 134.
[33] ibid art 135(c).

registered where it infringes prior rights such as those of an indication of origin or a protective designation of origin.[34]

5. Procedure and Requirements for Registration

5.1 GIs

The registration of GIs and designations of origin in Morocco involves two institutions: the Moroccan Industrial and Commercial Property Office (OMPIC) and the National Commission for Distinctive Signs of Origin (NCDO).

Umbrella Law No 17-97 does not explicitly provide who may introduce the demand for the registration of a designation of origin or GI in Morocco. It is, however, accepted that a grouping must make the request for the registration of a GI and designation of origin. For GIs and designations of origin for food, agricultural, and fish products under Law No 25-06 on food, applicants may be producers and/or transformers grouped in an association, cooperative, or any other professional group, local authorities, or interested public institutions. Individuals and other legal entities may join the application.[35] Applications under Umbrella Law No 17-97 are filed with the OMPIC, while applications under Law No 25-06 on food are filed with the Ministry of Agriculture. A foreign grouping must be represented by a Moroccan agent.

There is no standard application form under Umbrella Law No 17-97. Applicants may, however, rely on the provisions of Law No 25-06 on food for guidance as to the content of the application. Applicants must provide a list of specifications stating the name of the product; delimitations of the geographical area, proof that the product originates from the region, proof of the link between the quality and characteristics and the geographical origin, characteristics of the product, methods of production, references of the certification organisms, labelling specifications, agreement of participants to keep records for control purposes, a control plan for the certification organisms, and any other requirements with regard to hygiene and quality.[36]

Every application under Umbrella No 17-97 is inputted in the national register of GIs and designations of origin. The application is published for opposition for two months as of publication date. The owner of a protected trade mark, GI, or designation of origin may oppose the application within two months from publication through a declaration. The opponent must state the existence of its rights and the reasons behind the opposition.

---

[34] ibid art 137(d).
[35] Law No 25-06 on food, art 8.
[36] ibid art 9.

In an opposition procedure under Umbrella Law No 17-97, the OMPIC is the relay between the applicant, the opponent, and the relevant governmental authority. The OMPIC receives all oppositions and forwards them to the relevant governmental authority. The OMPIC also informs the applicant or its agent by registered letter and invites them to respond within two months of receiving the letter. Any reply received by the OMPIC from the applicant or its agent is promptly forwarded to the relevant governmental authority. The opponent is also informed and allowed fifteen days to present its observations. The relevant governmental authority decides on the opposition and provides a reasoned decision. The decision is communicated to the OMPIC, the applicant, and the opponent.

The opposition procedure concludes where

a) the opponent has lost its legal standing, i.e., it is no longer the owner of a protected trade mark, GI, or designation of origin;
b) the opposition has become devoid of purpose following a mutual agreement of the applicant and the opponent. In this case, the agreement shall be sent by the opponent to OMPIC by registered letter with acknowledgement of receipt; or
c) the application is withdrawn.[37]

Where there has been no opposition to the published application or if the opposition is rejected, the GI or designation of origin is entered in the national register and published.

In the case of an application under Law No 25-06 on food, the application is published to allow the NCDO, which is established under the government authority in charge of agriculture, to draw a list of producers of the same type of goods but situated outside of the relevant geographical area and to allow for declarations of opposition by interested parties, both within two months of publication.[38] The declarations are only receivable where they prove that the requested sign does not conform to the definitions provided under the law or that the requested denomination conflicts with a plant variety or animal breed or is a name that has become generic or homonymous with a published denomination. The NCDO comments on the acceptability of the application, taking into account the declaration of oppositions received. The NCDO comments on both local and foreign applications. The Ministry of Agriculture and Fisheries has the final word on the application but considers the comments from the NCDO. The grant of a sign is published in the *Official Bulletin*.

The registration procedure for handicrafts is rather similar to Law No 25-06 on food. An application for a GI for a handicraft must be brought by producers and/or transformers grouped in an association, cooperative, or any other professional

---

[37] Ibid, art 182.2
[38] ibid art 12.

group, local authorities, or interested public institutions. Individuals and other moral entities may join the application after the application has been filed.[39] A draft list of specifications, which follows closely the list of specifications provided under Law No 25-06 on food, must be provided. The National Commission for distinctive signs for handicrafts publishes the application. The aim is to draw a list of producers of the same type of goods and allow for opposition declarations by interested parties within two months of publication. The declarations are only receivable where they prove that the requested sign does not conform to the definitions provided under the law.[40] The Commission comments on the application, taking into account the declaration of oppositions received. The Ministry of Handicrafts decides to grant or refuse an application. The grant of a sign for handicrafts is published in the *Official Bulletin*.

5.2 Collective and certification marks

The application procedure for a collective or certification mark is highly similar to a trade mark application but must also include a copy of the regulations governing their use, duly certified by the applicant. The regulations must state the common characteristics or qualities of the goods or services the mark is to designate, the conditions under which the mark may be used, and the persons authorized to use it.[41] The regulations may be provided together with the application or within three months from the date of the application. A certification mark may only be applied for by a legal entity that is neither the manufacturer, importer, or seller of the product or services.

Applications for both collective and certification marks are received by the OMPIC and examined on absolute grounds and for formal requirements. The application will not be examined on relative grounds, although the opposition procedure allows objections based on relative grounds. An opposition must be initiated within two months of the publication of the application. For a collective or certification mark, the opposition is heard and decided upon by the OMPIC.

6. Term of Protection

6.1 GIs

There is no set limit on the validity of a GI or designation of origin. A designation of origin or GI recognized under Law No 25-06 on food may, however, never become generic or fall in the public domain.[42]

---

[39] Law No 133-12 (n 13) art 6.
[40] ibid art 11.
[41] Umbrella Law No 17-97, art 170.
[42] Law No 25-06 on food, art 33.

The owner of a GI or a designation of origin may bring an action for nullity against an improperly registered trade mark.[43]

6.2 Collective and certification marks

A collective and certification mark is valid for ten years as from the filing date and renewable indefinitely. At any time, the owner of a collective or certification mark may communicate in writing to the OMPIC any change in the rules governing the mark. Such changes are entered in the National Register of Trade Marks.

7. Rights of the Owner and Enforcement Mechanisms against Infringers

7.1 GIs

Any infringement of the rights of the owner of a GI or a designation of origin constitutes an offence. Under Umbrella Law No 17-97, the direct or indirect use of a false or misleading indication concerning the origin of a product or service, or the identity of the producer, manufacturer, or trader, or the direct or indirect use of a false GI or designation of origin, or the imitation of a GI or a designation of origin, even if the true origin of the product is indicated or if the designation is used in translation or accompanied by expressions such as 'kind', 'manner', 'imitation', or similar, is considered unlawful.[44] Such infringements also constitute the offence of counterfeiting. These offences are punishable by two to six months' imprisonment and/or a fine of 50,000–500,000 MAD.

Usually, a criminal procedure will start through a complaint filed with the authorities (most likely the Royal Gendarmerie or the police). While a registered GI or designation of origin is necessary for a criminal complaint brought by the registered owner, the public action brought by the public prosecutor may apply to an unregistered GI and designation of origin outside of any complaint.[45] A raid will then be conducted, and the case will be forwarded to the Public Prosecutor. Once the case has been forwarded to the Public Prosecutor, an action for damages in the context of a civil action ancillary to the criminal action may also be brought by any injured party; natural or legal person; association or trade union; and in particular by producers, manufacturers, or traders who can correctly identify

---

[43] Umbrella Law No 17-97, art 161.
[44] ibid art 182.
[45] Mohamed Jaouhar, 'Le droit marocain des indications géographiques et des appellations d'origine' (2018) 57 REMADEG 24.

their products or services with the indication or designation in question or their representatives without prejudice to the right of recourse to civil action or the right to claim protective measures. Surprisingly, article 202 of Umbrella No 17-97, which provides for who may sue for counterfeiting, excludes the owner of a GI or designation of origin from such a possibility. Therefore, it must be assumed that an action for counterfeiting of a GI or designation of origin is only open for public action.

The offence of counterfeiting may also be prosecuted as a civil claim. In this case, the right owner must file a seizure petition before the court where the infringing goods are, requesting the appointment of a bailiff. Once the petition has been granted, the bailiff shall proceed with the seizure, with or without the real detention of counterfeit goods (*saisie contrefaçon*). The main case must be filed before the Tribunal of Commerce within thirty days of the seizure.

Umbrella Law No 17-97 also provides for the offence of unfair competition. Unfair competition is constituted by any act of competition contrary to honest practices in industrial or commercial matters. These include indications or claims the use of which, in the course of trade, are likely to mislead the public as to the nature, method of manufacture, characteristics, or suitability for use of the goods.[46] Acts of unfair competition may only give rise to civil action so as to put an end to the infringement and obtain damages.[47]

When an action for counterfeiting or unfair competition is filed in court, its president, ruling in summary proceedings, may prohibit, on a provisional basis, under penalty, the continuation of the alleged infringing acts or make such continuation subject to the provision of guarantees intended to ensure the compensation of the right owner or the beneficiary of an exclusive right of exploitation. This prohibition shall be ordered against a party to the infringement action or, where appropriate, against a third party to prevent an act of infringement and the introduction into commercial channels of counterfeit products. The request for prohibition or the provision of guarantees is allowed only if the action on the merits appears to be serious and has been brought within a maximum of thirty days from the day the owner became aware of the facts on which it is based. The judge may make the prohibition conditional on the provision by the claimant of guarantees to ensure the possible compensation of the defendant if the infringement action is later found unfounded.[48]

It is the court where the defendant is domiciled that is competent. A civil or criminal action is time-barred after three years from the date of the events giving rise to them. Introducing an action for damages in the context of a civil action ancillary to the criminal action suspends the limitation period of the criminal action.

---

[46] Umbrella Law No 17-97, art 184.
[47] ibid art 185.
[48] ibid art 203.

Those condemned for counterfeiting or an act of unfair competition may, in addition to a fine and/or imprisonment, be deprived for up to five years of the right to belong to a professional chamber. Final judicial decisions are published.

Those who use or apply without the necessary certification a distinctive sign registered under Law No 25-06 on food are punishable by a fine of 50–50,000 MAD.[49] The same penalty applies to anyone using

- a) a label for products bearing a GI or designation of origin where the label could create confusion in the mind of the consumer as to the nature, identity, qualities, or real origin of the product;
- b) an indication for sale, labelling and advertisement that is likely to mislead the consumer on the origin or the characteristics of the product or to undermine the specificity of the GI or designation of origin;
- c) a mode of presentation likely to mislead the consumer as to the real origin of the product, in particular by making believe that it benefits from a distinctive sign of origin or quality;
- d) a GI or designation of origin for an unrelated product so as to misappropriate or weaken the reputation of the said distinctive signs of origin and quality.[50]

The sanctions under Umbrella Law No 17-97 and Law No 25-06 on food apply without prejudice to the penalties provided for under Law No 13-83 on the repression of fraud in goods.[51] Sanctions under Umbrella Law No 17-97 also apply without prejudice to the sanctions provided under Law No 25-06 on food.[52] Law No 13-83 on the repression of fraud in goods provides for imprisonment of between six months and five years and/or a fine of 1,200–24,000 MAD in case of fraud or falsification on the substance or quality of the product. The court may further order the publication of the judgment in newspapers and on the door of the relevant outlet. In case of recidivism within five years of condemnation, the court must pronounce a sentence of imprisonment and the publication of the condemnation.[53] The same penalties are applicable where the offender has misled, or attempted to mislead, on the nature, the substantial qualities, the composition, and the content in useful principles of any goods or on their kind or origin when, according to convention or usage, the designation of the kind or origin is the main motivation for contracting.[54]

---

[49] Law No 25-06 on food, art 37.
[50] ibid art 38.
[51] Umbrella Law No 17-97, art 231.
[52] Law No 25-06 on food, art 38.
[53] Law No 13-83 on the repression of fraud in goods, art 1.
[54] ibid art 4.

7.2 Collective and certification marks

The provisions relating to counterfeiting of GIs and/or designation of origin apply to collective and certification marks.

8. Customs Enforcement

It is possible for the owner or representative of a GI, a designation of origin, a collective, or certification mark to file a preventative border protection application. This allows Moroccan customs to detain any counterfeit goods being imported, exported, or in transit at all the ports of entry in Morocco. This procedure is quite effective.

The right holder may file a preventative customs recordal by providing to customs, among other things, proof of its right, a power of attorney (where a representative files the application), and information on genuine and counterfeit goods. Once the application for customs recordal is accepted by customs, all the services in the ports of entry in Morocco are notified, and instructions will be given to them to suspend and seize products suspected to be counterfeited. The validity period of the customs recordal is one year, renewable every year.

Upon seizure of goods suspected to be counterfeits, customs shall immediately inform the right holder via a letter of the existence of the suspected counterfeit products. The declarant or holder of the goods is also informed. To prevent the release of the detained goods, the right holder must either find an agreement with the importer within ten working days or institute legal proceedings. The latter entails requesting a formal order from the president of the tribunal of commerce of the place of the importation of the suspended goods to undertake a descriptive seizure by a bailiff at the port of entry within a maximum delay of ten days from the date of notification. The bailiff report will be the legal ground for initiating civil proceedings. Within thirty days from the date of descriptive seizure, the right holder must institute a court action as to the merit before the tribunal of commerce, requesting the destruction of the seized products, the payment of damages, and/or the publication of the judgment in two newspapers. The right holder may further request an order for the infringer to cease the importation and/or commercialization of the infringing goods.

Customs may, in theory, also suspend, on its initiative (*ex officio*), the clearance of goods suspected to be counterfeit. The procedure shall be the same as described above.[55] In practice, *ex officio* suspensions are rare, and right holders are better off filing a preventative customs recordal.[56]

---

[55] Law on Industrial Property, art 176.4.
[56] More information may be found on customs enforcement in Morocco in Marius Schneider and Vanessa Ferguson, *Enforcement of Intellectual Property Rights in Africa* (OUP 2020) 560–65.

9. Bilateral Agreements

Since January 2015, an agreement on the mutual protection of agri-food products with GIs has been in force between Morocco and the European Union (EU). The agreement covers some 3,200 European products (processed agricultural products, wines, spirits, and aromatized wines) and thirty Moroccan products. All names covered by the agreement are directly and automatically protected since the agreement's entry into force. The names listed are protected against any direct or indirect commercial use; any misuse, imitation, or evocation of the product; any other false or misleading indication as to the provenance, origin, nature, or essential qualities of the product; or any other practice liable to mislead the consumer as to the true origin of the product. The EU and Morocco must enforce the protection provided for by appropriate administrative and legal action through their public authorities. They must also enforce such protection at the request of an interested party. Such protection goes beyond what is provided for under the TRIPS Agreement.

During the negotiations, the issue arose as to whether goods registered in Morocco but originating from Western Sahara could be protected under the agreement. Western Sahara is a disputed territory: while Morocco has claimed authority over it since 1975, the United Nations classifies Western Sahara as a non-self-governing territory and does not recognize Moroccan control. The contested products are the *Camel cheese from the Sahara*, which benefits from the agricultural label since 2018, and the *Camel milk from the Sahara*, benefiting from a GI since 2017. The geographical delimitation of these products is situated entirely in the disputed Western Sahara.[57]

The Court of Justice of the European Union ruled that no EU Trade or Association Agreement could be applied to Western Sahara because it has a 'separate and distinct status' from Morocco.[58]

Morocco also signed a free trade agreement (FTA) with the United States on 15 June 2004. The Agreement entered into force on 1 January 2006.[59] Under the FTA, Morocco and the United States must provide that the owner of a registered trade mark shall have the exclusive right to prevent all third parties not having the owner's consent from using, in the course of trade, identical or similar signs, including GIs, for goods or services that are related to those goods or services in respect of which the owner's trade mark is registered, where such use would result in a likelihood

---

[57] Western Sahara Occupation Watch, 'UE et la reconnaissance' (*Western Sahara Occupation Watch*, 30 March 2018) <https://wsrw.org/fr/archive/4149>.
[58] Case C-104/16 p*Council of the European Union, Belgium (intervening) and ors (intervening) v Front populaire pour la libération de la saguia-el-hamra et du rio de oro (Front Polisario)* [2016].
[59] Office of the United States Trade Representative, 'Morocco Free Trade Agreement' (*Office of the United States Trade Representative*, nd) <https://ustr.gov/trade-agreements/free-trade-agreements/morocco-fta>.

of confusion. A likelihood of confusion is presumed when using an identical sign, including a GI, for identical goods or services.[60] The FTA also touches on the definition of a GI, which is similar to the one under TRIPS, and the requirements for the registration of GIs, including the publication of the application for opposition and the possibility to cancel a registration.[61] Additionally, the FTA provides for the relationship between GIs and trade marks. It shall be a ground for refusing protection or recognition of a GI where the GI is likely to be confusingly similar to a trade mark that is the subject of a good-faith pending application or registration or the GI is confusingly similar to a pre-existing trade mark, the rights to which have been acquired in the territory of the country through use in good faith.[62] Thus, the FTA provides the principle of 'first-in-time, first-in-right' application.

---

[60] FTA, art 15.2(4).
[61] ibid art 15.3(1).
[62] ibid art 15.3(2).

15
Nigeria

Located in West Africa with a coastline on the Gulf of Guinea, Nigeria is bordered by Niger, Chad, Cameroon, and Benin. Nigeria is 923,768 km². With more than 218 million inhabitants in 2022, Nigeria is the most populous country in Africa and the seventh most populous country in the world. English is the accepted official language in Nigeria and is used by the administration, in court, in schools, and the business environment. The working week is from Monday to Friday, and the national currency is the Nigerian Naira (NGN).

Since the discovery of oil in 1956, Nigeria has become Africa's biggest oil exporter. Oil accounts for about 80 per cent of the country's export earnings and around 50 per cent of total government revenues.[1] As such, Nigeria is particularly vulnerable to any drop in the oil price. Nigeria also holds the largest natural gas reserves in the continent and is endowed with significant natural resources, such as coal, tin, and zinc. Agriculture remains a vital industry, accounting for approximately 20 per cent of the gross domestic product (GDP) and employing over 36 per cent of the country's workforce, making it the largest employer in Nigeria.[2] Other important industries are financial services, information and communication technology, and consumer goods.

Since the rebasing of its GDP in 2014, whereby Nigeria updated the sectors factored in its GDP calculation, Nigeria has become the largest economy in Africa.[3] It alone contributes approximately 20 per cent of the African continent's GDP.[4] Today, Nigeria is ranked third in Africa with regard to the number of millionaires in the country.[5] Twenty-three per cent of the country accounts for middle class and this percentage is growing. However, income inequality in Nigeria is high; over 40 per cent of the population lives under the country's poverty line.[6]

---

[1] World Bank, 'The World Bank in Nigeria: Overview' (*World Bank*, 31 March 2023) <www.worldbank.org/en/country/nigeria/overview>.

[2] Taiwo Oyaniran, 'Current State of Nigeria Agriculture and Agribusiness Sector' (*Pwc*, September 2020) <www.pwc.com/ng/en/assets/pdf/afcfta-agribusiness-current-state-nigeria-agriculture-sector.pdf>.

[3] Uri Friedman, 'How Nigeria Became Africa's Largest Economy Overnight' (*The Atlantic*, 8 April 2014) <www.theatlantic.com/international/archive/2014/04/how-nigeria-became-africas-largest-economy-overnight/360288>.

[4] Persianas, 'Overview of Nigeria' (*Persianas*, nd) <www.persianasgroup.com/the-market/overview-of-nigeria/#:~:text=23%25%20of%20the%20Nigerian%20population,diversified%2C%20sustainable%20and%20competitive%20economy>.

[5] Afrasia, *Africa Wealth Report* 2021 (NWWealth 2021) 6.

[6] World Bank, 'Nigeria Releases New Report on Poverty and Inequality in Country' (*World Bank*, 28 May 2020) <www.worldbank.org/en/programs/lsms/brief/nigeria-releases-new-report-on-poverty-and-inequality-in-country#:~:text=The%20National%20Bureau%20of%20Statistics,naira%20(%24381.75)%20per%20year>.

Still, Nigeria remains one of the most attractive retail markets for foreign companies in Africa. Private consumption expenditure in December 2020 amounted to USD 80.125 billion.[7] The growing upper and middle class, combined with a young population exposed to international trade marks, has created a strong market for high-quality branded products.[8] In 2021, Nigeria was the twenty-fourth importer of champagne in the world, South Africa being the number one importer in Africa.[9]

Importers in Nigeria will find themselves in the company of numerous international brands. The formal retail space is rapidly expanding, with surfaces multiplying more than ten times in twelve years from 30,000 m^2 in 2005 to 326,958 m^2 in 2017.[10] However, still over 80 per cent of shopping in Nigeria is carried out in informal retail spaces such as corner shops, local markets, and street vendors. There is no doubt that as more people move to urban areas and as customers get a taste of the more comfortable environment in formal retail, the latter will grow.

Although not yet a threat to brick-and-mortar retailers, e-commerce is growing in Nigeria, with transactions valued at USD 13 billion in 2019 and expected by the Ministry of Communication and Technology to increase to USD 154 billion by 2025.[11] Jumia, Africa's biggest e-commerce platform and the first unicorn[12] in Africa was founded in the capital city of Lagos in 2012. E-commerce growth in Nigeria is, no doubt, enabled by the large percentage of youth in the population (around 70 per cent of Nigeria's population is under the age of thirty), an internet penetration rate of 50 per cent in 2021, and the savvy manner in which e-commerce retailers have adapted themselves to the Nigerian market, such as accepting payment on delivery for goods ordered online.

No domestic products are registered as geographical indications (GIs) in Nigeria. However, numerous products have been highlighted as potential GIs. These include Sokoto Red Goat Skin, Ijebu Garri, Yaji (Dry Pepper), Nsukka Yellow Pepper, Aso Oke, Awori Mat, Fura, etc. It is only possible to list some potential products as it has been estimated that Nigeria has about 10,000 potential products.[13]

---

[7] CEIC, 'Nigeria Private Consumption Expenditure' (*CEIC*, nd) <www.ceicdata.com/en/indicator/nigeria/private-consumption-expenditure#:~:text=Nigeria%20Private%20Consumption%20Expenditure%20was,USD%20bn%20for%20Sep%202020>.

[8] Persianas (n 4).

[9] Jaco Maritz, 'Africa's Biggest Champagne Importers—Nigeria, Ghana, Congo among Top 10' (*How We Made It in Africa*, 28 April 2022) <www.howwemadeitinafrica.com/africas-biggest-champagne-importers-nigeria-ghana-congo-among-top-10/142855>. This ranking would likely be higher if black market sales were taken into account.

[10] Olajide Olutuyi, 'Is the Retail Sector Nigeria's Next Big Industry?' (*Financial Nigeria*, 16 February 2018) <www.financialnigeria.com/is-the-retail-sector-nigeria-s-next-big-industry-blog-329.html>.

[11] ASENDIA, 'How Nigeria Is Leading the Way in the Emerging African Ecommerce Market' (*ASENDIA*, 20 March 2019) <www.asendia.co.uk/asendia-insights/how-nigeria-leading-way-emerging-african-ecommerce-market>.

[12] A unicorn is a privately held start-up company valued over USD 1 billion.

[13] WIPO and Africa International Trade & Commerce Research, 'The importance of geographical indications to the sustainable development of Nigeria' (*WIPO and Africa International Trade &*

1. Legal Framework

The Nigerian legal system is based on the English common law. Other sources of law include customary law and *Shariah* law. The first set of courts is the inferior courts. Found in every local government, these courts are called magistrates' courts in Southern Nigeria and hear both civil and criminal cases based on the jurisdiction allowed under the state law establishing the court. In northern Nigeria, these courts are called district courts and have specified jurisdiction. Above the magistrate or district court are the high courts, consisting of the Federal High Court, the State High Court, and the High Court of the Federal Capital Territory. The State High Court has unlimited civil and criminal jurisdiction except for matters within the enumerated jurisdiction of the Federal High Court. The State High Court hears appeals from decisions of magistrates' or district courts. Above the High Courts is the Court of Appeal, which has divisions across the country. The Supreme Court is the highest court in Nigeria. Its decisions are final and binding upon all other courts. In Nigeria, there is one type of legal practitioner, which is a lawyer. Every lawyer is admitted to the bar as both a barrister and a solicitor. Lawyers thus have a right to conduct and take part in court proceedings and sign and file legal documents.

2. Domestic Legislation on GIs

Nigeria acceded to the Paris Convention for the Protection of Industrial Property of 1883 in July 1963, although the Convention still needs to be domesticated as required by section 12 of the 1999 Constitution of the Federal Republic of Nigeria (as Amended). Nigeria is a party to neither the Madrid Agreement for the Repression of False or Deceptive Indications of Source on Goods of 1891 nor the Lisbon Agreement for the Protection of Appellations of Origin and their International Registration of 1958. Nigeria is not a party to the Madrid Protocol Concerning the International Registration of Marks of 2007. Nigeria is a member of the World Trade Organization (WTO).[14]

Commerce Research, 13 August 2020) <www.wipo.int/edocs/mdocs/mdocs/en/wipo_webinar_wno_2020_4/wipo_webinar_wno_2020_4_gi.pdf>.

[14] The extent to which TRIPS provisions are directly applicable in Nigeria is debatable. In *Fan Milk International A/S v Mandarin Oriental Services BV* (Suit No FHC/ABJ/CS/791/2020) & *Fan Milk Inter-national A/S v Mandarin Oriental Services BV* (Suit No FHC/ABJ/CS/792/2020), both before the Federal High Court of Nigeria (Abuja Judicial Division), the Court held that the provisions of TRIPS are not binding and cannot be relied upon in court as they have not been domesticated in Nigeria. In the earlier case of *Procter and Gamble Company v Global Soap and Detergent Industries Limited* [(2012) LPELR-8014(CA), whilst being unable to confirm executive or legislative ratification of the TRIPS Agreement, the Court of Appeal, however, applied the underlying principle of TRIPS to the case.

There is no specific legislation regarding GIs currently in force in Nigeria. This applies to both domestic and foreign GIs. There have been numerous talks, papers, and seminars over the years as to the potential benefit of a *sui generis* GI regime for Nigerian products, more so given the diversified agricultural production of the country. In February 2022, members of the Nigerian Technical Working Group (TWG) on GIs met to consider their first draft of a bill for the protection of GIs. The TWG comprises representatives from the Ministry of Agriculture, the Ministry of Trade, and the Nigerian Bar Association, amongst others. The first draft protects all types of products as GIs but excludes services, an omission some stakeholders lamented. The draft provides for the setting up of several positions, such as the Technical Evaluation Expert, who will assist the Registrar in examining the GI applications, make policy recommendations, and give technical advice to the Registrar. A GI Board must also be established to advise the Minister of Industry, Trade, and Investment on significant appointments. The bill is still a work in progress and will only be sent to the Ministry of Justice once approved. If approved, the draft shall be sponsored to the National Assembly as an Executive Bill.[15] It will then follow the normal legislative process.

Since no *sui generis* law has yet been passed, GIs are currently protected under the Trademarks Act of the Federal Republic of Nigeria 1990 (TMA) as certification marks. Wine and spirits, however, also benefit from an additional layer of protection under the National Agency for Food and Drug Administration and Control Act 1993 (as Amended) Wine Regulations 2019 (Wine Regulations) and the National Agency for Food and Drug Administration and Control Act 1993 (as Amended) Spirit Drinks Regulations 2019 (Spirit Regulations). The Wine and Spirit Regulations are, however, not as explicit as article 23 of the WTO Agreement on Trade-Related Aspects of Intellectual Property Rights (TRIPS). Under the Wine Regulations, a clear indication of the country of origin must be shown on the wine's information panel, and the name of every wine shall indicate its accurate nature. Under article 5(1) of the Spirit Regulations, the name of the spirit drink shall be presented in a manner as to protect the GIs and geographical designation of the spirit drink. Categories of spirits drinks are further linked to the geographical origin. For example, *Scotch Whisky* is whisky distilled and matured in Scotland qualifying in accordance with the laws applicable thereto in Scotland, while *American/Rye Malt Whisky* shall be whisky distilled in the United States as whisky in accordance with the laws applicable thereto in the United States.

---

[15] Chijioke Okorie, 'Nigeria's Quest for Its Own Statute for the Protection of Geographical Indications Gains Momentum' (*The IPKat*, 17 March 2022) <https://ipkitten.blogspot.com/2022/03/guest-post-nigerias-quest-for-its-own.html>.

3. Registration of GIs Domestically

In the absence of a *sui generis* system, a GI can be registered in Nigeria via the trade mark regime as a certification mark. A certification mark is defined as 'a mark adapted in relation to any goods to distinguish in the course of trade goods certified by any person in respect of origin, material, method of manufacture, quality, accuracy or other characteristic, from goods not so certified'.[16] A certification mark is thus applied only to goods and not to services. A certification mark is registrable in Part A of the register. Collective marks are not available in Nigeria.

4. Registrability of Names

A certification mark may consist of a device, brand, heading, label, ticket, name, signature, word, letter, numeral, or any combination thereof, the shape of goods, their packaging, and any combination of colours.[17] Contrary to trade marks, the TMA contains no explicit prohibition as to the particulars for a name, sign, device, or word to be registered as a certification mark.[18]

5. Procedure and Requirements for Registration

The Trade Marks Registry, headed by the Registrar, is the relevant trade mark authority. An application for a certification mark is made online to the Registrar. The applicant, who cannot be the person who trades in the goods to be certified, must provide its name, description, and trade or business address. Where the applicant is a body corporate, the type and country of incorporation must also be stated. The applicant needs not be a citizen of, or domiciled in, Nigeria. However, the applicant must provide an address of service in Nigeria that can be easily reached. In practice, many foreign applicants choose to be represented by an authorized agent or an attorney by filing a signed power of attorney with the Trade Marks Registry. The applicant must also specify the class and specifications of goods for which the registration is sought. Nigeria is a single-class country, and multi-class applications are not allowed.

At filing, or upon being required to do so by the Registrar at any time before a decision has been rendered on the application, the applicant shall send to the Registrar a case setting out the grounds on which it relies in support of its

---

[16] TMA, s 43(1).
[17] ibid s 67(1).
[18] For example, ibid s 9(1)(d) prohibits registration of a word or words that is a geographical name according to its ordinary signification.

application, the draft regulations for governing the use of the mark, and prescribed Form 34.[19] The draft regulation shall include provisions as to the cases in which the proprietor is to certify the goods.

The Registrar shall consider the draft rules and report to the Minister of Industry, Trade, and Investment. The Registrar may communicate observations on the sufficiency of the case or the suitability of the draft regulations. The applicant may modify either of these documents.

When authorization to proceed with an application has been given, the Minister shall consider the application with regard to the following matters:

a) whether the applicant is competent to certify the goods in respect of which the mark is to be registered;
b) whether the draft rules are satisfactory; and
c) whether in all the circumstances the registration applied for would be to the public advantage.[20]

The Minister may also require or permit provisions to be inserted in the regulations, such as provisions conferring a right of appeal to the Registrar against any refusal of the proprietor to certify goods or to authorize the use of the trade mark in accordance with the rules.

The Minister may either direct that the application shall not be accepted or direct the Registrar to accept the application and approve the rules, either without modification and unconditionally, or subject to any condition or limitations, or to any amendments or modifications of the application or of the rules which the Minister thinks requisite, having regard to any of the matters aforesaid. Where the Minister provides for conditional approval, the Minister shall, prior to its decision, allow the applicant an opportunity to be heard.

With the concurrence of the Registrar, the applicant may forward the draft rules to the Minister for its consideration before obtaining the authorization to proceed. The Minister may, however, reconsider its decision if any amendment or modification is made afterwards to the application or in the draft regulations.

A trade mark application is examined in Nigeria on absolute and relative grounds. The trade mark may be accepted absolutely, accepted conditionally, or refused. The trade mark will be refused on absolute grounds where it is not distinctive; it is deceptive or scandalous, contrary to law or morality or in any way disentitled to protection; or contains some prohibited words and/or symbols. The Registrar shall inform the applicant of its objections to the trade mark in writing. An applicant whose application has been rejected on absolute grounds may make written or oral representations to the Registrar or may amend the proposed trade mark application.

---

[19] Trade Marks Regulations, reg 42.
[20] TMA, First Schedule, s 5.

Upon receipt of an application, the Registrar will undertake a search among the registered marks and pending applications to ascertain whether there is on record in respect of the same goods or description of goods any marks identical with the mark applied for or so nearly resembling it as to render the mark applied for likely to deceive or cause confusion. The Registrar may cause the search to be renewed at any time before the acceptance of the application but is not bound to do so. Other relative grounds on which a trade mark application may be refused include the fact that the applicant is not the true proprietor of the applied trade mark and that the trade mark contains restricted words and/or restricted symbols such as the Geneva Cross. The Registrar shall inform the applicant of its objections to the trade mark application in writing. An applicant whose application has been rejected on relative grounds may argue against the refusal, limit the specification, or impose some other kind of limitation on the trade mark.

The Registrar may also accept the application subject to the imposition of certain conditions, amendments, disclaimers, modifications, or limitations. In case of conditional acceptance, the Registrar shall inform the applicant in writing. Should the applicant object to the proposed conditions, amendments, disclaimers, modifications, or limitations, the applicant shall, within one month from the date of the communication, apply for a hearing or communicate its considered objections in writing.

Where the application has been rejected or subject to a conditional refusal and the applicant has objected to the refusal or the conditions imposed through a hearing or in writing, the Registrar shall communicate its decision to the applicant in writing. If the applicant is unsatisfied by the decision of the Registrar, the applicant may, within one month, require the Registrar to state in writing the grounds and the materials used by it in arriving at the decision. The applicant has a right of appeal before the court.

When an application for a certification mark has been accepted, whether absolutely or subject to conditions or limitations, the Registrar shall cause the application as accepted to be advertised in the *Trade Marks Journal*. The publication shall contain all conditions and limitations to which the application has been accepted.

Any person may give notice to the Registrar of its opposition to the registration within two months from the date of the publication. No extension is allowed. The notice shall include a statement of the grounds upon which the opponent objects to the registration. The notice shall be accompanied by an unstamped duplicate, which the Registrar shall send to the applicant. Within one month of receiving the notice of opposition, the applicant shall send to the Registrar its counterstatement by way of statutory declaration. Should the applicant fail to do so, the applicant shall be treated as having abandoned its application. Within one month of receiving a duplicate of the counterstatement from the Registrar, the opponent shall file a Statutory Declaration providing evidence to support the opposition. Upon receipt of the aforementioned Statutory Declaration, the applicant must file its own Statutory Declaration within one month. The opponent, again, has a right of reply. The Registrar may hear both parties, and after giving due consideration to the evidence placed before it, the Registrar will decide subject to what conditions or limitations, if any, registration is to be permitted. The decision of the Registrar may be appealed before the court.

Where a trade mark has been accepted, and there has been no opposition or the opposition failed, the Registrar shall issue the certificate of registration upon payment of the sealing fees. The rules concerning the certification mark shall be open for inspection by the public.

6. Term of Protection

A certification trade mark is valid for seven years at the first instance and is renewable thereafter for subsequent periods of fourteen years.

A mark may be removed from the register where

a) the mark was registered without any *bona fide* intention of use and that has been in fact no *bona fide* use by the proprietor in relation to the goods;[21]
b) up to one month before the date of the application a continuous period of five years or longer has elapsed during which the trade mark was registered but not used.[22]

Other reasons for cancellation include

a) the mark is used in a manner other than the permitted use or in such a way as to cause deception confusion;
b) the proprietor or registered user misrepresented or failed to disclose facts material to the application or that circumstances have materially changed since the date of registration; or
c) that the registration ought not to have been granted having regard to rights vested in the applicant by virtue of a contract the performance of which he is interested in.[23]

The rules deposited in respect of a certification mark may, on the application of the registered proprietor through the prescribed form (Form 35), be altered by the Registrar, with the consent of the Minister.[24] The Minister may cause an application for its consent to be advertised in any case where it appears to it expedient so to do and where the Minister causes an application to be advertised if, within one month from the date of the advertisement, any person gives notice to the Minister

---

[21] TMA, s 31(2)(a).
[22] ibid s 31(2)(b).
[23] ibid s 34(5).
[24] ibid First Schedule, s 3(1).

of opposition to the application, the Minister shall not decide the matter without giving the parties an opportunity of being heard.

On application of any person concerned or of the Registrar, the Minister may make such order as it thinks fit for striking out or varying any entry in the register relating to a certification trade mark or for varying the deposited rules on the ground that

a) the proprietor is no longer competent, in the case of any of the goods in respect of which the trade mark is registered, to certify those goods;
b) the proprietor has failed to observe a provision of the deposited rules to be observed on his part;
c) it is no longer to the public advantage that the trade mark should be registered; or
d) it is requisite for the public advantage that the rules should be varied if the trade mark remains registered.[25]

The Registrar shall rectify the register and the deposited rules in such matter to give effect to the order given by the Minister.

7. Rights of the Owner and Enforcement Mechanisms against Infringers

The registered proprietor of a certification trade mark has the exclusive right to the use of the trade mark in relation to the registered goods and the right to sue for or institute an action for any infringement of the trade mark.[26]

The right to the use of a certification trade mark shall be infringed by any person who, not being the proprietor of the trade mark or a person authorized by it under the rules and using it in accordance therewith, uses a mark identical with it or so nearly resembling it as to be likely to deceive or cause confusion, in the course of trade, in relation to any goods in respect of which it is registered, and in such manner as to render the use of the mark likely to be taken either as

a) being used as a trade mark; or
b) in a case in which the use is upon goods or in physical relation thereto or in an advertising, circular, or other advertisement issued to the public, as importing a reference to some person having the right either as proprietor or by its authorisation under the relevant rules to use the trade mark or to goods certified by the proprietor.[27]

---

[25] Ibid, First Schedule, s 4(1).
[26] ibid s 43(3).
[27] ibid s 43(4).

Using a certification mark in ways outside of the conditions or limitations entered on the register does not constitute an infringement of a certification mark.[28]

Where a certification trade mark is identical or nearly resembles another registered trade mark, the use of any of those marks in accordance with its registration shall not constitute an infringement.[29]

The registered owner of a certification mark may thus institute civil proceedings for any unauthorized use against an infringer. Such proceedings are heard before the Federal High Court. Civil remedies are available and may be classified as pre-trial or post-trial remedies. Among the pre-trial remedies available to a registered trade mark owner are preliminary (interim and interlocutory) injunctions to preserve its rights pending a final determination by the court as well as an Anton Pillar court order. An Anton Pillar order allows access to the defendant's premises by the claimant, its solicitors, law enforcement agents, and bailiffs to seize infringing goods or documents. The owner may request post-trial remedies, including a final injunction restraining future acts of infringement; damages or accounts for profit; costs; and the delivery of infringing articles for destruction. Damages are calculated according to what 'the law will presume to be the natural or probable consequence of the act complained of'.[30] A claimant may request an account for profit in lieu of damages. Both cannot be requested at the same time. With regard to the payment of costs, the infringer may be condemned to the payment of specific costs where these are expressly proven, otherwise, the court shall, at its discretion, quantify the costs recoverable.

Unregistered marks are protected under the common law doctrine of a passing off whereby a person passes off goods as another person's goods.[31] The successful claimant in an action for passing off may recover damages. Succeeding in a passing-off action is not easy, with the plaintiff having to prove goodwill or reputation, misrepresentation by the defendant to the public, and damage suffered or likely to be suffered.[32] The correct court to institute proceedings for passing off of an unregistered mark is the Federal High Court.

Criminal prosecution is the concern of the Police and Attorney General (AG). The AG's power may be delegated to the Director of Public Prosecution. The relevant laws for the criminal prosecution of infringing trade mark use are the Merchandise Marks Act Cap M10 Laws of the Federation of Nigeria 2004 (MMA) and the Trade Malpractices (Miscellaneous Offences) Act.[33] Under the MMA, any person who

---

[28] ibid s 43(5).
[29] ibid s 43(6).
[30] *Beech Group Limited v Esdee Food Product Nigeria Limited* [1999] FHCLR 477.
[31] TMA, s 3.
[32] *Banire v NTA-Star TV Network Ltd* [2021] LPELR-52824 (CA).
[33] The only criminal offence under the TMA concerns the falsification of the register and false representation of a mark as registered under ss 60 and 61, respectively.

a) forges any trade mark;[34] or
b) falsely applies to goods any trade mark or any mark so nearly resembling a trade mark as to be calculated to deceive; or
c) makes, disposes of, or has in its possession any die, block, machine, or other instrument for the purpose of forging, or of being used for forging, a trade mark; or
d) applies any false trade description to goods;[35] or
e) causes any of these things mentioned to be done,

shall unless it proves that it acted without intent to defraud, be guilty of an offence.[36]

Any person who sells, or exposes for, or has in its possession for sale or any purpose of trade or manufacture, any goods or things to which any forged trade mark or false trade description is applied, or to which any trade mark or mark so nearly resembling a trade mark as to be calculated to deceive is falsely applied, shall be guilty of an offence unless it proves either

a) that, having taken all reasonable precautions against committing an offence, it had at the time of the commission of the alleged offence no reason to suspect the genuineness of the trade mark, mark or trade description, and that, on demand made by or on behalf of the prosecutor, it gave all the information in its power with respect to the persons from whom it obtained such goods or things; or
b) that otherwise it had acted innocently.[37]

An offender under the MMA shall be liable

a) on conviction before a High Court to imprisonment for a term of two years and/or to a fine;
b) on summary conviction before a Magistrate Court to imprisonment for a term of six months or to a fine of NGN 100;
c) in any case, to forfeit every chattel, article, instrument, or thing by means of or in relation to which the offence has been committed.[38]

---

[34] MMA, s 4 provides that a person is deemed to forge a trade mark where, without the assent of the proprietor of the trade mark, its makes that trade mark or a mark so nearly resembling that trade mark as to be calculated to deceive or it falsifies any genuine trade mark, whether by alteration, addition, effacement, or otherwise.
[35] The MMA explicitly includes any description, statement, or other indication, direct or indirect as to the place or country in which any goods were made or produced as a trade description: ibid s 2(1).
[36] ibid s 3(1).
[37] ibid s 3(2).
[38] ibid s 3(3).

Under the Trade Malpractices (Miscellaneous Offences) Act, any person who labels, packages, sells, offers for sale, or advertises any product in a manner that is false or misleading or is likely to create a wrong impression as to its quality, character, brand name, value, composition, merit or safety commits an offence and is liable to a fine of not less than NGN 50,000.[39] The Attorney General will commence prosecution under this Act following a report made to it by the Special Trade Malpractices Investigation Panel.

Individual offenders under the Wine Regulations mentioned at section 3 may be liable on conviction to imprisonment for a term not exceeding one year and/or to a fine not exceeding NGN 50,000. Corporate offenders are liable to a fine not exceeding NGN 100,000. The same penalty is applicable under the Spirits Regulations.

8. Customs Enforcement

There is no formal recordal mechanism available with customs in Nigeria. Right holders may, however, start an informal collaboration with customs by first training the officers of the Nigerian Customs Service and thereafter signing a memorandum of understanding with customs. This will usually make customs more sensitive to counterfeits of the particular brand.

Several options are available where right holders are aware of the importation of counterfeits in the country. Right holders may lodge a complaint containing information as to the specific shipment with customs. Right holders may also obtain a court order from the Federal High Court and present it to customs for enforcement. Once the suspected goods have been detained, customs will contact the right holder and allow it to inspect the goods. It is not clear exactly how long customs may retain the goods. However, it is advised that the right holder be responsive. Customs will destroy detained counterfeit goods. The right owner may be permitted to be present where the enforcement action was initiated by its application, required by a court order, or customs deems it necessary.[40]

9. Bilateral Agreements

There are no bilateral agreements between either the European Union or the United States and Nigeria specific to GIs.

---

[39] Trade Malpractices (Miscellaneous Offences) Act, s (1)(a).
[40] More information may be found on customs enforcement in Nigeria in Marius Schneider and Vanessa Ferguson, *Enforcement of Intellectual Property Rights in Africa* (OUP 2020).

16
South Africa

South Africa is at the southern tip of Africa with access to both the Atlantic Ocean and the Indian Ocean. It shares its borders with Namibia, Botswana, Zimbabwe, and Eswatini and surrounds Lesotho. At 1,22 million km², South Africa is the ninth largest country on the continent. In 2022, its population was estimated at 59,89 million. There are eleven official languages in South Africa, with isiZulu having the largest percentage of home speakers amongst the different languages. However, English, one of the official languages in South Africa, is the most spoken and used language for business and commerce. English and Afrikaans are the only languages of record in the country's courts. The working week is from Monday to Friday, and the national currency is the South African rand (ZAR).

With a gross domestic product (GDP) of USD 369 billion in 2020, South Africa remains a dominant economic player in Africa.[1] The second largest economy in Africa, South Africa has traditionally been driven by the primary sector, particularly mining and agriculture. South Africa has the world's fifth-largest mining sector having regard to its GDP,[2] while the agricultural sector contributes to around 10 per cent of the country's total export earnings.[3] Although it has a robust agricultural sector, South Africa imported USD 6.3 billion in agricultural and food products in 2020. Its top five food suppliers are Eswatini, Argentina, the United Kingdom, France, and China.[4] Nowadays, the country's economy is also driven by the tertiary sector, including trade, tourism, manufacturing, and financial services.

As a reflection of the strength of the South African economy, there are twice as many millionaires in South Africa as in any other African country. There is a sizable number of high-net-worth individuals.[5] Income inequality, however, remains

---

[1] Prinesha Naidoo, 'South Africa's Economy Is $37B Bigger than Previously Thought' (*AlJazeera*, 25 August 2021) <www.aljazeera.com/economy/2021/8/25/south-africas-economy-is-37b-bigger-than-previously-thought>.

[2] Brand South Africa, 'SA's Key Economic Sectors' (*Brand South Africa*, 2 January 2018) <https://brandsouthafrica.com/78205/economic-sectors-agricultural>.

[3] International Trade Administration, 'South Africa—Country Commercial Guide: Agricultural Sector' (*International Trade Administration*, 9 November 2021) <www.trade.gov/country-commercial-guides/south-africa-agricultural-sector>.

[4] World Integrated Trade Solution, 'South Africa Food Products Imports by Country in US$ Thousand 2020' (*World Integrated Trade Solution*, nd) <https://wits.worldbank.org/CountryProfile/en/Country/ZAF/Year/2020/TradeFlow/Import/Partner/by-country/Product/16-24_FoodProd>.

[5] Carin Smith, 'These Are the Reasons Why the Super Wealthy Still Find SA Attractive' (*News24*, 23 December 2020) <www.news24.com/fin24/economy/south-africa-these-are-the-reasons-why-the-super-wealthy-still-find-sa-attractive-20201223>.

a significant concern in the country: South Africa, with the highest Gini coefficient in the world, is the world's most unequal society. While 10 per cent of the population form part of the upper class, over 50 per cent live in poverty.[6]

South Africa has, without a doubt, one of the most sophisticated and modern formal retail landscapes in sub-Saharan Africa. The country has almost 2,000 shopping malls covering over 24 million m^2.[7] In fact, the next frontier for retail in South Africa is online shopping. In 2020, e-commerce in South Africa grew by 66 per cent, in part due to the COVID-19 pandemic and the resulting lockdown.[8] The expansion of e-commerce in South Africa will no doubt be facilitated by a high internet penetration rate (64 per cent in January 2021[9]) and the widely accepted use of banks. Financial institutions bank and service around 75 per cent of the population.[10]

South Africa has no specific geographical indication (GI) legislation but adopts a common law approach of using various statutes to protect its noteworthy agricultural products. These statutes are the Merchandise Marks Act[11] (MMA), the Agricultural Product Standards Act[12] (APSA), the Trade Marks Act[13] (TMA), and the Liquor Products Act[14] (LPA). For example, the terms 'Rooibos', 'Red Bush', 'Rooibostee', 'Rooibos Tea', 'Rooitee', and 'Rooibosch', as well as 'Honeybush', 'Heuningbos', 'Honeybush Tea', and 'Heuningbos Tee' are protected under section 15 of the MMA. Once a term is decreed under section 15 of the MMA, it is protected in perpetuity and subject to criminal (as opposed to civil) sanction. In addition, the decree is at no cost to producers.[15] The APSA and its accompanying regulation protect agricultural products, excluding liquor, intended for sale in South Africa. South African products enjoying protection as a registered South African GI or designation of origin may use the official South African GI and designation of origin logos. Other goods, such as the Karoo Certified Meat of Origin are protected as a certification mark under the TMA. Finally, certain alcoholic

---

[6] Niemah Davids, 'Inequality in South Africa Is a "Ticking Timebomb"' (*University of Cape Town*, 21 May 2021) <www.news.uct.ac.za/article/-2021-05-21-inequality-in-south-africa-is-a-ticking-timebomb>.

[7] Bindy, 'Retail in Africa: Facts and Emerging Trends' (*Bindy*, nd) <https://blog.compliantia.com/retail-in-africa-interesting-facts-and-emerging-trends>.

[8] Luke Daniel, 'SA's Online Retail Has More than Doubled in Two Years—But the Best Is Probably Over' (*News24*, 17 May 2021) <www.news24.com/news24/bi-archive/sas-online-retail-has-more-than-doubled-in-two-years-but-the-best-is-probably-over-2021-5>.

[9] Simon Kemp, 'Digital 2021: South Africa' (*Datareportal*, 11 February 2021) <https://datareportal.com/reports/digital-2021-south-africa>.

[10] Oxford Business Group, 'South African Banks Making Efforts to Reach and Integrate the Unbanked Population' (*Oxford Business Group*, nd) <https://oxfordbusinessgroup.com/analysis/final-20-reaching-unbanked-population-complex-task>.

[11] Act No 17 of 1941.

[12] Act No 119 of 1990.

[13] Act No 194 of 1993.

[14] Act No 60 of 1989.

[15] Cobus Jooste, 'The Rooibos Rush' (*Anton Mostert Chair of Intellectual Property*, 6 August 2013) <https://blogs.sun.ac.za/iplaw/2013/08/06/the-rooibos-rush>.

products, including wine, alcoholic fruit beverages, spirits, and grape-based liquor, are protected under the Liquor Products Act (LPA). South African wines must further abide by the Wine of Origin scheme. A wine bottle bearing the term 'Wine of Origin' or 'W.O.' is produced only from grapes sourced from a specific demarcated area. Wines may further be demarcated based on their areas of origin, whether a single vineyard, estate wine, ward, district, or region. The Wines and Spirits Board will certify the wine according to the region from which the wine originates. The scheme is only relevant with regard to the origin of the grapes and does not touch on yield, size, or cultivating practices.

In May 2021, *'Rooibos'/'Red Bush'* became the first African product registered as a protected designation of origin (PDO) in the European Union.[16] Its protection outside of South Africa was, however, fraught with attempts to monopolize the term. In 2013, an investment company attempted to trade mark twelve terms involving the words 'Rooibos tea' and 'Rooibos' in France.[17] Both Rooibos suppliers and the South African Minister of Trade and Industry got involved, and the attempt to register the trade mark was ultimately unsuccessful. In the United States, 'rooibos' is now a generic term. One company had successfully registered the term 'rooibos' in the United States and, in 1994, started sending cease-and-desist letters to other commercial entities using the term 'rooibos' and requesting the payment of compensation. Those entities included South African companies. It was only in June 2005, following a number of lawsuits and mounting legal fees, that the United States company agreed to abandon exclusive trade mark rights over the term 'Rooibos'. Rooibos is now part of the public domain and free for anyone to use in the United States.[18]

Other noteworthy products that have, over the years, been highlighted as having the potential to be protected as GIs include Camdeboo Mohair, Klein Karoo Ostrich, South African Olive Oil, and Boland Waterblommetjies (the stems, leaves, and flowers of *Aponogeton distachyos*).

1. Legal Framework

South Africa has a mixed legal system combining Roman-Dutch civil law, English common law, customary law, and religious personal law. Sources of law are the statutes and regulations enacted by national and provincial governments,

---

[16] Gerardo Fortuna, 'Commission Awards Historic EU Protection for African Food' (*EURACTIV*, 1 June 2021) <www.euractiv.com/section/agriculture-food/news/commission-awards-historic-eu-protection-for-african-food>.

[17] David Smith, 'South Africa Fights to Protect Rooibos Tea Name after French Trademark Bid' (*The Guardian*, 25 July 2013) <www.theguardian.com/world/2013/jul/25/south-africa-rooibos-tea-france>.

[18] World Intellectual Property Organization (WIPO), 'Disputing a Name, Developing a Geographical Indication' (*WIPO*, nd) <www.wipo.int/ipadvantage/en/details.jsp?id=2691>.

jurisprudence, and common law. Magistrate courts are courts of first instance. They are either district courts (also called ordinary magistrates' courts) or regional courts. Regional magistrates' courts only deal with criminal cases, whereas the district courts deal with criminal and civil cases. The more serious criminal matters are heard before the regional magistrates' courts. District courts are competent for civil disputes (usually claims for less than ZAR 100,000). They are found in all nine provinces. High Courts hear both civil and criminal matters. Found in all nine provinces, some of the High Courts serve as Provincial Division High Courts, in which case they sit as review and appeal courts in civil and criminal matters from the courts of first instance or from the High Court within its jurisdiction. The High Court is the court of first instance for intellectual property matters other than patents. All appeals, criminal or civil, are heard by the full bench of Judges of the High Court (three judges) or before the Supreme Court of Appeal, except for labour and competition matters. A decision by the Supreme Court of Appeal can only be amended by the court itself or the Constitutional Court. The Constitutional Court is the highest court in South Africa and only hears constitutional challenges.

South African legal professionals are either advocates or attorneys. Advocates can appear in any court, while attorneys are heard in all the country's lower courts. Subject to certain requirements, attorneys may acquire a right of audience before the High Court, Supreme Court of Appeal, or Constitutional Court.

2. Domestic Legislation on GIs

South Africa acceded to the Paris Convention for the Protection of Industrial Property of 1883 in October 1947. South Africa is a party to neither the Madrid Agreement for the Repression of False or Deceptive Indications of Source on Goods of 1891 nor the Lisbon Agreement for the Protection of Appellations of Origin and their International Registration of 1958. South Africa is not a signatory to the Madrid Protocol Concerning the International Registration of Marks of 2007.

South Africa is a member of the World Trade Organization (WTO).

South Africa does not have a *sui generis* GI legislation. GIs are protected under various statutes and their corresponding regulations. The relevant statutes include the MMA, the APSA, the TMA, the LPA, and the Protection, Promotion, Development and Management of Indigenous Knowledge Act. The MMA is mainly concerned with the marking of merchandise, coverings in or with which merchandise is sold, and the use of certain words and emblems in connection with business. Section 15, whereby marks may be declared by the Minister of Trade, Industry and Competition to be prohibited, is of particular interest to GI protection.

The APSA is concerned with the control, sale, import, and export of agricultural products. APSA is a *sui generis* protection system of GIs for agricultural products. Of particular interest to the protection of GIs is Regulations 10 February 2023 relating to the protection of geographical indications and designation of origins used on agricultural products intended for sale in the Republic of South Africa under the Agricultural Product Standards Act (GI Regulations).[19] The Regulations apply to the use and sale of registered GIs and designated designations of origin on agricultural products in South Africa, whether primary or processed product. Liquor, including wine and spirits, is excluded from the ambit of GI Regulations. The Regulations give effect to international agreements regarding the protection of foreign GIs and designated designations of origin in South Africa, such as the European Union (EU)–South African Development Community (SADC) Economic Partnership Agreement (EPA).

The third relevant legislation is the TMA, which specifically mentions GIs and provides for the registration of certification and collective trade marks.

The LPA regulates the sale and production of certain alcoholic products, including wine, alcoholic fruit beverages, spirits, and grape-based liquor. It is a *sui generis* system for protecting wines and certain spirits and is more akin to an administrative product approval scheme. Under section 13A of the LPA, the minister of agriculture, taking into account the Republic's international obligations or agreements with other countries, may, by notice in the *Government Gazette*, restrict the use of specified geographical names in connection with the sale or export of a specified liquor product on such conditions as specified in the notice. The notice shall also apply where the geographical name concerned is used in conjunction with an indication of the true origin of the liquor product, is translated, or is accompanied by an expression such as 'kind', 'type', 'style'. 'imitation', or any similar expression.[20]

Finally, the Protection, Promotion, Development and Management of Indigenous Knowledge Act[21] focuses on the protection of indigenous knowledge. As traditional knowledge is not the focus of the book, the chapter does not dwell on the Act.

3. Registration of GIs Domestically

3.1 Prohibited marks

As there are no rules restricting the use of 'prohibited marks' under section 15 of the MMA to local GIs, a foreign GI could, in theory, be protected under section 15. The Minister of Trade, Industry and Competition may, after investigation, issue a notice declaring the use of a mark to be prohibited either absolutely or

---

[19] Agricultural Products Standard Act: Regulations: Protection of geographical indications used on agricultural products intended for sale in South Africa. No R447 of 2019.
[20] LPA, s 13A(2). There are further labelling requirements for wine, including on their indication of origin. These labelling requirements concern wines produced and sold in South Africa.
[21] Act No 6 of 2019.

conditionally. Under section 15 of the MMA, the Minister of Trade and Industry can prohibit either absolutely or conditionally any mark, word, letter, or figure or any arrangement or combination thereof, in connection with any trade, business, profession, occupation or event, or in connection with a trade mark, mark, or trade description applied to goods. A notice proposing the prohibition of particular terms together with Rules of Use is published in the *Gazette*. Thereafter, any interested person may submit their representations on the proposed prohibition to the Registrar of Trade Marks within thirty days of the publication of the notice. Once final, the Minister decides upon any withdrawal, amendments, and qualifying of any notice if the circumstances so require. There are no official fees attached to acquiring this protection, nor any renewal deadline.

Since the power to declare a prohibited mark lies with the minister, and there is no formal application process, it rather being a political, societal, and economic issue, this chapter does not discuss further the process behind being declared a prohibited mark.

3.2 GIs and designations of origin

GIs and designated designations of origin applied to agricultural products intended for sale in South Africa are protected in South Africa under the GI Regulations.[22] Under the GI Regulations, a GI is a name that identifies an agricultural product as originating in a specific region or place (locality) or in exceptional cases a specific country, whose specific quality or other characteristics are essentially or exclusively due to its geographical region, and of which at least one of the production steps take place in the defined geographical area. A designation of origin is a name that identifies an agricultural product as originating in a specific region or place (locality) or, in exceptional cases, a specific country, whose specific quality or other characteristics are essentially or exclusively due to the particular geographical environment with its inherent natural and human factors and where all production steps take place in the defined geographical area.

The GI Regulations separate GIs and designations of origin into three categories: a South African GI and designation of origin, which identifies an agricultural product as originating in the Republic of South Africa; a foreign GI and designation of origin, which identifies an agricultural product intended for sale on the South African market but originating from a foreign country; and a registered foreign GI and designation of origin, which is a foreign GI and designation of origin that forms part of an international agreement and which is registered under the GI Regulations.[23]

---

[22] GI Regulations, reg 2(1).
[23] ibid reg 1.

A registration procedure applies to domestic and foreign GIs or designations of origin. A different procedure is in place for foreign GIs and designations of origin, which form part of international agreements to which South Africa is a party/signatory and which concern the protection of GIs or designations of origin.

Imported agricultural products presented for sale under a registered foreign GI or designation of origin, as well as a registered foreign GI or designation of origin that forms part of an international agreement, may show GI or designation of origin logos, designations, and acronyms approved for use for such purpose by the competent authority in the country of origin concerned.[24]

3.3 Collective and certification marks

Under the TMA, a sign or indication which may exclusively serve, in trade, to designate the geographical origin of the services may not be registered as a trade mark and, if registered, is liable to be removed from the Register.[25] The Supreme Court of Appeal in *Century City Apartment Property Services CC and another v Century City Property Proprietors' Association* held that this provision serves a public interest permitting all to use such descriptive signs freely by preventing them from being reserved to one undertaking alone because they have been registered as trade marks. Section 10(13) further precludes registration of trade marks that are confusing and deceptive regarding geographical origin. However, where the geographical name is used in such a fanciful manner that it could not connote geographical origin in the mind of the consumer, the geographical name may be registered as a trade mark. One example is the registration of the trade mark 'Antarctica' for jams. Customers cannot be confused into believing that the fruits are grown or the jams produced in Antarctica. Instead, a GI may be protected either as certification marks or as collective trade mark.

Registration as a certification or collective trade mark is open to both foreign and local applicants. A certification mark is defined as

> a mark capable of distinguishing, in the course of trade, goods or services certified by any person in respect of kind, quality, quantity, intended purpose, value, geographical origin or other characteristics of the goods or services, or the mode

---

[24] ibid reg 18(4).
[25] TMA, s 10(2). *Century City Apartment Property Services CC and another v Century City Property Proprietors' Association* 2010 (3) SA 1 (SCA) para 31. The court further cites a judgment by the European Court of Justice, *Windsurfing Chiemsee Produktions-und Vertriebs GmbH v Boots-und Segelzubehor Walter Huber and Franz Attenberger* [1999] ETMR 585 at para 26:

> it is in the public interest that they [geographical names] remain available, not least because they may be an indication of the quality and other characteristics of the categories of goods concerned, and may also, in various ways, influence consumer tastes by, for instance, associating the goods with a place that may give rise to a favourable response.

or time of production of the goods or of rendering of the services, as the case may be, from goods or services not so certified.[26]

A collective mark is defined as 'a mark capable of distinguishing, in the course of trade, goods or services of persons who are members of any association from goods or services of persons who are not members thereof'.[27]

While the law on collective and certification marks refers to both goods and services, a review of the various means to protect a GI shows that the focus is on goods, the particular type of goods depending on the particular means of protection.

4. Registrability of Names

4.1 GIs and designations of origin

Under the GI Regulations, which are limited to the protection of GIs and designations of origin used on agricultural products intended for sale in the Republic of South Africa, a South African GI or designation of origin may not be considered for registration where the name

a) is identical to an existing registered GI or registered designation of origin for the same agricultural product originating from the same or similar geographical origin;
b) falsely communicates to the consumer that the agricultural product concerned originates from a specific region, place or locality, although its quality, reputation or other characteristic is attributable to another region, place or locality from which it truly originates;
c) is generic and cannot identify the place of production and given quality, reputation, or other characteristics attributable to the place of production. The genericity of the term shall be assessed by taking into account all relevant factors, particularly the opinion of producers and consumers, especially those in the region from which the name originates;
d) is identical to a customary name of a plant variety or an animal breed existing in the Republic of South Africa and is likely to mislead the consumer as to the true origin of the agricultural product;
e) is wholly or partially homonymous (i.e., having the same spelling or sounds) with an existing registered GI and is likely to mislead consumers (exception applies);

---

[26] TMA, s 42(1).
[27] ibid s 43(1).

f) is identical or similar to the name of a trade mark used in the Republic of South Africa on the same or similar agricultural product (exception applies); and
g) is intended to be used in translation or is accompanied by words or expressions such as 'kind', 'type', 'style', 'imitation', 'method', 'as produced in', or any similar words or expressions.[28]

In the case of a homonym, the Executive Officer of the Minister of Agriculture may consider the registration of the homonym as a GI or designation of origin, keeping in mind the need to ensure the equitable treatment of the producers of the agricultural product(s) concerned to which the GI or designation of origin relates, that there is a clear distinction between the use of the homonymous name registered subsequently and the use of the name already entered in the Register, and that consumers are not misled about to the true origin of the agricultural product concerned.[29]

In the case of a GI or designation of origin that is similar or identical to a trade mark used in South Africa for the same or similar agricultural products, the Executive Officer may register the GI or designation of origin where the owner of a trade mark has consented to the registration and the Executive Officer considers that the GI or designation of origin may coexist with the trade mark. The Executive Officer shall at least consider the proposed GI's or designation of origin's history of use in good faith in South Africa and the legitimate interests of the trade mark owner and third parties.[30]

Under the GI Regulations, a foreign GI or designation of origin, excluding foreign GIs or designations of origin that form part of international agreements, may not be considered for registration where the name

a) is not protected, or has ceased to be protected or has fallen into disuse in its country of origin;
b) is identical to an existing registered South African GI or designation of origin for the same agricultural product;
c) is generic and cannot identify the place of production and given quality, reputation, or other characteristics attributable to the place of production. The Department of Agriculture shall consult the competent authority in the concerned country to establish whether the name is generic in the country
d) is identical to a customary name of a plant variety or an animal breed existing in the Republic of South Africa and is likely to mislead the consumer as to the true origin of the agricultural product;

---

[28] GI Regulations, reg 4(1).
[29] ibid reg 4(1)(e).
[30] ibid reg 4(1)(f).

e) is wholly or partially homonymous with an existing registered GI and is likely to mislead consumers. The Department shall consult the competent authority in the concerned country to establish if the Executive Officer may consider the registration of a homonymous name;
f) is identical or similar to the name of a trade mark used in the Republic of South Africa on the same or similar agricultural product(s). The Department shall however consult the competent authority in the concerned country to establish if the applicant or applicant group has obtained the written consent from the South African trade mark owner to register the proposed name. The Department may also consult the trade mark owner in South Africa to establish whether it has consented in written to the registration of the proposed name; or
g) is intended to be used in translation, or is accompanied by words or expressions such as 'kind', 'type', 'style', 'imitation', 'method', 'as produced in', or any similar words or expressions.[31]

These restrictions do not apply to foreign GIs or designations of origin forming part of international agreements.

4.2 Collective and certification marks

The TMA does not provide for any particular restriction as to the types of marks or signs that may be registered as certification or collective marks. To be registered as a collective or certification mark, the mark must respect the conditions laid out generally for trade marks in sections 9 and 10 of the TMA.

5. Procedure and Requirements for Registration

5.1 GIs and designations of origin

A South African group's application for registration as a GI or designation of origin shall be submitted electronically to the Executive Officer.[32] An application for registration as a GI or designation of origin by a group from outside the Republic of South Africa, excluding foreign GIs or designations of origin that form part of international agreements, shall be submitted electronically to the Executive Officer designated by the Minister of Agriculture via the specific government department or other entity designated by such government department in the foreign country

---

[31] ibid reg 6(1).
[32] ibid reg 4(1).

as responsible for the registration and protection of GIs or designations of origin.[33] The application for both GIs shall be at least in English and shall include

a) Name of the applicant producer or group of producers[34] and contact details, i.e. physical address, e-mail address and telephone number;
b) Composition of the group as well as the details about the business interests of the producer or group of producers in the defined geographical area.
c) The name of the proposed GI or designation of origin to be registered. Where the GI or designation of origin is not in English, a translation of the proposed GI or designation of origin into English shall be provided.
d) Proof that the proposed GI or designation of origin is not a generic name; does not correspond with the customary name of a plant variety or an animal breed in South Africa that is likely to mislead the consumer as to the true origin of the agricultural product; and is not identical or similar to the name of a trade mark used in South Africa on the same or similar agricultural products. Where the group has obtained prior written consent from the owner of a trade mark for its co-existence with a GI or designation of origin on the same or similar agricultural products, the necessary proof shall be included in the application.
e) The following specifications regarding the agricultural product: the type of agricultural product; a description of the product's main physical, chemical, microbiological and organoleptic (where applicable) characteristics. Existing quality and/or compositional requirements prescribed in the regulations published under the APSA for the agricultural product concerned shall always be considered. A description of the production process/method, and any processing or preparation that takes place in the defined geographical area. Proof that the agricultural product originates in the geographical area, which shall include the history of the product and its traceability.
f) A definition of the geographical area.
g) Details demonstrating the link between the quality or characteristics of the agricultural product and the geographical environment; or where appropriate, the link between a given quality, the reputation or other characteristics of the agricultural product and its geographical origin.[35]

For a domestic GI or designation of origin, the applicant shall also provide a summary of the critical elements of control (ie minimum product specifications and any other information deemed necessary) that the designated assignee will use

---

[33] ibid reg 6(1).
[34] Under the GI Regulations, a producer is defined as one who produces, processes, or prepares agricultural products in a defined geographical area as well as exercises controls the standards of production and minimum product specifications: ibid reg 1.
[35] ibid regs 4(2) and 6(2)(a).

to verify compliance during inspections.[36] Joint applications designating a transborder geographical area are also registrable, subject to the minimum product specifications for the use of the proposed name having been negotiated and agreed upon by the Department and the competent authorities of the countries concerned, together with proof that the name for which registration is requested is registered, in use, and protected in the transborder countries concerned.[37]

For foreign GIs or designations of origin, the applicant must, in addition, prove that the GI or designation of origin is still in use and is protected in the country of origin. The applicant must provide the name and contact details of the certification body nominated to verify compliance with the provisions of the product specification. If the GI or designation of origin is in use, an example of the GI or designation of origin logo, designation and/or acronym that will appear with the GI or designation of origin either on the container and/or outer container of the agricultural product, or in an advertisement related to the agricultural product concerned must further be provided.[38]

A joint application for registration by several groups is possible where the proposed name designates a trans-border geographical area or is a traditional name connected to a trans-border geographical area.[39]

The application date for registration as a GI or designation of origin shall be the date upon which the Executive Officer receives the first application. The first application received by the Executive Officer has priority over any subsequent application for registration of an identical GI in respect of the same agricultural product and having the same or similar geographical origin.[40]

The Executive Officer shall, within a period not exceeding sixty days from the date of application, evaluate the information submitted and determine whether all the required conditions have been respected. The Executive Officer may correct any error of translation or any obvious spelling error in the application and shall notify the applicant group in writing to remedy the same. The Executive Officer may, where necessary, request additional information from the applicant group. The written request must be done within a reasonable time and the process completed within the sixty-day period. In the case of the South African GI or designation of origin, the Executive Officer may further visit the applicant group in the geographical area concerned to confirm the completeness and veracity of the information submitted and request that the designated assignee for the product accompany it on the visit. The visit must also take place within the sixty-day period. Finally, the Executive Officer may consult persons with specialized knowledge

---

[36] ibid reg 4(4).
[37] ibid reg 4(5) and (6).
[38] ibid reg 6(2).
[39] ibid reg 6(3).
[40] ibid reg 8.

and experience about any matter relating to the application within the sixty-day period.[41]

Once satisfied as to the conditions and truthfulness and completeness of the information received, including the submission of requested additional information, the Executive Officer shall publish a Notice in the *Government Gazette* to inform all interested parties of its intention to register the proposed GI or designation of origin and inform all interested parties that the most important elements of the product specification and its linkage to the geographical area concerned are available on request. The Executive Officer shall further, in the notice, invite any written objections to the proposed registration of the GI or designation of origin within a period not exceeding sixty days from the date of publication of the notice. Any interested party may motivate a request to the Executive Officer in writing to consider an extension of time for a period not exceeding thirty days.[42]

Any producer, group of producers, or other person asserting a legitimate interest may object in writing to the proposed GI or designation of origin registration within the allowed time on the grounds that

a) The proposed GI or designation of origin does not meet the definition for 'geographical indication' or 'designation of origin' respectively;
b) The proposed GI or designation of origin is a generic name;
c) The minimum proposed product specifications are inadequate or impractical for the defined geographical area;
d) The proposed registration would conflict with a trade mark, or a wholly or partially homonymous name in use.[43]

Any grounds for objection shall be duly substantiated.

Upon receipt of the objection, the Executive Officer shall write to the applicant group. The applicant group shall, within a period not exceeding thirty days, furnish the Executive Officer with a counter-statement of the grounds on which the group relies for the application. Failure to submit a counter-statement within the prescribed time limit will lead to the rejection of the application. A copy of the counter-statement shall be shared with the objector. The Executive Officer may, on request, give both parties an opportunity to be heard. If deemed necessary, the Executive Officer may consult persons with specialized knowledge and experience about any matter relating to the objection received to the registration of the proposed name. The Executive Officer shall, after considering all information, counter-statements, arguments, and any other relevant information presented to

---

[41] ibid reg 9.
[42] ibid reg 10.
[43] ibid reg 11(1).

it, decide, within a period not exceeding thirty days, whether to reject or register the proposed GI or designation of origin.[44]

Where the application for registration has not been opposed within the prescribed time period, or the application for registration has been opposed but the objection has been resolved in the applicant group's favour, the Executive Officer shall register the foreign GI by entering the GI in the electronic Register. The Executive Officer shall further inform the competent authority in writing of the registration.

Foreign GIs and designations of origin that form part of international agreements and concern agricultural products intended for sale in the Republic of South Africa follow a distinct procedure from domestic and foreign GI or designation of origin. Foreign GIs and designations of origin that form part of international agreements and concern agricultural products intended for sale in the Republic of South Africa do not need to be registered. The Executive Officer enters such GIs and designations of origin in the Register.[45] Where necessary, the Executive Officer may further request the competent authority in the foreign country to provide additional information, including the name of the registered GI or designation of origin; the type of agricultural product, the product specification or a summary of the critical elements of control (ie minimum product specifications and any other information deemed necessary) that will be used to verify compliance during inspections, the name of the country of origin, and the date of registration.[46]

Any addition of a name to the list of registered foreign GIs or designations of origin that form part of an international agreement and which fall within the scope of the GI regulations shall be done in accordance with the procedure provided for in such international agreement or as otherwise mutually agreed between the Republic of South Africa and the country concerned.[47]

5.2 Collective and certification marks

The Companies and Intellectual Property Commission (CIPC) is responsible for registering certification and collective marks in South Africa. An application for a certification and collective mark shall be made on Form TM1. The application shall be dated and signed by the applicant(s) or itsduly authorized agent. The application shall be in triplicate, and a separate and distinct application is required for each class of goods or services and for each separate mark. If a firm or partnership files the application, it may be signed in the name or for and on behalf of the firm or partnership by any one or more members or partners thereof. If the application is

---

[44] ibid reg 11(3)–(5).
[45] ibid reg 13(2).
[46] ibid reg 7(1).
[47] ibid reg 7(3).

made by a body corporate, it may be signed by any authorized person. Every application to register a mark shall contain a representation of the mark. Where a trade mark or application contains a word or numeral other than in roman characters, a transliteration and/or translation to the satisfaction of the Registrar of each such word or numeral shall be endorsed on Form TM1. Where a trade mark contains a word in a language other than an official language of the Republic, the Registrar may ask for a translation thereof, and if he or she so requires, such translation shall be endorsed on Form TM1.

The application for the registration of a certification mark shall, in addition, be accompanied by a statement of case and evidence (which must be couched in affidavit format) by the applicant whereby the applicant states that it does not carry on business in similar goods and services and the rules governing the use of the mark. This must include the conditions for use, the circumstances in which the proprietor will certify the goods/services, which characteristics the goods or services must comply with in order to be certified, and a sanction clause against abuse or misuse. The rules may be amended before or after registration of the trade mark.[48]

For a collective mark, the application for registration must be accompanied by rules governing the use of the mark. The rules shall specify the persons authorized to use the mark; the conditions of membership of the association; and, when applicable, the conditions of the use of the mark, including any sanctions against misuse. These rules can be amended either before or after registration.

Thereafter, the application for certification and collective marks shall proceed as an ordinary application. Importantly, both marks must pass the threshold of being registrable trade marks as per sections 9 and 10 of the TMA, that is capable of distinguishing and not consisting exclusively of a sign or an indication that may designate the kind, quality, or quantity of the goods.

On or after the receipt of any application for the registration of a trade mark, the Registrar shall furnish the applicant with an acknowledgement containing the official number and date of the application. The Registrar shall then undertake a search amongst registered marks and pending applications to ascertain whether there are on record any mark that may conflict with the applied mark.

The Registrar may accept; accept subject to such amendments, modifications, conditions or limitations; provisionally refuse; or refuse the application. The Registrar shall inform the applicant in writing within a reasonable period from the date of the application of its decision. If the trade mark is accepted subject to conditions, modifications, or amendments, the Registrar may, on application by the applicant, state in writing the grounds for its decision. If the applicant objects to such conditions, modifications, or amendments, the applicant shall, within three months from the date of notice of conditional acceptance, submit arguments in

---

[48] CIPC, 'Guidelines on the Examination of Trade Mark Applications: Insight into the Practice of the Office of the Registrar of Trade Marks (Version 3A, CIPC 2019) 30.

writing or apply for a hearing or an extension of time. Failure to do so will result in the application being deemed abandoned. If the applicant has no objections to the Registrar's conditions, modifications, or amendments, the applicant shall, within three months, so notify the Registrar in writing or apply for an extension of time. Failure to do so will result in the application being deemed abandoned. If objections exist as to the acceptance of the mark, a statement of the objections shall be sent to the applicant in writing. Unless the applicant submits arguments in writing within three months of the date of the statement or applies for a hearing or an extension of time, the application is deemed to be abandoned. If the trade mark is refused, the Registrar may, on application by the applicant, state in writing the grounds for its decision.

When an application for registration of a collective or certification mark has been accepted, the application is advertised once in the *Patent Journal* by the applicant in the form and wording required by the Registrar. Any interested person may, within three months from the date of the advertisement of an application in terms, or within such further time as the Registrar may allow, oppose the application. [49]

In cases of interlocutory applications on trade mark application matters, the Registrar can render decisions, enjoying powers equivalent to a judge of the High Court. Otherwise, in contested matters such as those that cannot be adequately decided in affidavit, the Registrar may either refer the matter to the High Court or make such an order as is deemed just and expedient. In practice, for the past ten years, the Registrar, relying on section 59(2) of the TMA, has referred all defended oppositions (and cancellations) to the High Court for determination due to a lack of resources to adjudicate the matters.

Any party to the opposition proceedings before the Registrar may appeal to the Gauteng Division of the High Court against any decision or order pursuant to such proceedings.

When any person objects to any order or decision of the Registrar, it may apply on Form TM2, within three months of the date of the Registrar's order or decision, or such further time as the Registrar may allow, requiring the Registrar to state in writing the grounds of its decision and the data used by it in arriving at it. The date of such statements shall be deemed to be the date of the Registrar's order or decision for the purpose of appeal. All written reasons for decisions and judgements of the Registrar may be published in the *Patent Journal* within three months from the date of signing by the Registrar if the Registrar so directs. In practice, this is not done.

Where an application has not been the subject of an opposition, or has been the subject of a failed opposition, the Registrar shall register the trade mark as on the date of the lodging of the application for registration and issue a certificate.

---

[49] TMA, s 21.

However, where it appears to the Registrar, having regard to matters that came to its notice after acceptance of an application, that the trade mark has been accepted in error, it may withdraw the acceptance and proceed as if the application had not been accepted.

6. Term of Protection

6.1 GIs and designations of origin

The Register containing the list of all registered GIs and designations of origin, including those that form part of international agreements, shall be open for inspection to the public on the Department's website.[50] There is no provision regarding the term of validity of those GIs or designations of origin or a requirement to renew a GI or designation of origin. The Executive Officer shall, however, cancel the registration of a registered GI or designation of origin at the request of the producer or group of producers for whom the name is registered where the registered GI or designation of origin is no longer used and where during inspections, it is established that the producer or group of producers no longer ensures compliance with the product specifications. A foreign registered GI or designation of origin, including a foreign GI that forms part of an international agreement, shall be cancelled when it is no longer protected or has fallen into disuse in its country of origin.[51] Where the registration of a GI is cancelled, the Executive Officer shall remove the name and other related details from the Register and publish a notice in the *Government Gazette*.[52]

Where any group wishes to amend its product specification, the group shall follow the same procedure as for an application to register a GI or designation of origin.[53] The only exceptions relate to the nomination of a new certification body for registered foreign GIs and designations of origin and labelling and packaging changes for all GIs and designations of origin as long as the existing regulatory labelling and packaging requirements and restrictions are complied with.[54]

Where there is any change in the status of foreign GIs or designations of origin that form part of international agreements and that fall within the scope of the GI regulations, the competent authority in the country concerned must inform the Executive Officer in writing and within a reasonable time.[55] An application to amend the product specifications of a registered foreign GI or designation of origin

---

[50] GI Regulations, reg 14(3). In practice, the authors were unable to find said Register.
[51] ibid reg 16(1).
[52] ibid reg 16(3).
[53] ibid reg 15(1).
[54] ibid reg 15(4).
[55] ibid reg 7(2).

that forms part of an international agreement shall be done in accordance with the procedure provided for in such international agreement or as otherwise mutually agreed between the Republic of South Africa and the country concerned.[56]

Once written confirmation has been received from the Executive Officer that the proposed amendment to the product specification has been accepted and that the Register was amended, the producer or group of producers shall, within reasonable time, amend their product specification accordingly and ensure that the amendment is implemented.[57]

When the product specification of a registered GI has been amended in accordance, the agricultural product in question may continue to be produced, packaged, labelled, and presented for sale (marketed) under the previous product specification for a period not exceeding twelve months following the publication of the amendment in the *Government Gazette*.[58]

6.2 Collective and certification marks

A collective or certification mark is valid for ten years and may be renewed indefinitely.

An application for the amendment of the rules of a registered collective and certification mark or the rules accompanying an application for the registration of a collective and certification mark shall be made on Form TM2. The amendment shall be indicated by showing in square brackets all words to be omitted and by underlining all words to be added. A copy of the application shall be sent to all persons authorized to use the mark. The applicant shall file a copy of the amended rules within one month of the approval of the rules by the Registrar. If the applicant fails to file a copy of the amended rules within the stipulated time, the application for amendment shall be deemed abandoned.

7. Rights of the Owner and Enforcement Mechanisms against Infringers

When a term is protected under the APSA, the Minister of Agriculture sets out by notice in the *Gazette* the conditions and prohibitions related to the use of the term. Terms protected under the APSA will be names of any commodity of vegetable or animal origin or produced from a substance of vegetable or animal origin and which consists wholly or partially of such substance. Such prohibitions shall apply

---

[56] ibid reg 15(2).
[57] ibid reg 15(5).
[58] ibid reg 20(2).

where the geographical name is used in connection with an indication of the true origin of the product; in translation; or together with the words 'kind', 'type', 'style', 'imitation', or such similar words or expressions.[59] Under the APSA, it is prohibited to make a false representation, whether through the name, word, expression, reference, particulars, or indication, either by itself or in conjunction with any other verbal, written, printed, illustrated, or visual material, that a product has certain characteristics relating to, for example, its nature, its origin, or place of production.[60] The minister may also prohibit the sale of a prescribed product unless the product is sold according to the prescribed class or grade; the product complies with the prescribed standards regarding the quality, class, grade, or the prescribed requirements in connection with the packing, marking, and labelling of that product; or unless that product is packed, marked, and labelled in the prescribed manner or with the prescribed particular.[61] The contravention of these conditions and prohibitions constitutes an offence punishable by a fine not exceeding ZAR 8,000 and/or imprisonment for a period not exceeding two years for a first conviction. In the event of a second or subsequent conviction, the offender is liable to a fine not exceeding ZAR 16,000 and/or imprisonment for a period not exceeding four years.[62]

Under the GI Regulations, any direct or indirect commercial use of a registered GI or designation of origin in the Republic of South Africa is prohibited on similar agricultural products not covered by the registration and on dissimilar agricultural products where such use exploits the reputation of the protected name. This prohibition applies in particular where the registered name is imitated, alluded to, or translated or the registered name is accompanied by words or expressions such as 'kind', 'type', 'style', 'imitation', 'method', 'as produced in', or any similar words or expressions. In the latter case, the use of these words or expressions, together with the registered name, is permissible when specifically allowed for in an international agreement.

This prohibition also applies to any false or misleading indication or depiction as to the agricultural product's true origin, provenance, manufacturing process, nature, or essential characteristics on a container, an outer container, a notice board and/or in an advertisement thereof; to any illicit use of a specific or unique shape of the registered GI or designation of origin; to any use of a container or packaging that could create a false impression regarding the origin of the agricultural product; to any illicit use of a GI or designation of origin logo; and to any illicit use of the following designations: 'Protected Geographical Indication', 'Registered Geographical Indication', 'Republic of South Africa Geographical

---

[59] APSA, s 6A.
[60] ibid s 6.
[61] ibid s 3(1)(a).
[62] ibid s 11(2)(a) and (b).

Indication', 'South African Geographical Indication', 'Protected Designation of Origin', 'Registered Designation of Origin', 'Republic of South Africa Designation of Origin', 'South African Designation of Origin' and the corresponding acronyms 'PGI', 'RGI', 'RSA-GI', 'SA-GI', 'PDO' , 'RDO', 'RSA-DO', or 'SA-DO'.[63] The prohibition also applies where the agricultural product protected by a registered GI or registered designation of origin is used as an ingredient in the manufacture of another foodstuff unless the conditions in regulation 19 have been met.[64] Under regulation 19, a registered GI or registered designation of origin may be indicated as part of or in close proximity to the product name/designation of a foodstuff incorporating agricultural products benefiting from such registered name, as well as in the labelling, presentation, and advertising relating to that foodstuff where specific conditions are met. The foodstuff in question should not contain any other 'comparable ingredient', that is any other ingredient that may partially or totally replace the ingredient benefiting from the registered GI or designation of origin. If an ingredient comparable to a registered GI or designation of origin has been incorporated into a foodstuff, the registered name of the GI or designation of origin may appear in the list of ingredients only. The ingredient should preferably be used in sufficient quantities to impart an essential characteristic to the foodstuff concerned. Any emphasis regarding the presence of the ingredient should be subject to the requirements on Quantitative Ingredient Declarations (QUID), as specified in the regulations published under the Foodstuffs, Cosmetics and Disinfects Act, 1972 (Act No 54 of 1972).[65] The Executive Officer may grant written exemption, either entirely or partially, from these provisions on such conditions as it deems necessary.[66]

An agricultural product that fails to meet the requirements for the use of a registered GI or designation of origin but which has been legally presented for sale (marketed) under such name for at least five years prior to the publication of a Notice of application for registration in the *Government Gazette* may continue to be produced, packaged, and labelled under such name for a period not exceeding two years following the aforementioned publication and presented for sale (marketed) for a period not exceeding three years following the aforementioned publication.[67]

Designated assignees shall, while exercising their mandate in the trade for the agricultural product(s) they were appointed for, ensure that all GIs or designations of origin, including registered foreign GIs and designations of origin that form part of international agreements, enjoy the necessary protection. Designated assignees shall take the appropriate action against any transgressions.[68]

---

[63] GI Regulations, reg 3(2).
[64] ibid reg 3(2)(a)(iv).
[65] ibid reg 17(1).
[66] ibid reg 3(1).
[67] ibid reg 20(1).
[68] ibid reg 21(6).

Any person who contravenes or fails to comply with these provisions of the GI Regulations shall be guilty of an offence and, upon conviction, be liable to a fine not exceeding the maximum provided under the Adjustment of Fines Act No 101 of 1991 and/or imprisonment as provided under section 11(2) of the APSA.[69]

Under the MMA, a trade description is defined as an indication as to the place or country of manufacturing or production of goods or as to the mode of manufacturing or producing any goods. It includes any mark or the like that, according to custom in trade, is taken to serve as indication of place of manufacturing or production of goods.[70] Being broad in nature, the protection offered under the MMA may also covers GIs and, to at least a substantial extent, covers GI protection as required by the WTO Agreement on Trade-Related Aspects of Intellectual Property Rights (TRIPS). The protection further corresponds with the protection of indication of source under the Paris Convention.

Under the MMA, it is further an offence to use prohibited marks under section 15 or to fail to comply with any condition prescribed in the notice.[71] Upon conviction, a person shall be liable, in the case of a first conviction, to a fine not exceeding ZAR 5,000 for each article to which the offence relates and/or to imprisonment for a period not exceeding three years. In any other case, the offender shall be liable to a fine not exceeding ZAR 10,000 for each article to which the offence relates and/or imprisonment for a period not exceeding five years. Upon conviction, the court may further order the confiscation of all or any part of the goods in respect of which the offence was committed. The confiscated goods shall be disposed of as the Minister of Trade and Industry may direct.

GIs may further be protected under the Consumer Protection Act, which stipulates in section 29(b)(i) that a producer, importer, distributor, retailer, or service provider must not market any goods or services 'in a manner that is misleading, fraudulent or deceptive in any way, including in respect of . . . (i) the nature, properties, advantages or uses of the goods or services'. This includes misrepresentation as to the origin of the goods as decided in the case of *Long John International Ltd*, where the court found that 'Ben Nevis Scotch Whisky', being a liqueur, was misrepresenting itself as Scotch whisky through the label and get-up and was substantially misleading customers.[72] The owners of a GI could therefore use this section to prevent false representations as to characteristics for which the GI is well known or has a strong reputation.

A GI owner may also pursue civil remedies where its rights are infringed, in particular relying on unfair competition. The owners of both registered and unregistered GIs may rely on South African common law, which classifies misleading or deceiving the public in respect of the origin of goods as an act of unlawful

---

[69] ibid reg 21.
[70] MMA, s 1.
[71] ibid s 15(3).
[72] *Long John International Ltd v Stellenbosch Wine Trust (PTY) Ltd and others* 1990 (4) SA 136.

competition. The plaintiff must prove that there was an unlawful act and that such act was attributable to the wrongdoer's fault. Such conduct must result in or constitute a false representation that causes, or is likely to cause, confusion or deception of a substantial number of consumers. In addition, this false representation must result in financial loss to the plaintiff. Such an action is, however, only available to those who trade or have a business activity in South Africa, as they are otherwise not considered a competitor.[73] Upon recognition of an act of unfair competition, the High Court may order an interdict and/or payment of damages.

Alcoholic drinks benefit from an additional layer of protection under the LPA. It is forbidden to use

> any name, word, expression, reference, particulars or indications in any manner, either by itself or in conjunction with any other verbal, written, printed, illustrated or visual material, in connection with the sale of a liquor product, in a manner which conveys or creates, or is likely to create, a false or misleading impression as to the nature, substance, quality, composition or other properties, or the class, cultivar, origin, age, identity, or manner or place of production of that liquor product.[74]

Infringement of section 12(1) of the LPA will result in a fine not exceeding ZAR 8,000 and/or imprisonment for a period not exceeding two years upon the first conviction and a fine and/or imprisonment for a period not exceeding four years for any subsequent conviction. In *Milestone Beverage CC and others v The Scotch Whisky Association and others*, the Supreme Court of Appeal held that the appellant had infringed section 12 of the LPA by selling a spirit being represented as a whisky or Scotch whisky or a whisky with a Scottish connection with an alcohol content of 43 per cent or 43.5 per cent when it was not, in fact, whisky and had a lower alcohol content. The misrepresentation of the product through the use of tartan, a Scottish clan name, a heavily crested label, and the prominent display of the term 'Whisky' also led to a finding of unlawful competition by the court.[75]

Finally, certification or collective marks may be protected under the relevant provisions of the TMA. The following constitutes infringement of a certification or collective mark:

> a) the unauthorized use in the course of trade in relation to goods or services in respect of which the mark is registered, of an identical mark or a mark so nearly resembling it as to be likely to deceive or cause confusion;

---

[73] *Tie Rack plc v Tie Rack Stores (Pty) Ltd and another*, 1989 (4) SA 427 (T).
[74] LPA, s 12(1).
[75] *Milestone Beverage CC and others v The Scotch Whisky Association and others* (1037/2019) [2020] ZASCA 105.

b) the unauthorized use of a mark which is identical or similar to the mark registered, in the course of trade in relation to goods or services which are so similar to the goods or services in respect of which the mark is registered, that in such use there exists the likelihood of deception or confusion;
c) the unauthorized use in the course of trade in relation to any goods or services of a mark which is identical or similar to a registered mark, if such mark is well known in South Africa and the use of the said mark would be likely to take unfair advantage of, or be detrimental to, the distinctive character or the repute of the registered mark, notwithstanding the absence of confusion or deception.[76]

The *bona fide* use by a person of any *bona fide* description or indication of the kind, quality, quantity, intended purpose, value, geographical origin, or other characteristics of its goods or services, or the mode or time of production of the goods or the rendering of the services, does not constitute a trade mark infringement where it is consistent with fair practice.[77]

Upon a mark being infringed, the High Court may order an interdict, an order for removal of the infringing mark from all material, and, where the infringing mark is inseparable or incapable of being removed from the material, an order that all such material be delivered up to the proprietor and damages. The mark owner may also, in lieu of damages, opt to receive a reasonable royalty, which would have been payable by a licensee for the use of the mark concerned.[78]

However, the owner of a certification or collective mark may not interfere with or restrain the use by any person of a trade mark identical with or nearly resembling it where that person or its predecessor in title has made continuous and *bona fide* use of that trade mark from a date anterior.[79]

8. Customs Enforcement

South African customs may seize and detain counterfeit or suspected counterfeit goods at the time of importation, exportation, removal in transit, and on goods under Customs Control in a Customs and Excise Warehouse. Collective and certification marks and marks prohibited under section 15 of the MMA are subject to automatic customs enforcement. To enforce a GI, a right owner would be required to invoke the normal remedies available for preliminary injunctive relief on an urgent basis.

---

[76] TMA, s 34(1).
[77] ibid s 34(2).
[78] ibid s 34(3).
[79] ibid s 36.

A preventative customs recordal may be filed with South African customs, the South Africa Revenue Service (SARS), in the prescribed format. Information to be provided includes a power of attorney, an indemnity form, proof of intellectual property (IP) rights, and a letter confirming minimum quantities for which customs action is required. The National Coordinator: Intellectual Property Rights at SARS will examine the application. An application is usually approved within seven days of submission. If the application is rejected, reasons shall be provided, and the applicant will be allowed to rectify the application. Once accepted, the application is valid for two years of the date of approval or the expiry of the IP right.

When suspected goods are detained, a notice of detention is sent to the importer, the exporter, and the right owner. There is no specified time as to how long a detention may last. It must, however, be for a reasonable time. When the goods are confirmed as counterfeits, a formal complaint must be lodged for the formal seizure of the consignment in terms of the Counterfeit Goods Act[80] and to obtain the required search and seizure warrant. Once the seizure notice has been issued, the right holder must lodge either criminal or civil proceedings within the statutory time limits. For criminal proceedings, the right owner must lodge a complaint with the South African Police Services within three calendar days, and the State will confirm within ten working days its intention to institute criminal prosecution. For civil proceedings, the right owner must notify the importer or exporter of the intention to institute civil proceedings within ten working days of issuance of the seizure notice. The right owner then has ten working days to institute legal proceedings. Failure to respect these time limits will lead to the release of the goods. Detained goods remain under the control of customs until an order of the court to return, release, or destroy the goods.[81]

9. Bilateral Agreements

As a wine- and spirit-producing country, South Africa has been the focus of much attention by the European Union (EU), desirous of securing protection of some of the names for wine and spirits protected in Europe as GIs but used for local South African wine and spirits. South Africa and the EU (then the European Community) signed an agreement on trade in wine within the context of the Agreement on Trade, Development and Cooperation between the Community and South Africa on 11 October 1999 and which came into force on 28 January 2002. [82] South Africa had to phase out *Port* and *Sherry* within eight years of the

---

[80] Act No 37 of 1997.
[81] More information may be found on customs enforcement in South Africa in Marius Schneider and Vanessa Ferguson, *Enforcement of Intellectual Property Rights in Africa* (OUP 2020) 749–55.
[82] Michael Blakeney, 'Legal Infrastructure for the Protection of GIs' in Michael Blakeney and others (eds), *Extending the Protection of Geographical Indications: Case Studies of Agricultural Products in Africa* (Routledge 2012) 57–58.

signature of the agreement for non-SACU SADC countries,[83] five years on all export markets, and twelve years for the South African domestic market.[84] New denominations approved by South Africa and Europe would be used for the products on the South African market. Additional layers of protection for EU GIs were obtained later in the year. South Africa also agreed to protect the full list of GIs for wines as provided in Annex 2 of the agreement. The agreement on trade in spirits contained rather similar provisions. The agreement on trade in spirits protects European origin terms and phases out the terms 'Grappa' and 'Ouzo' within five years as from 1 January 2002.[85] In return, the EU provided €15 million of aid to restructure the South African wine and spirits industry and increased the import quota for South African wines and spirits. Under TRIPS, using the reclaimed terms would have been permissible as used for more than ten years prior to 15 April 1994 or in good faith to this date.[86] The bilateral agreement was one of the few ways in which the EU could reclaim those terms. It is no secret that the fact that the EU is among the most important trading partners for South Africa played a major role in adopting this agreement.

In June 2016, an EPA was signed between the European Union and six SADC countries: South Africa, Botswana, Lesotho, Mozambique, Namibia, and Swaziland. The EU–SADC EPA also includes a bilateral protocol on the protection of GIs and the trade in wines and spirits, between South Africa and the EU. Under the bilateral protocol, the EU will protect 105 GI names from South Africa, of these, 102 wine names, such as *Paarl* and *Stellenbosch*, and three non-wine agricultural products, such as *Honeybush*, *Rooibos*, and *Karoo Meat of Origin*. In exchange, South Africa will protect 251 EU names, which are spread over the categories of wines, spirits, and food.[87] The protocol, however, does not affect products currently produced in South Africa but bars new entrants from using protected names.[88]

---

[83] The non-SACU SADC countries are Angola, Comoros, Democratic Republic of Congo, Madagascar, Malawi, Mauritius, Mozambique, Seychelles, United Republic of Tanzania, Zambia, and Zimbabwe.

[84] For the purpose of the Wines and Spirits Agreement, the South African domestic market is defined to cover SACU (Botswana, Eswatini, Lesotho, Namibia, and South Africa): art 9 of the Agreement between the European Community and the Republic of South Africa on Trade in Wine referring to ANNEX X of the Agreement on Trade, Development and Cooperation between the European Community and Its Member States, of the one part, and the Republic of South Africa, of the other part—Protocol 1 concerning the definition of the concept of 'originating products' and methods of administrative cooperation—Protocol 2 on mutual administrative assistance in customs matters—Final Act—Declarations.

[85] European Commission, 'Commission Welcomes Conclusion of EU–South Africa Wine and Spirits Negotiations' (*European Commission*, 21 January 2002) <https://ec.europa.eu/commission/presscorner/detail/en/IP_02_99>.

[86] A Van der Merwe, 'Geographical Indication Protection in South Africa with Particular Reference to Wines and the EU Connection' (2008) 33(1) J Jurid Sci 115.

[87] SADC–EU EPA Outreach South Africa, 'SADC–EU Economic Partnership Agreement: Geographical Indications' (2017) 8.

[88] SAPA, 'Rooibos Protected in EU Trade Pact' (*TimesLIVE*, 21 July 2014) <www.timeslive.co.za/politics/2014-07-21-rooibos-protected-in-eu-trade-pact>.

The South African ratification process of the EPA was concluded in Parliament on 30 August 2016 through the General Notice 722 of 2016 on Prohibition of the use of Geographical Indications of the European Union in connection with the sale of Liquor Products. The new agricultural market access agreement (which includes the protection of GI names) took effect on 1 November 2016.

On the basis of a Transition Agreement signed with the United Kingdom, products included in the EU bilateral protocol remain protected after completion of BREXIT. Similarly, UK GIs will remain protected in South Africa.[89]

---

[89] Rooibos Council, 'Rooibos Continues to Enjoy GI Protection in UK Post BREXIT' (*Rooibos Council*, nd) <https://sarooibos.co.za/rooibos-continues-to-enjoy-gi-protection-in-uk-post-brexit>.

17
Conclusion

The desire to protect the names (and sometimes the external characteristics)[1] of high-quality products elaborated or produced in a specific locality using local know-how from imitations by outsiders and other copiers is nothing new. Throughout history and in various corners of the world, producers have tried to protect 'their' products, developed through decades, and even centuries, of effort and tradition from imitators. While this desire for protection is shared by many countries, reaching common ground on how best to protect the names and characteristics of these high-quality origin products has proven more challenging. The first international agreements on the protection of products with characteristics linked to their geographical origin administered by the World Intellectual Property Organization (WIPO), such as the Madrid Agreement for the Repression of False or Deceptive Indications of Source on Goods of 1891 and the Lisbon Agreement for the Protection of Appellations of Origin and their International Registration (Lisbon Agreement) of 1958 were far from popular, with low levels of adhesion. Today, these agreements still have few contracting states.

The Agreement on Trade-Related Aspects of Intellectual Property Rights (TRIPS), under the auspices of the World Trade Organization (WTO), upset the *status quo* by making it compulsory for all WTO members to protect geographical indications (GIs) in their national legislation. Contrary to the Lisbon Agreement, under the TRIPS Agreement, states may choose how to protect signs or expressions used to indicate that a product's characteristics are attributed exclusively or essentially to the natural and human factors of the country, region, or specific place from which the product originates. The TRIPS Agreement allows states to protect GIs through *sui generis* laws, trade mark laws, unfair competition laws, or modalities focusing on business practices, including administrative product approval schemes. As shown in Part II of the book, states have taken full advantage of this leeway. While Algeria, Morocco, Botswana, Egypt, Mauritius, and the Organisation Africaine de la Propriété Intellectuelle (OAPI) have adopted a *sui generis* system of protection, treating GIs as an independent category of intellectual property, other

---

[1] Under European Union (EU) law and practice, Regulations (EU) Nos 510/2006 and 1151/2012 prohibit not only the use by a third party of a registered name but also the reproduction of the shape or appearance characterizing a product covered by a registered name where that reproduction is liable to lead the consumer to believe that the product containing that reproduction is a product covered by that registered name. See Case C-490/19 *Syndicat interprofessionnel de défense du fromage Morbier v Société Fromagère du Livradois SAS* ECLI:EU:C:2020:1043, paras 40–41.

states, such as Angola, Ethiopia, Kenya, and Nigeria, provide for the protection of GIs through the trade mark system. South Africa adopts a common law approach, using various statutes and corresponding regulations to protect its noteworthy agricultural products. The Democratic Republic of Congo's legislation provides for the *sui generis* protection of GIs as appellations of origin, although practical implementation remains doubtful. In countries that have adopted a *sui generis* system, this registration system often cohabits with certification and/or collective marks. In countries such as Mauritius, GI owners may thus choose to register their sign or name as a GI, a collective, or a certification mark. In Botswana, GI owners may register their sign or name as a GI or a collective mark. Most countries also provide for unfair competition rules, although the bar to a successful suit is often higher with more stringent requirements.

There are numerous advantages to protecting GIs through a *sui generis* system as opposed to registration through the trade mark system. These include the possibility to tailor the legislation to suit the country's objectives by providing specific rules. A country may, for example, elect in its legislation to provide that GI names may never become generic, thereby eliminating any risk of genericide domestically. This is the case in Morocco. The law could further provide for the indefinite registration of GIs, thereby removing renewal fees and reducing the administrative burden for right owners. This is the case at the OAPI.

The *sui generis* registration of GIs may, in addition, offer solutions to the issue of prior-registered trade marks that contain or reproduce later-in-time GI names. Under the trade mark system, the principle of 'first in time, first in right' means that a previously registered trade mark takes precedence over a subsequent GI. A *sui generis* law could, however, provide for the superiority of the GI over the trade mark under certain conditions or for the intermediary solution of coexistence. In Botswana, section 82 of the Industrial Property Act thus provides that the rights over a registered mark cannot prevent a third party from using a registered GI in the course of trade.

The current generic status of 'rooibos' in the United States is an excellent example of the difficulties faced by GIs in a trade mark system. Where no grouping is sufficiently organized and financially secure to oppose opportunistic trade mark registrations, unrelated third parties may register and monopolize a GI. This is especially true in countries where the GI may be less well known, and public uproar is unlikely. The registration of the word 'rooibos' by an American 'entrepreneur' in the United States led to the monopolization of the term in the United States to the detriment of South African *Rooibos* farmers. It also led to a prolonged costly legal battle, which only ended with the parties agreeing that the word 'rooibos' would be a generic term in the United States. This prejudices South African *Rooibos* producers, who would no doubt have benefited economically from a monopoly on the term *Rooibos* in the United States. The difficulties posed by a trade mark system are further illustrated through Ethiopia's efforts to register 'Sidamo' for coffee and the resulting battle with Starbucks in the United States. It is unlikely that without the vocal public outcry, Starbucks would have agreed to withdraw its earlier application for the trade mark 'Shirkina Sun-Dried Sidamo'.

It is also possible to include in a *sui generis* law *ex officio* procedures whereby the Intellectual Property (IP) Office must automatically reject any trade mark that is identical or confusingly similar to a GI. This reduces enforcement costs for GI owners. For example, in Morocco, the law provides that no mark may be registered if it contains the name of a GI or a designation of origin. This is a formal requirement and will lead to the rejection of any conflicting application by the IP Office. A *sui generis* GI system also allows lawmakers to craft provisions that go beyond protecting GIs from misuse for similar products or the addition of terms such as 'like' or 'style'. The concept of evocation, as developed by the European Union (EU), is a good example. Evocation occurs when 'the consumer is confronted with the name of the product, the image triggered in its mind is that of the product whose designation is protected'.[2] Evocation may even occur through the shape or appearance characterizing a product. Evocation allows GIs a broad scope of protection against acts that are not necessarily actionable under trade mark law or even unfair competition. This has allowed for an expansive scope of protection.

In some countries, the registration of GIs entails a high level of government involvement, which might be particularly advantageous for small actors. The government may take on a variety of roles, from assessing the suitability of specific products for registration as GIs to organizing training sessions and evaluating the technical information on the production specification to ensure its adequacy. At the OAPI level, the organization has taken on a developmental agency role, identifying possible GIs and setting up a comprehensive scheme for each potential GI, codifying the rules and mechanisms underlying the GI. In Algeria, a specialized subcommittee of the National Labelling Committee examines any demand for the registration of an appellation of origin or GI for agricultural products or products of agricultural origin and elaborates a specification chart with the applicant. The National Labelling Committee is attached to the Ministry of Agriculture and regroups representatives from the public service, farmers, producers, transformers, distributors, artisans, and consumers. In contrast, in a certification or collective mark system, the applicant is solely responsible for crafting the mark and the relevant specifications with limited governmental involvement.

Creating a GI would have proven an insurmountable task for many small producers: drafting a product specification or regulations of use is a highly technical exercise that could prove difficult, time-consuming, and expensive for small producers. This may result in their exclusion to the benefit of more prominent actors who can devote the time and financial resources to participate meaningfully in the

---

[2] Case C-87/97 *Consorzio per la tutela del formaggio Gorgonzola v Käserei Champignon Hofmeister GmbH & Co KG and Eduard Bracharz GmbH* ECLI:EU:C:1999:115, para 25.

project. Similarly, the drawing of the geographical region to ensure that every relevant actor is included and the continued mobilization of a group of producers are challenging tasks. The involvement of the government with qualified technicians and other experts specifically employed to ensure the successful registration of a GI may guarantee that the process comes to fruition with a fair and satisfying result for all. At the OAPI level, the registration of domestic GIs was only made possible following the heavy involvement of the organization and external donors. Set up by the OAPI and financed by the *Agence française de développement* (AFD), the *Projet d'Appui à la Mise en Place des IG dans les Etats Membres* (PAMPIG), running from 2010 to 2014, identified potential GIs from a list of products sent to the OAPI by the member states' ministries of agriculture. Four GIs were selected from the list. PAMPIG surveyed the sector, identified the actors, wrote the terms of reference for local consultants, and supported the producers' organization in preparing its marketing strategy and drafting its specification chart.

States, as external and impartial actors, are probably best placed to ensure that producer associations truly reflect the diversity of producers. Power dynamics based on gender disparity and historical discrimination may impact representativeness and participation in a producers' association. The state may thus ensure that such disparities and discrimination do not impact the composition of the association. Some countries, such as Uganda, explicitly provide for the need for an association representative of all players in the industry.[3]

Often, government expertise will extend beyond the creation of the GIs to international marketing, product development, and enforcement. The OAPI thus signed a contract of objective and performance with the producer group for *Penja Pepper* to ensure the development and efficient management of the GI.[4] In Morocco, cooperatives and economic interest groups receive state subsidies to cover the external, third-party quality-control costs by independent bodies over agricultural GIs.[5] In African countries, where GIs are new and small producers may have limited means, the government's heavy involvement may be the only realistic way of successfully registering a GI.[6]

The trade mark regime, whereby GIs are protected as certification or collective marks, also has its advantages over a *sui generis* system. A certification or collective

---

[3] Monique Bagal and others, *Manual for Geographical Indications in Africa* (2nd edn, European Union Intellectual Property Office 2023) 45.

[4] OAPI, 'L'OAPI et le Groupement IGP Poivre de Penja: Le contrat de confiance' (*OAPI*, nd) <www.oapi.int/index.php/en/component/k2/item/522-l-oapi-et-le-groupement-igp-poivre-de-penja-le-contrat-de-confiance>.

[5] Bagal (n 3) 52, 86.

[6] The authors are aware of other advantages often linked to *sui generis* system, such as the costless registration of a GI compared to the costs for trade mark registration. Although the producer might not directly pay out the costs of a GI registration, there are undoubtedly costs associated with creating a GI. In addition, in some countries, such as Mauritius, a fee must be paid to register a GI. The authors have therefore purposefully decided to exclude this advantage.

mark can be more inclusive than a *sui generis* system, often with less stringent requirements. While a certification or collective mark may apply a region-specific requirement, this is not an obligation and ensures greater inclusion. The ability to include all coffee producers, not just those growing coffee in the namesake regions, was one of the determinants for Ethiopia to adopt trade marks for its coffee rather than *sui generis* GIs. Furthermore, the standards under a *sui generis* GI may simply be too much to bear for small producers: small producers may not have the capacity to comply with more stringent production methods or with the requirement to maintain detailed records. This is particularly true for disadvantaged or low-literacy communities. This is a genuine concern, and one must be wary of major actors in an industry pushing for the creation of a *sui generis* GI as it could lead to the exclusion of the smaller players. The exclusion of small players could be unintentional. The main aim could be to obtain a premium price rather than to reduce competition. Still, the result remains the same: the exclusion of small producers. Reduced government involvement in the creation of a certification or collective mark also translates into less public spending. One may argue that there is no need for public spending on a sign that will benefit only a small proportion of the population while raising the price for the rest. In a certification or collective mark system, those who directly benefit from the sign are responsible for the costs associated with creating and maintaining the sign. This includes drafting production standards, ensuring respect by users of the mark, promoting the mark, and enforcing the mark against counterfeiters. Finally, a collective or certification mark owner may also take advantage of the Madrid System for the international registration and maintenance of the mark.[7] A GI is often associated with a desire to enter foreign markets, and the Madrid System provides a cheap and effective way of doing so.

There is no right or wrong way to protect GIs. Both the *sui generis* system and the trade mark system have advantages and corresponding disadvantages. Through both systems, collective actions may result in economies of scale for producers and boost earnings. Every country should choose the system most likely to result domestically in the advantages often associated with protecting high-quality origin goods such as rural development and price premium. This is the position adopted by many developed countries and which developing countries, including African states, should adopt. The EU has been a major proponent of the strong protection of GIs as this aligns with its interests. As home to the original producers of certain world-famous goods, it is understandable that the EU likes to control the use of the names of these products as this directly benefits European producers. European producers will do best where they benefit from a monopoly over the product's

---

[7] Madrid Agreement Concerning the International Registration of Marks (as amended on 28 September 1979) <www.wipo.int/wipolex/en/treaties/textdetails/12599> and Protocol Relating to the Madrid Agreement Concerning the International Registration of Marks (as amended on 12 November 2007) <www.wipo.int/wipolex/en/treaties/textdetails/12603>.

name. Further, with many European countries, such as France and Italy, having strong agricultural ties, protecting rurality through a high level of protection for GIs is a significant objective of the EU. On the opposite side of the spectrum, the United States and Australia benefited from migrants bringing in recipes, methods of production, and the corresponding names from Europe. Producers in those countries are currently using names of GIs to sell their goods, and any restrictions on the use of those terms could prejudice those producers. The United States and Australia thus favour a trade mark system that ensures that the prior rights of their producers are respected and that all who wish to use those names may do so subject to the respect of certain conditions.

Developing countries should adopt a similar domestic-focused approach in choosing which system to adopt. African countries must consider which products they want to protect and the costs associated with adopting a particular system. Where the product's geographical origin is already an important differentiator in the market, a *sui generis* system could be the best fit from a marketability perspective. A *sui generis* system could further allow a newly registered GI to cohabit with previously registered trade marks incorporating the GI and prevent the GI from ever becoming generic. Even where the product's geographical location does not yet invoke images of quality, a *sui generis* system may still be a good fit. Countries should assess the marketability of the product and region: will they be able, cost-effectively, to create an impression of high quality and exceptionalism for customers? The type of products should also be considered. Data from Europe have shown that wines and spirits account for the majority of the earnings of GI products. In addition, GIs for wines and spirits benefit from enhanced protection under the TRIPS Agreement. Where a developing country produces quality wines and spirits, a *sui generis* system might be most appropriate.

On the other hand, if the producers of the relevant product are spread out across the country or in different regions, the trade mark system might be best. The trade mark system is also most suitable where the focused group comprises small land owners or artisanal manufacturers who might find it easier to abide by the rules of a certification or collective mark rather than a GI.

Attachment to traditional methods should also be considered. GIs are particularly appropriate for protecting traditional techniques: divergence from old methods is frowned upon, making a GI particularly appropriate to protect ancestral and traditional knowledge. The level of innovation in the sector is therefore an essential consideration in choosing the type of protective mechanism. Compared to *sui generis* GIs, collective and certification marks allow for more adaptability to innovative production methods, which could increase production levels. Many African states, such as Kenya, aim for a higher level of industrialization to boost development and ensure food security. The impact of a GI, which could solidify traditional practices with, at times, low production and productivity levels, must be considered. Is the premium afforded by the GI sufficient to counteract any benefits that improved production methods and an increased production level would have brought?

Countries must also consider the impact of climate change. Climate change is a significant threat to pursuing production using the techniques and calendar of the past. Climate change affects plant cycles, and producers may need to adapt their farming and production methods to better reflect this reality. The increase in temperature and changing patterns of rainfall impact crops that might become less resistant or whose taste may change. For wines protected under a GI, changing the grape variety or adapting the wine composition to the evolving taste of each variety of grapes is no easy task. All these run the risk of falling foul of the specification chart. In time, winemakers will face even more difficult questions: as the temperature increases, can they move their production to another region whose climate better reflects the former climate in the region while still holding on to the notion of *terroir*?

Creating a *sui generis* system also involves higher public costs as opposed to the trade mark system. While most countries already have a system for registering trade marks and may register collective or certification marks with little additional reworking, creating a *sui generis* system for GIs will necessarily involve higher costs. At the same time, it is vital to remember that it is not necessary for developing countries to create an organizational structure as complex and comprehensive as that in the EU. A more straightforward system could work just as well for a country with few GIs. Registration and renewal fees could further contribute to offsetting the costs of creating a *sui generis* system. The entity bearing the costs is also an important consideration. In the *sui generis* system, the government bears most of the costs. In contrast, in a certification or collective mark, members of the right holder organization bear most of the costs, whether through admission and renewal fees or certification costs. Given the low means of some producers, the state may be the most appropriate entity to bear these costs.

The ability of African countries to freely choose the most appropriate system may soon be limited, since the African Continental Free Trade Area (AfCFTA) protocol on intellectual property provides that all state parties must protect GIs under a *sui generis* system, which may be complemented by additional protective mechanisms including certification marks, collective marks, or unfair competition laws.[8]

Under these circumstances, we can expect more and more African countries to offer the concurrent possibility of registering GIs under the *sui generis* system and the trade mark system. This is the approach already taken by some countries, including Mauritius. Mauritius offers the *sui generis* system, the certification mark, and the collective mark, in addition to affording protection of names and signs

---

[8] Draft AfCFTA Protocol on IPRs, art 9(1).

under the laws on unfair competition. It is up to rights holders to choose which system works best for them.

The African Union has been audacious enough to impose a *sui generis* system for GIs on all signatories of the AfCFTA. Hopefully, the African Union will dare to propose a pan-African system for the unitary registration of GIs on the continent. History has shown that a unitary approach benefits economic integration and development. The OAPI and the EU are good examples of unitary registration systems that have shaped perceptions of the importance of IP rights, including GIs. In the case of the EU, unitary IP rights were an important tool for the completion of a single market, which is also the aim behind the adoption of AfCFTA. A unitary registration system for GIs would accelerate the creation of a single and liberalized market for goods and promote regional value-chain development, agricultural development, and food security, all objectives of the AfCFTA.

The creation of a GI, whether under a *sui generis* system or a trade mark law system, is not the be-all and end-all. For economic value to accrue from the GI to the producers and the surrounding community, it is necessary to put in place an ongoing quality-monitoring system and, most importantly, an effective enforcement programme. Quality monitoring is at the core of a successful GI. Quality monitoring is necessary to continuously secure high prices and ensure the long-term viability of the GI. Consumers will only be willing to pay a premium for consistent quality. In Egypt, the Cotton Egypt Association goes as far as using DNA testing to separate genuine from counterfeit Egyptian cotton.[9]

Quality monitoring must be coupled with enforcement mechanisms to ensure that the products bearing the GIs respect the specification charts. The registration of a GI can only prevent freeriding by outsiders if effective enforcement mechanisms are present. Otherwise, copycats will take advantage of the reputation of the GI, thereby lowering economic gains for rightful producers while eroding consumer confidence in the quality and reputation of a GI. Much may be learned from successful past experiences in enforcing trade mark rights. Effective enforcement requires trained market inspectors with the power to seize infringing products and fine offenders. The authorities and judges need to be trained to understand issues related to IP and GIs.

In Africa, increasingly high-quality local products are registered as *sui generis* GIs, certification, or collective marks. As we have seen in the chapters in Part B of this book, most of the countries surveyed have legal provisions to enforce the rights of *sui generis* GIs, collective or certification marks owners. Legal proceedings are, however, often lengthy and costly.

The difficulties are compounded where the infringing acts occur outside of the 'home' country of the GI. *Penja Pepper* is only the second protected geographical

---

[9] Egyptian Cotton, 'Who Is Cotton Egypt Association? Protecting Our Luxury Cotton' (*Egyptian Cotton*, nd) <www.cottonegyptassociation.com/about-egyptian-cotton/cotton-egypt-association>.

indication (PGI) in Europe from Africa. There do not seem to be any agencies or lawyers tasked with monitoring the PGI in Europe and ensuring that products sold as *Penja Pepper* in Europe are *Penja Pepper*. Marketing of the PGI in Europe may thus inadvertently benefit counterfeiters. Policing the use of a GI abroad remains an issue, particularly for bulk commodities such as coffee and cacao, where origin differentiation is not so meaningful to consumers. Although GIs may have been registered for such goods, manufacturers, distributors, and sellers may be using the names of the product as an indication of provenance rather than a GI. One typical example is the use of the name 'Kenya' on coffee which may or may not be solely from Kenya, although the certification mark 'Coffee Kenya: So rich, so Kenyan' has been registered in Kenya. This use could arguably be deemed to dilute the reputation of the product but is harder to enforce as there is neither false indication nor an attempt to benefit from the GI's reputation.[10] While foreign aid may be available for creating a GI, much less aid is available for GI enforcement. Few international aid agencies would finance long-running court cases, even though a GI lacking enforcement mechanisms is one whose added value will only with difficulty trickle down to the rightful actors.

A successful GI requires a strong marketing campaign and an effective enforcement mechanism to be sustainable and profitable.

As consumers clamour for products with a story, respectful of traditions and the local culture, African states, with their rich history, are uniquely placed. African farmers and producers have much to offer, and the growing interest in origin products may therefore represent a boon for African rural communities. African states must therefore choose wisely the most appropriate system domestically while also considering the possibility of regional or continental collaborations, where appropriate and beneficial. The AfCFTA protocol on intellectual property limits the choice available to its member states by providing that every member state must protect GIs through a *sui generis* system. Hopefully, such an obligation will push African states towards creating better synergies on the topic through a continental or regional *sui generis* registration system. It remains to be seen whether this obligation under the AfCFTA protocol will have a real impact. Still, registration is not the be-all and end-all: the various advantages associated with a GI will rarely come solely through registration. It is hoped that states, donors, and development agencies will invest significantly in the marketing and enforcement of African GIs locally and abroad. With the appropriate tools and support, African products are poised to conquer the hearts of consumers.

---

[10] Bagal (n 3) 45.

Index

For the benefit of digital users, indexed terms that span two pages (e.g., 52–53) may, on occasion, appear on only one of those pages.

African, Caribbean, and Pacific (ACP)–EU Partnership Agreements 29–31
  Cotonou Agreement 29–30
  Economic Partnership Agreements (EPAs) 30–31
African Continental Free Trade Area (AfCFTA) 27–28, 233, 234
  protocol on intellectual property 28, 235
  Agenda 2063 27
  Continental Strategy 25–27
African Intellectual Property Organization (OAPI) 25, 55–57
  bilateral agreements 71
  customs enforcement 70–71
  legal framework 57–58
  logo 57
  membership 55
  PAMPIG 26, 56, 229–30
  PAMPIG II 57
  procedure and requirements for registration
    certification marks 63–64
    collective marks 63–64
    GIs 61–63
  regional legislation on GIs 58–59
  registrability of names
    certification marks 60
    collective marks 60
    GIs 60
  registration 60
    certification marks 59–60
    collective marks 59–60
    GIs 59
  rights of the owner and enforcement mechanisms against infringers
    certification marks 67–70
    collective marks 67–70
    GIs 66–67
  term of protection
    certification marks 65–66
    collective marks 65–66
    GIs 64–65

African Regional Intellectual Property Organization (ARIPO) 7, 25
  geographical indications 53
  applications for registration 20
  legislation on GIs 51
  Register of GIs 49
  registration of GIs 51–52
  membership 53
  protocols 47–48
    Banjul Protocol 50–51
Agenda 2063 27
AIPPI 40
Algeria
  background 73–76
  bilateral agreements 85
  customs enforcement 84–85
  domestic legislation on GIs 77
  e-commerce 74
  economy 73–74
  legal framework 76
  procedure and requirements for registration
    appellations of origin 79–81
    collective marks 81
  registrability of names
    appellations of origin 78–79
    collective marks 79
  registration
    appellations of origin 77–78
    collective marks 78
  rights of the owner and enforcement mechanisms against infringers 82–84
  term of protection
    appellations of origin 81–82
    collective marks 82
  wine industry 74–75
Angola
  background 87–88
  bilateral agreements 95
  customs enforcement 94–95
  domestic legislation on GIs 89–90
  e-commerce 87–88

Angola (*cont.*)
  economy 87
  legal framework 88–89
  procedure and requirements for registration 91–93
  registrability of names 90–91
  registration 90
  rights of the owner and enforcement mechanisms against infringers 93–94
  term of protection 93
Appellation d'origine contrôlée (AOC) 1–3
appellations of origin 8–10
ARIPO *see* African Regional Intellectual Property Organization

bilateral agreements
  Algeria 85
  Angola 95
  Botswana 108
  Democratic Republic of Congo 116
  Egypt 127
  Ethiopia 140
  Kenya 157–58
  Mauritius 171
  Morocco 187–88
  Nigeria 200
  OAPI 71
  South Africa 224–26
Botswana
  background 97–98
  bilateral agreements 108
  customs enforcement 107–8
  domestic legislation on GIs 99
  e-commerce 97–98
  legal framework 98–99
  procedure and requirements for registration
    collective marks 102–3
    GIs 101–2
  registrability of names
    collective marks 100–1
    GIs 100
  registration
    collective marks 100
    GIs 99–100
  rights of the owner and enforcement mechanisms against infringers
    collective marks 105–6
    GIs 104–5
    unfair competition 106–7
  term of protection
    collective marks 104
    GIs 103–4

certification marks 6–7, 230–31
claw-back clauses 43–44

climate change 233
collective marks 6–7, 230–31
Cotonou Agreement 29–30
customs enforcement
  Algeria 84–85
  Angola 94–95
  Botswana 107–8
  Democratic Republic of Congo 115–16
  Egypt 126
  Ethiopia 139–40
  Mauritius 170–71
  Morocco 186
  Nigeria 200
  OAPI 70–71
  South Africa 223–24

definitions of GIs 8–10
  appellations of origin 8–10
  indications of source 8–10
Democratic Republic of Congo
  background 109–10
  bilateral agreements 116
  customs enforcement 115–16
  domestic legislation on GIs 111
  legal framework 110–11
  procedure and requirements for registration
    appellations of origin 113
    collective marks 113–14
    indications of source 113
    registrability of names 113
  registration
    appellations of origin 111–12
    certification marks 112
    collective marks 112
    indications of source 111–12
  rights of the owner and enforcement mechanisms against infringers
    appellations of origin 115
    collective marks 115
    indications of source 115
  term of protection
    appellations of origin 114
    collective marks 114
    indications of source 114
development and geographical indications 10–15
  creating demand and increasing awareness of products 13
  divergent approaches of the 'Old World' and the 'New World' 3–4, 7–8
domestic legislation on GIs
  Algeria 77
  Angola 89–90
  Botswana 99
  Democratic Republic of Congo 111

INDEX

Egypt 119–20
Ethiopia 133–34
Kenya 144–45
Mauritius 161
Morocco 176–77
Nigeria 191–92
South Africa 204–5

East African Community (EAC)–EU EPA 31
Economic Partnership Agreements (EPAs)
  EAC–EU EPA 31
  EU–SADC EPA 30–31
Egypt
  background 117–18
  bilateral agreements 127
  customs enforcement 126
  domestic legislation on GIs 119–20
  e-commerce 118
  legal framework 118–19
  procedure and requirements for registration
    certification marks 122–23
    collective marks 122–23
    GIs 121–22
  registrability of names 120–21
  registration
    certification marks 120
    collective marks 120
    GIs 120
  rights of the owner and enforcement mechanisms against infringers
    certification marks 124–25
    collective marks 124–25
    GIs 123–24
  term of protection 123
enforcement mechanisms 234–35
EPAs *see* Economic Partnership Agreements
Ethiopia
  background 129–32
  bilateral agreements 140
  Coffee Trademarking and Licensing Initiative 131–32
  customs enforcement 139–40
  domestic legislation on GIs 133–34
  e-commerce 130–31
  economy 129–30
  legal framework 132–33
  procedure and requirements for registration 135–37
  registrability of names 134–35
  registration 134
  rights of the owner and enforcement mechanisms against infringers 137–39
  term of protection 137
EUCariforum 29
European Union (EU)
  EAC–EU EPA 31
  EU–SADC EPA 30–31
  evocation 36–37, 229
  free trade agreements 29, 31–32
  Protected Designation of Origin 4–6
  Protected Geographical Indication 4–6
  protection of GIs 231–32
  sales of GIs 14
evocation 36–37, 229

'First in Time, First in Right' (FITFIR) principle 39–41, 228
free trade agreements (FTAs)
  AfCFTA 27–28, 233, 234
    protocol on intellectual property 28, 235
  European Union 29, 31–32
  United States 32

genericity
  geographical indications considered as generic in other countries 42–45
Geneva Act 21

homonymous GIs 45

indications of source 8–10
International Association for the Protection of Intellectual Property (AIPPI) 40
international legal framework
  Geneva Act 21
  Lisbon Agreement 20–21, 39, 44–45, 227
  Madrid Agreement 20, 44, 227
  Paris Convention 19, 35
  see also TRIPS Agreement
International Trademark Association (INTA) 39–40

Kenya
  ACA enforcement 157
  background 141–43
  bilateral agreements 157–58
  domestic legislation on GIs 144–45
  e-commerce 142
  economy 141
  legal framework 143–44
  procedure and requirements for registration 146–48
  registrability of names 146
  registration 145
  rights of the owner and enforcement mechanisms against infringers 149–57
  term of protection 148–49

Lisbon Agreement 20–21, 39, 44–45, 227
Lusaka Agreement 47–48

Madrid Agreement 20, 44, 227
Mauritius
  background 159–60
  bilateral agreements 171
  customs enforcement 170–71
  domestic legislation on GIs 161
  e-commerce 160
  economy 159
  legal framework 160–61
  procedure and requirements for registration 163
    certification marks 164–65
    collective marks 164–65
    GIs 163–64
  registrability of names
    certification marks 162
    collective marks 162
    GIs 162
  registration 161–62
    certification marks 162
    collective marks 162
    GIs 161
  rights of the owner and enforcement mechanisms against infringers 167–70
  term of protection
    certification marks 166, 167
    collective marks 166–67
    GIs 165–66
Morocco
  background 173–75
  bilateral agreements 187–88
  customs enforcement 186
  domestic legislation on GIs 176–77
  e-commerce 174
  economy 173
  legal framework 175–76
  procedure and requirements for registration
    certification marks 182
    collective marks 182
    GIs 180–82
  registrability of names
    certification marks 179–80
    collective marks 179–80
    GIs 179
  registration
    certification marks 178–79
    collective marks 178–79
    GIs 178
  rights of the owner and enforcement mechanisms against infringers
    certification marks 186
    collective marks 186
    GIs 183–85
  term of protection
    certification marks 183
    collective marks 183
    GIs 182–83

Nigeria
  background 189–90
  bilateral agreements 200
  customs enforcement 200
  domestic legislation on GIs 191–92
  e-commerce 190
  legal framework 191
  procedure and requirements for registration 193–96
  registrability of names 193
  registration 193
  rights of the owner and enforcement mechanisms against infringers 197–200
  term of protection 196–97

OAPI *see* African Intellectual Property Organization
origins and evolution of geographical indications 1–3

PAMPIG 26, 56, 229–30
PAMPIG II 57
Paris Convention 19, 35
potential benefits of protecting GIs 7–8
procedure and requirements for registration
  Algeria 79–81
  Angola 91–93
  Botswana 101–3
  Democratic Republic of Congo 113–14
  Egypt 121–23
  Ethiopia 135–37
  Kenya 146–48
  Mauritius 163–65
  Morocco 180–82
  Nigeria 193–96
  OAPI 61–64
  South Africa 210–17
producers' associations 230
Protected Designation of Origin (PDO) 4–6
Protected Geographical Indication (PGI) 4–6

quality monitoring 234

registrability of names
  Algeria 78–79
  Angola 90–91
  Botswana 100–1
  Democratic Republic of Congo 113
  Egypt 120–21
  Ethiopia 134–35
  Kenya 146
  Mauritius 162
  Morocco 179–80
  Nigeria 193
  OAPI 60
  South Africa 208–10

registration
  Algeria 77–78
  Angola 90
  Botswana 99–100
  Democratic Republic of Congo 111–12
  Egypt 120
  Ethiopia 134
  Kenya 145
  Mauritius 161–62
  Morocco 178–79
  Nigeria 193
  OAPI 59–60
  South Africa 205–8
rights of the owner and enforcement mechanisms against infringers
  Algeria 82–84
  Angola 93–94
  Botswana 104–7
  Democratic Republic of Congo 115
  Egypt 123–25
  Ethiopia 137–39
  Kenya 149–57
  Mauritius 167–70
  Morocco 183–86
  Nigeria 197–200
  OAPI 66–70
  South Africa 218–23
'rooibos' 17–18, 203, 228–29

South Africa
  background 201–3
  bilateral agreements 224–26
  customs enforcement 223–24
  domestic legislation on GIs 204–5
  e-commerce 202
  economy 201
  legal framework 203–4
  procedure and requirements for registration
    collective and certification marks 214–17
    GIs and designations of origin 210–14
  registrability of names
    collective and certification marks 210
    GIs and designations of origin 208–10
  registration
    collective and certification marks 207–8
    GIs and designations of origin 206–7
    prohibited marks 205–6
  rights of the owner and enforcement mechanisms against infringers 218–23
    collective and certification marks 222–23
    GIs and designations of origin 219–22
  'rooibos' 17–18, 203, 228–29

term of protection
  collective and certification marks 218
  GIs and designations of origin 217–18
sui generis system of protection 3–6, 33, 227–28, 229, 232, 233
  use of *sui generis* system and the trade mark system 233–34

term of protection
  Algeria 81–82
  Angola 93
  Botswana 103–4
  Democratic Republic of Congo 114
  Egypt 123
  Ethiopia 137
  Kenya 148–49
  Mauritius 165–67
  Morocco 182–83
  Nigeria 196–97
  OAPI 64–66
  South Africa 217–18
trade marks
  advantages of the trade mark regime 230–31, 232
  overlap and conflicts between trade marks and GIs 33, 34–41, 46
    EU law 40–41
    evocation 36–37
    FITFIR principle 39–41, 228
    goods or services different from those for which the GI is registered 35–36
    later-in-time GI 37–39
    later-in-time trade mark 34–35
  use of *sui generis* system and the trade mark system 233–34
traditional knowledge 15
  definition of 15–16
  geographical indications, and 16–18, 232–33
TRIPS Agreement (WTO) 9–10, 21–22, 33, 34–35, 37–39, 44, 227–28
  GI section 22–24

unitary registration systems 234
United States
  certification marks 6–7
  free trade agreements 32
  US-Morocco FTA 32, 39–40

World Intellectual Property Organization (WIPO)
  International Bureau 20–21
World Trade Organization (WTO)
  TRIPS Agreement 9–10, 21–22, 33, 34–35, 37–39, 44, 227–28
  GI section 22–24